# ETHICS IN ISLAM

# ETHICS IN ISLAM

*By*

**Amir Ansari**

**2008**

**CYBER TECH PUBLICATIONS**
4264/3, Ansari Road, Daryaganj, New Delhi-110002 (India)
Ph.: 011-23244078. Fax: 011-23280028
E-Mail: cyberpublicationsdelhi@yahoo.com

**ETHICS IN ISLAM**

**Amir Ansari**



First Edition 2008



*Published by :*

**G.S. Rawat** for **Cyber Tech Publications**
4264/3, Ansari Road, Daryaganj, New Delhi-110002 (India)
Ph.: 011-23244078. Fax: 011-23280028
E-Mail: cyberpublicationsdelhi@yahoo.com

*Printed at :* **Amit Enterprises**, Maujpur, Delhi, (9810878184)

# Preface

Islam came on the scene, with a message, philosophy and code of conduct, perfect by all means, with its advent, the new faith revolutionised the contemporary world in a very short span of time. It also brought along with its beliefs and practices, a new culture, which gradually build a new civilization, now known as Islamic civilization.

Islam has made a great contribution to the development and growth of human civilization, education and intellect in particular and the whole society, in general. This well-known fact now that Muslims were leading the world of knowledge and wisdom, when Europe was still a dark continent, far behind in education and science. In the early era of Islam, the Muslims were in full command of the science and technology of the times. They not only unearthed, adopted and preserved the lost treasure of the Greek wisdom, but also promoted it to new heights. Muslim academics and scientists were among the leading lights of that period of history. They contributed a lot to the growth of all branches of knowledge, be that philosophy, logic, literature, geography, history, physics, chemistry, mathematics or medicine.

Islam is a scientific and progressive religion. All its teachings have a scientific and logical approach. Islam directs all its followers to learn, gain knowledge and master the arts and sciences of the contemporary world. Islam, as a living faith stands for spreading flight and eliminating darkness from the world. They contributed a lot to the growth of all branches of knowledge and thus enriched the new civilization.

This book, unique in its presentation, is perhaps first of its kind, to take all the great developments and changes over the centuries. All the significant aspects have been covered in these volumes. This multi-volume study is based on original (Holy Quran and traditions) and other authentic sources: Arabic, Persian and Urdu books and manuscripts. For further comprehension and comparative study, English books by Muslim scholars and as well as western writers have also been consulted at length. The painstaking research and thorough study of thousands of pages by a team of scholars over a period of time, has resulted in an authentic, comprehensive, exhaustive, exclusive, lengthy and still interesting work, which, is bound to fill a big vacuum in Islamic studies to fill a big vacuum in Islamic studies and as well as the treasure of knowledge about culture and civilization.

—*Author*

# Contents

# 1

# The Concept

Islam sees life in totality. All its areas whether politics or economics, social or religious, sex or others are to be governed and controlled by Divine Law. This leads to social solidarity or an edifice parts of which strengthen each other.

## MODERATE LEVEL

The outstanding feature of Islamic life is that it is free from extremes and justly balanced, for virtue is to avoid the extremes on either side. The message of God is: 'We have moulded you into a society justly-balanced that ye might be a pattern unto others, even as the Prophet has been a pattern unto you' (a: 143); 'You are the best of peoples evolved for mankind,, enjoining what is right, forbidding what is wrong (3:110).

Islam, thus, steers clear of the extremes in life and chooses for itself the middle path or the principle of moderation. Here it may be said that this is the same as the 'Golden Mean' of Aristotle. But there is a difference between 'the moderation or mean' as a principle and 'the mean' of Aristotle which he put forward as a rule. A rule is not a special order or command, it fluctuates with the collateral circumstances of each situation and is subject to flexible reason, while a principle is the command, not variable but to be obeyed by all. In Islam it takes the form of law and is law itself. Islamic law, not given to extremes, is no other than the law which adheres to the middle course and moderation in life.

We read in the Quran: 'And be moderate in thy pace' (31: 19). In all things we have to be moderate, we are not to be so niggardly as to keep back our wealth from the just needs of those who have a right to our help, nor is it becoming to be so lavish as to make ourselves destitutes: 'Make not thy hand tied (like a niggard's) to thy neck, nor stretch it forth to its utmost reach so that thou become blameworthy and destitute,' (17: 29). In our spending it is wise neither to be extravagant nor niggardly but strike a perfectly just balance between these extremes: 'Those who when they spend, are not niggardly, but hold a just (balance) between those extremes' (25: 67).Nothing in excess is allowed: 'Eat and drink but nothing in excess. Indeed He does not like; those who indulge in excesses' (7: 31). To indulge in excess is to transgress the limits ordained by God. Meticulous observance of Jaw is, therefore, essentially required and this has been well specified by the Prophet who says: 'What is lawful and unlawful is evident, yet there are some doubtful cases not known to many of the people. He who guarded himself against doubtful things saved his faith and himself from what is unlawful (Bukhari). Thus, to keep the mean is to observe the law strictly and discard what is doubtful. While the mean of Aristotle is fluctuating and subject to flexible reason and thus doubtful, the mean of Islam is free from doubt, justly balanced and without any excesses.

Islam never preaches self-abnegation, for that is the creed of Cynics, nor does it advocate repression of emotions practised by Stoics but only sets a limit to Hedonistic desires as a deterrent against the evils resulting from excesses, harmonious development of body and soul being the most desirable thing. Squandering and hoarding are both denounced, Usury or unjustifiable enrichment is forbidden, moderation or just mean enjoined.

## SYSTEMATIC LAW

'Islamic law is systematic, that is to say, it represents a coherent body of doctrines. Its several institutions are well put into relations with one another; the greater part of the law of contracts and obligations, for instance, is construed by analogy with the contract of sale. Furthermore, the whole of the law is permeated by religious and ethical considerations; each institution, transaction or obligation is measured by religious and moral rules, such as the prohibition of interest, the prohibition of uncertainty, the concern for the just mean or average (*mithl*)'. See, Schacht, *An Introduction to Islamic Law*, p. 201.

## THE ROOTS

*Adab* is an Arabic term meaning custom; it denotes a habit, an etiquette, a manner of conduct derived from people considered as models.

During the first two centuries following the emergence of Islam, the term '*adab*' carried ethical and social implications. The root *db* means marvellous thing, or preparation, feast. 'Adab in this sense was the equivalent of the Latin urbanites, civility, courtesy, refinement of the cities in contrast to bedouin uncouthness.' So adab of something means good manner of that thing. The plural is *adab*. *Adab al-Islam*, therefore, means the good manners adopted by Islam, derived from its teachings and instructions. It is in this sense that it will be used in this book.

Manners in many cultures other than the Islamic are determined by local conditions and are therefore subject to changes in those conditions. According to W. G. Sumner, 'From recurrent needs arise habits for the individual and customs for the group, but these results are consequences which were never conscious, and never foreseen or intended.'

## CONSCIOUS MANNERS

Islamic manners and customs are not in this sense 'unconscious'. They are derived from the two main sources of Islam, namely the Quran and the Sunnah, the Prophet's deeds, words and indirect commandments, and are therefore, in the strictest sense, divinely inspired.

The Quran and the Sunnah contain the broad principles needed to negotiate the problems that arise in human societies in different ages. As a complete way of life, Islam orders economic, political and devotional activity as well as manners relating to everyday human exchanges and routines. Islam is not confined merely to devotional and legal manners; it embraces criteria and values, attitudes, customs and manners in all reaches of human concern and relationship. As a portion of this whole, Islamic manners are derived from the broad objectives of Islam and reflect its broad ideas and values. *Adab al-Islam* should neither be conceived nor practised in isolation from the whole. Rather, their interrelation with other elements of Islam should always be kept in mind. Nor, likewise, should the different elements within adab al-Islam be treated as isolatable, for these too are closely interrelated. To give a single, conspicuous example: a Muslim is required to sleep early so that he may rise early for the Fajr (dawn) Prayer.

The divine inspiration of manners in Islam confers on them a religious character which motivates proper adherence. It does not follow from their religious character that every detail of these manners is obligatory. The prescribed manners of Islam vary, in fact, from the 'forbidden' to the 'recommended'. The former are upheld and enforced by law, the latter do not expose offenders to any formal trial or punishment except in the disapproval of other members of the Muslim community. A third group of manners are those which do not even lead to disapproval if one violates them.

Nor does it follow from the divine origin of Islamic manners that the system should be rigid and inflexible. Islam is not the sort of ideal that is impenetrable to human experience or inapplicable to existing world conditions. Rather, the nature of the system is such that it is flexible in many respects while stable in others, the element of flexibility being grounded in human reasoning to which Islam appeals and which may even be reckoned among its general sources.

The two basic sources of Islam, the Quran and the Sunnah, include, besides many detailed rules, general principles which ultimately govern all matters related to the various aspects of life, religious, social, economic, political, etc. None of these general principles are subject to historical change. But conditions do change. The means for deriving rules for new problems in new situations are provided for within Islam in Ijtihad. Ijtihad is, the disciplined use of independent individual reasoning to draw the necessary conclusions in accordance with the essence and spirit of Islam and in adherence to its immutable general principles. Thus, through the faith and diligence of qualified scholars, the detail of Islamic teachings can respond effectively to the problem of historical change. The teachings of Islam are, in fact, fully cognizant of human nature and human needs.

Islam acknowledges the realities of life and deals with them in the most practical way. There is then no impulse to abrogate or adjust the general principles of the faith in order to adapt them to particular conditions. The realism and practicability of Islamic manners is easily illustrated. For example, fasting the full lunar month of Ramadan is a primary obligation upon all Muslims, yet Islam understanding the vicissitudes of travelling exempts the traveller from fasting, requiring that he make up lost days when the hardship is over. Likewise, women who have recently given birth, or are in the monthly cycle, and those seriously ill, are similarly exempted. The five daily prayers are, again, a primary obligation, yet the traveller is permitted, according to some a Hadith, to combine certain of the five occasions of Salat and perform them together, also to shorten the four-rakat prayers to two-rakat prayers, known as qasr. Islam allows that the precise, final detail of the application of manners may differ, according to the fashions and circumstances of local groups, provided, of course, that the main principles of dress, of dietary laws, etc. are adhered to Islamic manners are meant to order daily life, to give it rhythm, dignity and serenity; they are not a set of snobbish or legalistic rituals to complicate daily life.

## ESSENTIAL FACTS

Islam determines every aspect of the life of a Muslim. This essential fact is very difficult for non-Muslims to grasp. For the believer, Islam gives the criteria for judging all of his behaviour and conduct; it determines his relationship with other individuals, with society as a whole, with the physical world, and it determines also his relationship to his own self. Many examples can be given of what in secular communities are the preserve of arbitrary individual will or the equally arbitrary demands of the social milieu. Food, for example, may be prepared only from what is allowed by Islam; a Muslim can make no use of, for example, pork. A Muslim woman may not uncover her feet in public because in Islam it is not permitted. Goods forbidden to a Muslim, such as wine, may not be exchanged as gifts. If a Muslim is invited to a wedding feast, he should (if physically possible) accept the invitation because it is obligatory to do so. Death-bed wishes may not be fulfilled if they contradict the teachings of Islam, such as a request to allocate an extra share of inheritance to one of the dead person's heirs, or to have his body cremated.

Adab al-Islam are a comprehensive code covering almost every aspect of social behaviour, a part of the complete way of life which is Islam. As the different parts of Islam make up an integral unity, the application of adab al-Islam in detachment from the rest will not bring about total realization of Islam, indeed it may, in certain respects, become meaningless. The customs and manners discussed in this book are considered suitable for Muslims: those who have a proper religious attitude will instinctively seek to observe the good manners commended or required by Islam.

The various aspects of Islam, ideological, spiritual, legal, social, economic, political, etc., are mutually consistent and supplement each other. For example, faith is essential as it instals in Muslims the spirit of observing the ethical, moral, legal and other prescriptions without external compulsion. Equally, voluntary observance of those prescriptions supports and enhances faith, opening up the path from devotion to social action, linking the two in a strong, stable bond. More specifically the unitary strength of Islam may be seen in, for instance, the manners concerning women, which follow from and sustain the Islamic concept of Muslim womanhood in an Islamic community.

The breadth of adab al-Islam contrasts sharply with the limitations of 'etiquette'. The manners of Islam are not merely rules of courtesy for various occasions, but cover the whole range of human relations from the simplest actions to the most elaborate of social occasions. The true purpose of Western 'etiquette' (even after it had been extended beyond royal circles to ordinary people) 'seems to have been the protection of the upper class'. By contrast, the true purpose of adab al-Islam lies in their religious character and nature. They derive from and sustain man's need to remember God in his daily routine; they are designed to keep up his remembrance of God and to help him act rightly and correctly. This is conspicuous in the invocations of God that accompany most everyday incidents of behaviour in Islam. A Muslim should start and end his day, when waking up and when going to sleep, by mentioning God.

He should thank and praise God when taking food and drink, when buying new clothes or other articles of use. Mentioning God is recommended even when relieving oneself. It is recommended to say, when entering the lavatory: 'In the name of Allah. Allah, in You I take refuge from demons', and on leaving the lavatory, ask for His forgiveness. Remembering God and asking Him for perfection and guidance are of special importance when travelling. It may be noted here that the major festivals in Islam are in fact collective celebrations of the successful completion of two principal religious obligations, namely, fasting in the month of Ramadan and Hajj (pilgrimage to Mecca).

One of the chief foundations of adab al-Islam is morality, the cornerstone of a nation's self-confidence and strength, as surely as corruption and immorality are one of the main causes of a nation's decline and disintegration. The insistence on morality often gives to the Islamic way of life an appearance of rigidity or puritanism; as one writer has noted: '...in regard to certain aspects of morality, Islam is more rigid and more puritan than certain other systems of life in our times.' But given the importance of morality to the health of a nation, normative Islam is surely right to block all ways leading to corruption, such as illicit sex and luxurious living. Material comforts should not be at the expense of human virtues, individual and collective; politics also (considered, in non-Islamic thought, as immoral or even amoral) must conform to the goals of Islam, the development of human character, the humanity of man.

The ideal of the humanity of man is grounded in the concept of Al-amal al-Salih or virtuous deeds. The term extends beyond what is normally understood as the 'religious' domain and covers a wide range of human activities (in relation to others, to the animate and inanimate environment) sanctioned within Islamic faith and law. The Prophet's life provides many concrete instances: to act justly between two people, to help a man onto his mount, to help load his belongings, to speak good words, to remove nuisances from paths or roads, to give food and water to stray dogs and cats, to be forward in greeting others, to visit relatives, etc.; even the act of making love within marriage is valued as a good deed. The most inclusive characteristics of the ideal Muslim personality are humility, modesty and simplicity or naturalness (lack of affectation). Pride and arrogance in any aspect of conduct are not accepted, as no individual is superior to another except in his degree of faith and contribution of good deeds.

Thus, clothes that show haughtiness, that flaunt social status, are forbidden. Manners in eating should demonstrate humility before the occasion as well as respect for the meal: leaning on a cushion while eating is forbidden. Sitting on the floor when eating is a sign of humility, and therefore recommended. Furnishings should show modesty and restraint; for example, the bed should not be set too high above the ground. Gait in walking, manner of address in greeting and in speech generally, should avoid any taint of arrogance.

## THE NATURALNESS

Islam requires and demands moderation and naturalness in all aspects of life, worldly and religious. Extremism, exaggeration, eccentricity and affectation, caprice and complicatedness are rejected. The insistence on a certain informality in adab al-Islam is intended to ease their use by the vast majority of the members of the Muslim society. Naturalness of manners is valued as a means of relieving social tension, of enabling and strengthening social relations.

Western 'etiquette' originated in the Royal courts of Europe, and was invented to meet 'the requirement of behaviour in courts and among aristocrats everywhere'. The meaning of etiquette was weakened when it spread to all classes. To this day Western etiquette varies from group to group. Members of so-called 'high society' observe more complicated and rigid forms of etiquette than the less well-to-do. This comes out of and helps sustain the class system.

Adab al-Islam, however, are different. They are not designed to divide society according to social classes. The rules, revealed through the Quran and the Sunnah, were not formulated by certain groups, i.e. the rich and powerful in order to subdue or distance other groups. Islam attaches great importance to the adherence of the whole of Muslim society to its adab. It does not consider these manners as the privilege or preserve of a certain group, but as a privilege open to every member of the

Muslim society. A variety of etiquette levels is non-existent in Islam.

The function of adab al-Islam in unifying Muslim communities, as well as being an expression of their unity, is clear. But adab al-Islam are not just about coherence or consistency of behaviour; they are about coherence or consistency of right behaviour. The notion of 'proper' conduct may not, in Islam, be separated from the notion of 'good' deeds, nor from 'faith' and 'devotion'. Faith and good deeds are both necessary in this world for a prosperous and ideal society in which there is mutual and shared responsibility. And in the Hereafter, faith and good deeds are the necessary conditions for forgiveness and salvation, for admission to Paradise. A large number of verses in the Quran link faith and good deeds as defining characteristics of a true Muslim.

## BROAD RELATIONS

In Islam, what is 'central' and 'essential' is determined by its broad relation to the goals of Islam, among which is the civilization or advancement of human society, the promotion of happiness and prosperity, material as well as moral. On examination, the prescriptions and prohibitions which form part of Islamic teachings will be seen to be not arbitrary decrees but an ordered system of commandments whose purpose (besides testing man's obedience and loyalty to God) is the advancement of man, according to a safe, proper and perfect course, at the individual, family and societal levels.

The details of adab al-Islam are not meaningless formalities, unwelcome to the individual because they are unrelated to the actual needs of his personal or social life. On the contrary, they directly address the different basic functions that concern all members of society at almost every moment of their lives. They are intended to concentrate attention on the central and essential, to rescue man from the peripheral and distracting. They distinguish means from ends and help individual and community to administer personal and collective resources effectively. It may be helpful to illustrate this general point by listing the basic human needs and functions as they are viewed within the perspective of adab al-Islam:

1. Clothes are primarily intended to protect the wearer against the climate, and to conceal parts of the body.
2. The purpose of housing is to provide shelter from the climate and to secure necessary privacy and safety.
3. Cleanliness, as well as protecting man from disease, expresses his humanity.
4. Adornment, make-up, etc. are a woman's means to look attractive and pleasant before her husband.
5. Speech is important as a means of communication, serving in the essential functions of exchange and relationship with other people, such as buying, selling, etc.
6. Humour reduces tension and relaxes people at a gathering.
7. Gifts are meant to express goodwill and to foster good relations with others.
8. Inviting others to eat, sharing food with others, makes and strengthens social bonds.
9. Social relations themselves are valued because they prevent or limit isolation of the individual. Social customs are valued because they create stability and harmony in social relations.
10. Graves are primarily for honouring the dead, but also to protect the living from the decaying corpse.
11. Animals, in direct relation to man, are intended to be used only for specific purposes such as provision of food, labour, transport. They are not meant to be used by man for his entertainment as, for instance, when animals are set against each other.

It will be immediately obvious that, without the restraint of adab al-Islam, all these means become ends, destroying a proper sense of values and priorities. Clothes, houses, parties, gifts, drain the resources of individual and community, as people (having lost sight of the true function of these things) spend money in a fruitless endeavour to prove to others their greater purchasing power; in their world the ability to waste goods is a proof of personal success and of the success of the society to which they belong. The consequences of self-adornment or amusement becoming ends in themselves can be measured in the fortunes devoted to these activities by the vast majority in Western countries and, by increasing numbers in Muslim countries. But the real cost of so defying the realities of human accountability under God's law, is the loss of the soul of each individual who hurries fretfully from one escapism to another, seeking to be always excited or distracted and, whenever he catches himself alone, feeling profoundly empty and wretched.

Adab al-Islam are designed to avoid such ungrateful waste of human potential, and encourage man to exercise that potential in full conformity with the true purposes and realities of his life. The rules of conduct for a Muslim life contain sound wisdom, whether viewed in religious, cultural, social, economic, psychological or even medical terms. It follows that, for a healthy, balanced life, individual and community should apply these rules comprehensively and conscientiously. Wherever they are applied, two things must always be borne in mind, namely kindness and consideration. Among the root meanings of 'Islam' (besides surrender or submission) is peace; a 'Muslim' is one who has submitted to the decrees of God, who has sought to make peace with God and His creatures. Moreover, the Prophet defines a 'Muslim' as one who does not harm others by hand or tongue.

***Kindness and Gentleness:*** According to a saying of the Prophet, kindness is required in every instance of Muslim conduct. One of the main ends of adab al-Islam is to train people to be kind and gentle in every matter and toward every thing. The following examples will illustrate:

1. Speaking should be loud enough to be audible to those addressed, never louder.
2. Bad or objectionable language should be avoided.
3. Laughter should not be characterized by loud or unpleasant sounds.
4. Weeping should be restrained and polite, not hysterically loud or abandoned.
5. Eating and drinking should be done at a gentle, dignified pace.
6. It is proper for a Muslim to restrain his anger, keeping himself within the bounds of courtesy.

7. Parents should give their children beautiful, meaningful names, and avoid names indicating difficulty and sadness.
8. Tenderness should be a most essential element in the love-making process.
9. Smiling at other people when meeting them is recommended.
10. Looking pleasantly at others while conversing with them is required as polite conduct.
11. It is necessary that a Muslim be gentle when criticizing others for something they might have done.

***Consideration for Others:*** Inflicting any kind of harm or offence physically, psychologically or morally must be avoided. In the Words of the Prophet, 'There should be neither harming nor reciprocating harm.' Anything done or said with disregard for others is not considered proper Muslim conduct. In fact, good behaviour in Islam depends to a large extent on showing consideration toward others. The contribution of adab al-Islam in this regard is enormous. Just a few examples will illustrate:

1. Disgracing or reviling others' beliefs, directly or indirectly, is forbidden.
2. The main principle governing one's behaviour on the road is to avoid harming, impeding or disturbing others, including such acts as spitting or making loud noises.
3. Reviling another or speaking of his mistakes is disapproved, even if a Muslim is reviled by him and even though his faults are spoken of by him.
4. Making jokes, using impolite or sarcastic terms at the expense of others, is prohibited. Character assassination through insinuation, backbiting and undesirable conjecture is also prohibited.
5. Distasteful expressions should be avoided while eating, as they might disturb or upset others.
6. In a group of three people, two should not talk privately as this might offend the third.
7. Reviling the dead is forbidden as this causes hurt to their living relatives.

8. In socializing with others, their comfort and well-being must be positively considered. For instance, neither a person's clothes nor mouth should smell badly; after eating onions or garlic, it is preferable that socializing is avoided.
9. To squeeze between two men in a mosque or to step on others while proceeding to a place, is forbidden, as this will annoy them.
10. To relieve oneself in still water, in the shade, on the road or in any public place, is forbidden, as this might prevent others from making normal use of such facilities and/or be a health hazard.
11. When shoes are taken off, they should be put in a place where they will not disturb others by their smell.
12. When sneezing, the mouth and nose should be covered; when yawning, the hand should cover the mouth; when speaking, one should not speak loudly, as this might annoy others. Even the sitting posture should be such as will not offend others, as does, for example, turning one's back to them.

***Role of Adab al-Islam:*** Among the main aims of adab al-Islam is to help in establishing and maintaining healthy social relationships. As will be seen, among the necessary attributes of the ideal Muslim personality, are honesty, respect for others, honouring one's word, restraint of anger, patience, modesty, kindness, etc. These virtues eliminate mistrust and create trust, the necessary foundation upon which alone sound relations can be built and developed.

In the Islamic view it is not enough simply to avoid doing harm to others, nor even to wish for others what you wish for yourself. What is required of Muslims toward each other is mutual responsibility and positive assistance.

As will be seen, formality in the manners of Islam is reduced to the barest possible minimum. This enables freer social intercourse, makes the social machinery run more smoothly and facilitates meetings and visits, for isolation is not recommended in Islam. Muslims are encouraged to meet each other, for that strengthens social bonds and defends the individual against the psychological consequences of social isolation. Moreover, Muslims are encouraged to meet frequently. It is the duty of the host to be hospitable and generous to his guest. Acceptance of an invitation to a meal is recommended and, in the case of an invitation to a wedding meal, acceptance becomes obligatory.

Visiting the sick, taking part in funeral processions, offering condolences to the bereaved, comforting and encouraging them, providing food for them, exchanging gifts with other members of the society, shaking hands when meeting or parting, sharing other happy occasions such as weddings and births, etc., are all ways to strengthen and develop social relations. Particular importance is attached to such exchanges between relatives and neighbours.

Islam has recommended Muslims to hold feasts from time to time and invite others to these occasions. It has also prescribed holding feasts on certain occasions such as weddings, births, the day of Sacrifice, etc. Eating together makes social ties stronger between members of a community irrespective of social status: this is why Islam disapproves of the feast to which the rich are invited and from which the poor are excluded and considers it the worst of feasts.

## SOCIAL RELATIONS

Social relations should be quite free of personal interest, and engaged in wholly for the sake of God. Thus, a Muslim should not accept a gift presented by someone who intends thereby to influence him favourably. Invitations given out of some personal interest, e.g. in the hope of personal popularity or in expectation of some return, should be rejected.

Social life is encouraged at a wider level, namely by meetings of the community as a whole. It is recommended that the five prayers prescribed in Islam be performed in congregation in the mosque. This provides the opportunity for a large number and variety of people to meet more than once each day. There is the weekly gathering on Friday to perform Friday prayer which, with certain exceptions, is obligatory upon every Muslim. Also, there are the two annual occasions to meet on the feast of Fitr (breaking the fast) and the feast of Adha (Sacrifice). Moreover, hundreds of thousands of Muslims from all over the world meet every year, for a few days during the pilgrimage season, in Mecca.

The mosque is an important centre where Muslims may discuss religious, social and political issues related to the community and the nation as a whole. Therefore personal matters (e.g. the announcement of lost articles, or other private business) should not be discussed in the mosque. As it is a place for public meeting it should be kept clean-that is the responsibility of every Muslim. Cleanliness and orderliness of the mosque contribute vitally to the success of social meetings held within it.

Personal cleanliness is an important factor when communicating with others, and Muslims are required to bath frequently and, where possible, use perfume, the more so when public occasions (the Friday congregation, for example, or the two Eid festivals, etc.) arise. Especially stressed are those areas of commonest contact, namely the face and hands, and above all the mouth, which deserves to be kept clean and pleasant-smelling because talking is so vital a factor in communication and contact with others.

## ABSOLUTE ONENESS

Islam is based upon *tauhid*, the absolute Oneness and Uniqueness of God, and rejects all kinds of polytheism whether primitive or evolved. The Shariah is, in fact, the embodiment of this concept, and its every detail springs from it. Adab al-Islam are consistent with tawhid, affirming and serving this most fundamental principle. Here are a few examples:

1. Names that mean being a slave of someone other than God, such as 'Abd al-Nabi (the slave of the Prophet), are forbidden.
2. Reviling natural phenomena, such as wind or rain, which are under God's command, is forbidden. So too is reviling one's fate, or the attribution of injustice to God.
3. Expressions or exclamations that contradict tawhid, that seem to ascribe partners to God, for example, 'What God wills and what so-and-so wills!' or 'I have no help except from God and you!', are strictly forbidden.

4. Slaughtering animals must be done only for the sake of God; if His name is not taken deliberately, or if some other name is taken instead, the meat of the animal becomes *Haram*, forbidden, the sacrifice void.
5. On the occasion of someone's death, expressions that contradict Islamic faith, such as, 'What will become of me now that our source of independence is gone' or 'He died a premature death', are forbidden.
6. Swearing by people or things other than God, His Names or Attributes, is forbidden.
7. A vow pledged for anything or anyone other than God, is null and void and should not be fulfilled.
8. A Muslim is required not to make absolute assertions without referring to God's will, and to say instead *Insha Allah* (If God wills).
9. To bow in respect to any person in not permitted, as bowing is reserved only for God in the act of prayer.
10. To refrain from travelling because some sort of supposed omen against it has been sighted, is forbidden, because this contradicts the principle of belief in destiny.
11. The purpose of visiting the cemetery, which is recommended in Islam, is to remind the living of death, thus influencing them to better their obedience to God and improve their conduct and behaviour in relation to others.
12. The Kaaba is the first house of God on earth. It was built by the Prophet Ibrahim and his son Ismail at Mecca in Arabia. Every Muslim faces the Qiblah in prayer the world over: it is a symbol of Muslim unity and of the unity of Islam. But it orients more than the Muslim's prayer. When animals are slaughtered they are made to face in the direction of the Qiblah; deceased Muslims are placed in the grave with their face towards the Qiblah. Even the design of the lavatory is connected with the Qiblah in that when relieving himself, a Muslim should avoid facing or turning his back to the Qiblah.

The contribution of Islamic manners to the unity and solidarity of Muslims will be discussed in greater detail in subsequent pages. Adherence to the manners of normative Islam will result in the eradication of many bidah that have penetrated into Muslim life. Bidah can be defined as an innovated belief or practice added to the original and authentic Islamic belief or practice.

It has been rejected by the Prophet saying, 'He who innovates something in this matter of ours that is not of it will have it rejected.' And also, '... Beware of matters newly introduced (in religion), for every innovation is an error and every error will lead to Hell-fire.'

Anything added and introduced into Islam is considered as bidah and is therefore rejected. The effect of innovations upon the various aspects of Islamic life is tremendously negative. They transform Islam from being a simple religion to one complicated and difficult to practise, which will lead gradually to the abandonment of at least certain aspects of Muslim life. Bidah should not be confused with Ijtihad which is the use of individual reasoning to draw conclusions from the Quran or the Sunnah in conformity with the general principles of Islam, and exercised only by qualified scholars.

As mentioned above, many non-Islamic elements have been introduced into the behaviour and manners of Muslims. Here are some examples:

1. Certain religious occasions have been introduced into Islam, such as those of the Prophet's birthday (Maulid), his Ascension (Miraj), and his Emigration (Hijrah).
2. Mentioning God's name audibly and reading the Quran aloud during a funeral procession.
3. Shaking hands following every congregational prayer.
4. The practice that after a certain number of days a bereaved family should prepare food and serve others. The correct Islamic conduct is for friends and relatives to prepare food for the bereaved since they are over whelmed by sorrow.
5. The practice of plastering and ornamenting graves.

***Psychological Aspect:*** One of the striking characteristics of adab al-Islam is that psychological factors are fully taken into consideration. A few examples are:

1. Divorce is highly discouraged during the woman's monthly period, as she is usually passing through a period of psychological tension.
2. Apart from the benefits of hygiene, cleanliness is prescribed in Islam because it refreshes and re-orientates body and mind. This is true in the case of performing ablution before prayer and washing the whole body after sexual intercourse and at the end of childbirth and menstruation. Those who have washed the body of a deceased person are recommended to bathe afterwards. The significance of this advice is that taking a bath in such situations helps to rid people of the psychological effects of those situations.

***Medical and Hygienic Aspects:*** Islam teaches Muslims to be always clean and pure. The daily manners of cleanliness and purity of body, place, clothes, etc., contribute enormously to the soundness of bodily health, as reliable medical evidence confirms, for cleanliness prevents the transmission of microbial diseases. 'Wudu' (the ablution) demanded of Muslims several times every day, as a necessary condition before prayer, requires washing those parts of the body that are generally exposed to dirt and dust.

Paring the nails (ordered by Islam) is to prevent the accumulation of dirt and impurities on fingers which are in constant use for eating and drinking, as well as shaking hands.

Cleaning the axillary and pubic regions from growing hair is also prescribed by Islam. It helps to keep the sweat glands functioning well and prevents the multiplication of the bacteria that would otherwise affect those sweat glands.

Among the impurities from which a Muslim should keep away and purify himself, his clothes, etc. are faeces and urine. The urine contains urea and other nitrogenous compounds which disintegrate into ammonia through the effect of bacteria, giving rise to unpleasant odour. Pinworms (oxyuriasis), viral hepatitis, ascariasis and taeniasisi are among the diseases transmitted mainly through swallowing the infective stage present in faeces.

The fact that the Muslim should not overeat, but should rather stop before his stomach is full, has medical as well as social and moral benefits. The stomach contains stretch receptors; when distended it can give rise to pain and discomfort, as well as more disabling ailments.

When drinking, the Muslim is advised not to breathe into the vessel, for carbon dioxide is present in the expired air in a higher percentage than in the inspired air, and high concentrations of carbon dioxide in the circulation negatively influence several physiological functions.

After drinking milk, the Muslim owes special thanks to God, for the benefit contained in it. Milk is considered adequate nourishment, a complete diet. It contains all the essential nutritional components: carbohydrates, fats, and proteins, in addition to many vitamins and minerals, mainly vitamin D, calcium, phosphate, deficiencies of which cause rickets, in children and osteomalacia in adults.

Slaughtering according to Islamic law provides meat that is clean of blood. Blood is known to be a good breeding ground for micro-organisms which can be the source of many diseases. Besides the health aspect, there is the cultural fact that many people feel disgusted, even ill, when they see meat with blood clotted or oozing amidst the meat fibres. Eating or drinking blood is forbidden in Islam.

Pork is also forbidden in Islam. Pigs are not selective about what they eat and can be fed on garbage, on food remnants. On this subject, Sake has observed: 'There are a good number of germs, parasites and bacteria that infest swine and live in its flesh which, when it is eaten, transmit diseases to man. Among these parasites are tapeworms, round worms, hook worms, fasciolopsis buski, paragonimus, clonorchis senesis and erysipelothrix rhnsiphathiac.' He goes on: 'In short, the pig, the supreme germ carrier, is the cause of many serious and fatal diseases, among them dysentery trichinosis, tape worm, round worm, hook worm, jaundice, pneumonia, suffocation, intestinal obstruction, acute pancreatitis, enlargement of the liver, diarrhea, emaciation, high fever, hindering the growth development in children, typhoid, lameness, heart trouble, abortion, sterility and sudden death.'

Drinking alcohol is prohibited by Islam. Although it has some beneficial effects, it leads to addiction with all its moral and physiological problems. Further, ingestion of large amounts causes irritation of the stomach and peptic ulcer formation. It also affects the liver and causes its inflammation, cirrhosis and ultimately liver failure.

The Muslim is required not to restrain a sneeze, rather to thank God for this blessing. Sneezing results from irritation of the mucous membrane of the upper respiratory tract and it leads to the expulsion of the irritating substance. Prevention of sneezing will retain the irritant which may then cause inflammation where it lodges. Covering the mouth when sneezing is recommended in order to prevent the transmission to other persons of bacteria which may be present in the upper respiratory tract of some individuals.

Circumcision, required of every male Muslim, has been increasingly carried out in some parts of the Western world on medical grounds. The prepuce (a quite redundant piece of skin), if not cut off, can accumulate dirt and organisms which encourage the growth of bacteria. This may be one of the factors causing cancerous changes in the female genital tract.

Sexual intercourse during menses, which is completely forbidden in Islam, is harmful for two reasons:

1. The cervix is opened during menses, and intercourse will facilitate the entry of bacteria into the uterus and the fallopian tubes leading to inflammation and formation of adhesions which can cause sterility.
2. The negative psychological effect on the man when he discovers blood on his sexual organ. This may create a sensation of disgust such as to inhibit proper sexual relations with his wife.

The wisdom behind the prohibition of anal intercourse is that it is a painful process and it stimulates the defecation reflex. In addition, the male sexual organ may be soiled with some faeces which may contain pathogenic micro-organisms, in turn causing urinary tract infection in the male.

During the menstrual period the female sexual hormones are disturbed, leading to psychological upset, mainly in the form of nervous tension and depression, and this may explain the changes observed in the behaviour of women during the menstrual period. It partly explains the wisdom of the exemption of women from prayer and fasting.

The fact that, according to Islamic injunctions, the corpse must be buried without delay, shows proper understanding of the dangers of putrefaction: dangers much greater in hot climates where no cooling facilities are available.

The wisdom behind forbidding Muslims to own dogs, except watch and hunt dogs whose place must be outside the house, is clearly seen in the fact that the saliva of dogs contain rabies virus which can be transmitted to man by biting or by contact with the dog's saliva through any cut in the skin. Echinococcus worm is found in the intestine of dogs; transmitted to man through food contaminated with dogs' excreta, it can lead to the formation of cysts primarily in the liver and lungs.

The observance of adab al-Islam is also essential to a healthy economy; extravagance is forbidden, thriftiness encouraged, even required. Money plays an important role in the life of a nation, both in times of peace and of war. As a store of value it serves as a reserve of ready purchasing power and medium of exchange. Money power is essential for the nation as a whole. The private individual is not absolutely free to spend any amount of money in any way he likes, as this leads to the destruction of this national power. Adab al-Islam give Muslims a religious motive for saving. In other words, it is the religious duty of every Muslim to abstain from extravagance, for Allah says in the Quran: 'Lo! the squanderers were ever brothers of the devil, and the devil was ever an ingrate to his Lord.'

Here are different aspects of Islamic life which demonstrate the importance that Islam attaches to a healthy economy:

1. Moderation in eating and drinking is required. No food, however little, should be wasted. Forbidding wastefulness saves a large amount of the national wealth, and directs it to more useful investments.
2. Moderation in dress is required. Clothes should not become an end in themselves, and spending large sums of money on clothes should be avoided.
3. Furniture and other household items should be of moderate price. Silver or gold should not be used in

domestic furniture or for utensils, or in any other items. Also silk or silk brocade should not be used in furniture or in men's clothes.

4. Large sums of money should not be spent on building lavish houses. Even extravagance in mosque buildings is forbidden. Ornamentation in both cases should also be avoided.
5. In Islam, the ideal wedding is that which involves the least expense and avoids the unnecessary things.
6. Funerals should also be inexpensive. Extravagance is forbidden. Coffins should not be used, unless to comply with special regulations or for health reasons.
7. Though generosity and hospitality toward guests is highly recommended in Islam, extravagance is forbidden.
8. Suspending work on Friday is not specifically prescribed in Islam except for about an hour to say the Friday prayers. Useful work should be continued, for to stop working for even a day may cause a loss to the national economy as a whole. Abandoning work on Friday is not encouraged, for the concept of the Sabbath does not exist in Islam. However, if Muslims have to have a day off, it should be Friday and not Saturday or Sunday.
9. Skill and thoroughness in every task entrusted to a Muslim is considered as his duty in Islam: according to the Hadith, 'Verily Allah has prescribed proficiency in all things.' A successful economy is obvious when industry and quality combine.

## DOMESTIC ASPECTS

The family 'provides the environment within which human values and morals develop and grow in the new generation; these values and morals cannot exist apart from the family unit. The family system and the relationship between the sexes determines the whole character of a society and whether it is backward or civilised.'

Because marriage and family are so important, it is not surprising that so large a number of Quranic verses and Prophetic Traditions are devoted to these two areas; these sources provide the basis and the details necessary for successful marriage and a morally sound, stable society.

1. A Muslim is recommended to marry at an early age. Marriage enlarges the circle of relatives by adding new ones through the marriage tie. Breast-feeding by foster nurses is permitted in Islam for it too enlarges the circle of the family with new-found relatives, called 'relatives in breast-feeding'.
2. Muslims are encouraged to make marriage an easy task. According to the Islamic view, the most blessed marriage is that which involves the least burden upon the bride and bridegroom.
3. Celebrating marriage has been made commendatory in Islam, for marriage is a social event.
4. Although singing is generally forbidden in Islam, it is allowed on the occasion of marriage.
5. Holding a wedding feast is recommended and rejection of the invitation, when it is possible to accept, is not allowed on this very special occasion.

Islam is concerned that marriages should succeed. They cannot do so unless properly founded. The conditions and recommendations for success are:

1. Full mutual agreement by the man and the woman to marry one another.
2. Common ground and understanding between the man and the woman are obviously necessary. A common conception of life, way of living and common ways of overcoming disagreements is needed, and all these are provided by the Islamic faith and Shariah. Therefore, the ideal husband and wife are those who adhere most to Islam
3. As preparatory steps towards marriage, Islam recommends that the man and the woman should have sufficient information about each other's knowledge and practice of Islam and that they should also see each other.
4. There is no room for any intent on either side to have a temporary marriage. Islam recognizes only the intention to have a lasting marriage.

5. To fulfil all the conditions in any marriage contract is considered by Islam as among the best of deeds and the highest of moral virtues. According to the Prophet: 'The most worthy conditions to be fulfilled by Muslims are those included in a marriage contract.'
6. Husband and wife are advised, in case of disagreements, to try to solve their problems without the interference of anyone else.
7. The husband-wife relationship if it is to succeed must be based upon mutual respect, understanding, cooperation, love and mercy.

A study of adab al-Islam shows the importance of marriage in Islam. The special relationship of husband and wife is recognized in adab al-Islam in the following ways:

1. Men are not allowed to wash the bodies of dead women, nor vice versa unless they are married to one another. In the case of a deceased wife the husband has the right to place her body in the grave.
2. Men and women are not allowed to see each other's private parts-even though they are related to each other by blood as brother and sister, or mother and children-except in the case of husband and wife.
3. Women are forbidden to mourn a deceased relative including even a brother or father for a period exceeding three days; but a widow may mourn for her dead husband for a period of four months and ten days.

The parent-child relationship also has an important place in the manners of Islam. According to the Prophet of Islam, Paradise lies at the feet of mothers. If good manners toward others are a form of politeness, they are an obligatory religious duty in the case of parents.

Strong kinship, affection, responsibility should not be confined to children and parents, but extended to all relatives. There is, first, the moral responsibility to visit relatives from time to time, to ensure that they do not feel neglected and ignored. Second, there is the financial responsibility upon those more able to assist their needy relatives. If a Muslim dies in debt, his relatives are recommended to discharge the debt as soon as they can. Allowing breast-feeding by a woman other than the mother, as mentioned earlier, enlarges the circle of relatives, and must be recognized and welcomed in mutual responsibility. Family feeling and responsibility are so stressed in adab al-Islam because the family is the formative ground of the whole range of human sentiments, and therefore the best foundation for a healthy, stable society is a healthy, stable family life.

***Norms of Sexual Behaviour:*** Islam recognizes sex as a portion of nature created by God, and nothing created by Him is evil or wrong if used and practised according to His commands.

There is no doubt that sex is necessary for the development of the individual's personality, and for the society as a whole. Sexual development is intimately connected with feelings of personal worth and the assurance of being loved. Sexual deprivation endangers mental health, hinders good relationships and creates inefficiency in the society. But sex can be a destructive force if not controlled and channelled through marriage. It will then be a force working against the individual, the institution of marriage and family, and the society as a whole. In fact, 'sex is capable of impelling individuals, reckless of the consequences while under its spell, towards behaviour which may imperil or disrupt the cooperative relationships upon which social life depends'.

Sexual behaviour, therefore, must be controlled. This, however, seems difficult, and may indeed be impossible in any society without the assistance of other elements and factors that help the individual to keep sexual desires in check. Islam provides a solution to this problem through the observance of the following rules of conduct:

1. Marriage should be made easy for every member of the society and opportunities for early marriage enhanced.
2. All factors and conditions that incite the individual to indulge his sexual desires outside marriage should be blocked.

   Adab al-Islam are vital here:

   (a) The body of the woman is of such a nature that it causes sexual excitement among men. Because this is so and not the other way about, Islam has forbidden all forms of nudity and exploitation of the female form. It prescribes a form of dress designed to cover the whole body except face and hands so as to protect the woman from the gaze of men and to protect men from exposure to her charms. There is no doubt that clothes convey inter-personal attitudes among which is that of sexuality.

(b) The separation of the sexes is necessary in Islam. This helps to ease sexual tension.

(c) A Muslim woman should not adorn her face with cosmetics nor use perfume outside the home. Such actions should be confined to her home and for her husband.

(d) Women are not allowed to bathe in a public bath used by men.

(e) When a woman speaks to a man other than her husband or relatives whom she is forbidden to marry (mahram), her speech should not be inviting, but should remain objective and crisp.

(f) Showing decorous shyness is also required of men, both in dress and personal conduct. If, by chance, a Muslim's gaze falls upon a woman, he should turn away his eyes: a second look is forbidden.

(g) Privacy in sexual relations is of the utmost importance in the Islamic view. Husband and wife are a mercy to each other, a garment and veil. It is forbidden for either husband or wife to discuss their sexual relations with others.

All the rules given above and others concerning sexual conduct are intended to enable men and women to benefit from the blessings of sex within marriage, and to enable the society to benefit from the blessings of marriage and secure family relations.

## FEMALES' STATUS

When Europe was plunged into its Dark Ages and debated on the nature of woman's soul, on whether or not it was human,

Islam had already declared men and women to be of the same origin and nature, equal before God and society, and promised like rewards or punishments for their good or evil deeds.

Islamic law is just and fair for both women and men. A woman in Islam has the right to hold property, and to manage her estates. She has the right to lease, or bequeath, or exploit property for her own benefit. Although a woman's main domain is the house, she is not excluded from making financial transactions such as selling and buying, lending and borrowing, investments, etc. In the different schools of law, women are judged legally competent and fully entitled to carry out any of these transactions.

There is no-difference between men and women concerning the penalties accorded under Islamic law whether for drinking alcohol, committing adultery, apostasy or murder.

Women in Islam enjoy the right to express their views freely, and to reject marriage proposals. The contemporary position of Muslim women in some parts of the Islamic world should not be adduced as evidence or argument against the concept and position of women in Islam. The following adab should remove any misunderstanding on this point:

1. The news of the birth of a girl should be welcomed exactly as the news of the birth of a boy is usually welcomed. It is against the teaching of Islam to convey congratulations on the birth of a boy, but to refrain from doing so on the birth of a girl. Islam stresses the importance of taking special care of daughters.
2. The Prophet exhorts men to treat women respectfully and gently, not to look down upon them as inferior, but to regard them as equals.
3. Women should be consulted in matters concerning them. The fact that in Islamic marriage there must be a guardian does not mean that he has the right to make the marriage decision. The woman alone has that right, to accept or refuse marriage, free from any pressure. If a girl is betrothed to someone without her consent, she then has the right to approve or disapprove the betrothal.
4. The woman in the role of mother is deeply honoured: we have noted above the Prophet's saying, 'Paradise lies

at the feet of mothers.' The one most deserving of loving care by a Muslim is his mother, who commands greater respect than even his father.

5. A married woman may retain her own family name and not necessarily relinquish it in favour of her husband's. This is a mark of respect.
6. Certain manners have been prescribed by Islam in order to protect sexual identity: viz. imitation by men of women in dress, gait, etc. or vice versa, is forbidden.
7. Safeguarding a woman's personality is required in Islam as long as her deeds are not contrary to Islamic teachings. A husband is not allowed to destroy his wife's personality and make it conform to his own.
8. A woman, during her monthly period, may be treated more gently and kindly. A menstruating woman is not considered dirty or sinful as is the case in some other religions and cultures.
9. It is the right of a woman to have sexual intercourse with her husband from time to time. If the husband had never been able to make love to her, then it is her right to have a divorce.
10. A good wife is considered by Islam to be the best asset in the world. She has an extremely important role in married life-she has responsibility for running the household and the regulation of its economy.
11. Islam requires that Muslim women maintain their cultural identity and do not imitate the manners of non-Muslim women in dress, shoes, etc. Such imitation is a clear indication of weakness.
12. In Islam, a woman's dress has to serve certain purposes among which is the protection of her honour and integrity. The difference between men's and women's dress is due to the difference between the male and female forms and the sexual effect of that difference. For the same reason, a woman may not undertake a journey unless accompanied by her husband or a mahram (a consanguine relative whom the law forbids her to marry).

## INDIVIDUAL TRAINING

Islamic manners train and educate the individual to control his passions and to respond to the voice of reason. They also educate him to exhibit qualities of patience, of being content and of self-dependence, that is, not seeking the help of others unless unavoidable. One of the most praised virtues in Islam is the ability to control one's anger and not react violently. In the words of the Prophet, a powerful human being is one who controls himself when he is angry.

Punctuality and self-discipline are also valued as most important characteristics of a good Muslim. The five daily prayers teach punctuality, and the month of fasting teaches sustained self-control.

The fruits of discipline are (a) moderation and (b) wise use of time. Moderation is one of the main aims of adab al-Islam, for it creates a life of balance and equilibrium, which is necessary if a man is to be of service to others (for how can anyone given to exaggeration or affectation ever be sufficiently free of himself to help others disinterestedly) and if he is to serve God in all that He commands? Time is a human measure of the value of the life God has given: one of the most crucial questions that every man will be asked on the Day of Resurrection is what use he made of his time. Therefore, it is the responsibility of every Muslim to make the best use of every minute, to weigh every grain, for his own interest and for the interest of the nation as a whole.

Adab al-Islam are prescribed so as to be in full conformity with the above-mentioned principle. The following clarify this point:

1. Muslim daily life begins at dawn before sunrise, and ends early just after Salat al-isha (the night prayer) that is, about one and a half hours after sunset.
2. Socializing for the sake of passing the time is disapproved. Although it is recommended that Muslims meet one another frequently, they should make use of these meetings to discuss useful matters.
3. Spending an unnecessarily long time eating should be avoided.

4. Moderation in speaking is required. Speaking at length or just for the sake of it is a bad habit and considered a waste of time: silence is preferable.

***Concern About Human Safety:*** It is notable that Islam concerns itself with the safety of individuals. Below are some familiar adab, but any conduct that assists in achieving this purpose and does not contradict the principles of Islam is considered as part of adab al-Islam. The following are recommended:

1. Before going to bed, one should make sure that doors are properly closed, food pots and drinking vessels covered, and all sources of fire extinguished or turned off.
2. Sleeping on the roof of a house where there is no protecting wall or in a lonely place with nobody else around in case of emergency, should be avoided. Also, mattress and pillow should be examined to ensure that no harmful insects have hidden under or inside them.
3. Before drinking from any vessel, one should check that nothing harmful has fallen into it.
4. Travelling should, as far as possible, be undertaken in company and not alone. No vehicle should be so parked as to obstruct, hinder or endanger others.
5. Before putting on shoes, they should be checked to ensure that no harmful insect has hidden in them during the night or while they have been in disuse.
6. Certain animals, considered pests, are harmful to man, and for that reason should be killed: examples are scorpions, mice and snakes.

## PRESERVATION OF UNITY

One of the great achievements of adab al-Islam has been their contribution to the unity of Muslim peoples who belong to different races, speak different languages, and inhabit different parts of the globe. The religious character of Islamic manners, derived from the Quran and the Sunnah, plays an important role in this respect. Thus a Moroccan who travels to Pakistan will not find it difficult to understand the manners of the people there, nor feel out of place. Muslim women from Egypt will not be astonished by the sight of Turkish women wearing Islamic dress. Members of the Islamic society reassert their solidarity on each occasion of each day that they adhere to the ways of doing things which constitute their very tradition. Adab al-Islam create common understanding among Muslims-they form a universal culture which gives shape and meaning to local cultures throughout the world. The local culture may well differ from one Islamic community to another. By contrast, the system of prayers, greetings, major festivals, dietary restrictions (e.g. on alcohol), the practice of Haram and halal, are elements of the universal Islamic pattern. Conspicuous too is the fact that everywhere Muslim women dress modestly and in most Muslim countries wear the proper Islamic dress. The local variations (e.g. in national dishes, such as biryani, popular in the Indian subcontinent, or in dress, such as the sari as worn by Muslims in India) are important in that they distinguish one group of Muslims from another-we are created in different nations, the Quran tells us, that we may know one from another-but they are completely insignificant in the sense that they do not diminish the Muslim character and Muslim identity of the particular group.

An important rule of adab al-Islam is the prohibition against imitating the manners of non-Muslim peoples. This should not be confused with seeking knowledge, in crafts, technology, science, etc. which has always been encouraged by Islam. Manners play a vital part in the maintenance of cultural identity. It is obvious that manners embodying a Muslim life should be distinguished from others by their own Islamic character.

Any intrusions of non-Muslim cultures into Muslim life do not mean that Islamic identity is being erased. This is because the Islamic way of life is so deeply ingrained that a Muslim cannot easily rid himself of it and it is so deeply ingrained because it is not a temporary improvisation of forms in response to a particular period of history but a stable structure of interrelated manners and ideals that conform to the unchanging realities of human relations between man and man, and between man and God. Let whoever doubts this consider the different states of Christianity and Islam in the Soviet Union, hated and suppressed alike by the ideology of Russian communism. No;

despite the economic and political disunity that prevails on the surface, the cultural strength and unity of Islam is still a reality throughout the Muslim world.

***Manners and Customs of Non-muslims:*** The tolerance shown by Muslims toward non-Muslims living in Muslim lands is without parallel. Islam affords protection to the religion and culture of every community within the Islamic state. Any conversion to Islam must be through free choice and conviction.

The life, property and honour of every non-Muslim individual is fully protected by Islam. Moreover, Islam has guaranteed full religious autonomy and limited judicial authority to its non-Muslim citizens. Non-Muslims have the following rights:

1. Full freedom of belief and worship, and independent religious and educational institutions.
2. Full autonomy concerning personal and family law including the rules of marriage and divorce though opposed to Islamic rules.
3. In financial, transactional and civil affairs, treatment equal to that of Muslim citizens, except in certain cases, e.g. drinking alcohol, for which they may not be punished, provided it is not done in public.
4. In social customs, non-Muslims are free to preserve their distinct character as expressed, for example, in modes of dress (as long as they do not contradict Islamic law), eating and diet.

The refusal of Islam to impose its own adab on non-Muslims has helped to avoid communal frictions and religious strife; European rule, by contrast, has exploited and exacerbated community differences for the sake of political or military advantage.

There are some restrictions upon Muslims concerning their social relations with non-Muslims. These restrictions are self-explanatory the religious occasions of non-Muslims are not part of a Muslim's faith, though it is a part of his Islam to tolerate them; it follows that he should not participate in them. Far from indicating fanaticism or intolerance these restrictions express a balance between tolerance, even respect, and the need to preserve the distinctness and stability of Muslim belief, practice and adab. The tolerance of Islam is particularly striking when compared to the intolerances inflicted upon Muslims in non-Muslim lands or under non-Muslim authority. For example, in the sixteenth century, following the collapse of Muslim rule, the Christian courts of the Inquisition burnt to death all Muslims who refused to abandon their faith and convert to Christianity. Muslims were forced to change their names, dress and customs and to behave according to Christian manners.

A further example from history is the case of the Jews who, in various parts of Christian Europe, were forced to change their clothes, names and customs to conform to Christian tradition, but who, in the Muslim world, were treated with a unique tolerance. They were allowed to practise and maintain their religious rituals and customs according to their own traditions. The golden age of Jewish literature took place during Muslim rule in Spain. When the Muslims left Spain, the Jews left with them.

The evidence of this difference in treatment is still to be found today. The Jews who have lived in the Muslim world, whether they are still living there or have migrated to Israel, have Jewish names, while those who lived or are still living in the Western world have Russian, English, German or French names.

## PRINCIPAL CODES OF CONDUCT

The Islamic day has a character perhaps surprisingly different from the day as it looks and is experienced in non-Islamic countries. It begins very early (i.e. after the Fajr prayer) and also ends very early (i.e. after the 'Isha' prayer). As the Islamic calendar is lunar, dates are determined according to the moon, not the sun, with the months moving round from year to year. Time is precious for the Muslim, and he must apportion each day wisely.

Quotidian problems and difficulties are put aside to observe the prayers at the five prescribed times and observing them mitigates the intensity of these problems, setting them into proper perspective. But since that perspective is Islam it applies throughout the day. For, unlike other religions, Islam influences a Muslim's conduct from the moment he rises until the moment he retires for the night. These influences of course vary in degree, the variations broadly classifiable into five categories:

1. What is permitted most actions fall into this category.
2. What is recommended.
3. What is disapproved or abhorred.
4. What is obligatory.
5. What is forbidden.

It is interesting to note that only a very small percentage of man's actions fall into the categories of obligatory and forbidden. The dividing lines between these five categories are flexible. What is forbidden under one set of conditions may become, under another, an exceptional set of conditions, permissible or even obligatory. For instance, Muslims are forbidden to eat pork. But if a Muslim finds himself faced with starvation and all that is available for him to eat is pork, then, to save his life, he is allowed to eat it.

The general rules that govern Muslim conduct have not simply been arbitrarily dictated; they are derived from the Quran and the Sunnah of the Prophet; both are divinely inspired and intended as a mercy to mankind. No Muslim may be taken to task if he commits a breach of Islamic tenets or laws, if there was an unavoidable and compelling reason resulting either from his own condition or from external compulsion.

Although practising Islam is not absolutely obligatory until the individual has passed the age of puberty, it is nevertheless recommended that children grow up in an Islamic atmosphere, thus facilitating their practise later. The principal characteristics and rules of Islamic manners for various aspects of life can be summarized as follows:

1. In almost everything, deliberation (and not haste) is required. A Muslim should consider how a matter may turn out; then, if the outcome appears worthwhile and good, he should carry on, otherwise he should refrain.
2. Kindness and gentleness in a Muslim's dealings with others are essential.
3. Cleanliness and purity of body, place, clothes, etc., should be one of the most conspicuous characteristics of Muslim life.

4. Beauty, elegance, orderliness are values for the Muslim to observe, and whenever possible to attain.
5. According to Islam, a good deed done with courtesy beautifies that deed; impudence, on the other hand, destroys the good in it.
6. All a Muslim's deeds should express an attitude of humility and not arrogance.
7. A Muslim is commanded to avoid any act that might harm himself or some other person, physically, mentally or morally.
8. In the daily life of a Muslim, silence is preferred to unnecessary speaking.
9. A Muslim should treat others as he would wish them to treat him. Like for others what he would like for himself. Good manners without consideration for others are an impossibility.
10. A Muslim should never order or ask anyone to do something that he would not do himself.
11. Favouring the right side or hand in things such as giving, taking, shaking hands, eating, drinking, walking, etc., and using the left hand for such things as cleaning oneself in the toilet, is recommended.
12. Eating, drinking and clothing oneself, etc., well, are allowed as long as the motive is not pride or arrogance. Life characterized by extravagance is abhorred.
13. Though extravagance is abhorred, this does not imply that a Muslim should not have money or not enjoy life. The effects of God's blessings upon him should be visible to others.
14. Being generous and not mean or avaricious is a virtue.
15. Gratitude to God should characterize a Muslim's life, whether He blesses or burdens him, and gratitude with patience and fortitude.
16. A Muslim must be always faithful.
17. In all aspects of life a Muslim must exercise moderation and be natural; unnaturalness and exaggeration are disapproved.

18. A Muslim should be self-sufficient and should seek the help of other Muslims only when it is urgent and necessary.
19. Copying or imitating other cultures and religions in any way is forbidden.
20. Obedience and carrying out another's orders or wishes may not contradict the teachings of Islam; if it does, the teachings of Islam must be given priority.
21. Maintaining sexual identity is most important. Imitation of men by women, or of women by men, in dress, manner of walking, etc. is forbidden.
22. One of the most pervasive characteristics of Islamic manners is discipline, leading to balance and harmony in the life of the individual and the community.
23. Flexibility and tolerance are also characteristics of adab al-Islam. Broadly speaking, any particular conduct is tolerated or accepted if it is civilized (i.e. considerate of others) and respectable (i.e. inoffensive to the individual and community) and provided it does not fall into the categories of the abhorred or forbidden.

**2**

# Routine Etiquettes

Islam, etiquettes cover all the following:

• *Purity and Neatness* • *Maintenance of Health* • *Dress* • *Eating and Drinking* • *Going to Bed and getting up* • *Walking* • *Travelling* • *Mourning and Grief* • *Fear and Panic* • *Rejoicing*

*Hadrat Jabir [R.A.A.] stated: "One day the Holy Prophet [S.A.W.] visited our home to see us. He [S.A.W.] beheld a man who had dishevelled his hair and was covered all over with dust. The Holy Prophet [S.A.W.] observed: "Has this fellow no comb with which to set his hair." And the Holy Prophet's [S.A. W] gaze fell on another man who was wearing very soiled garments. The Holy Prophet [S.A.W.] observed: "Can't this man procure even that thing with which to wash his clothes clean."*

*(Mishkat al-Masabih)*

## THE CLEANLINESS

Allah's favourites are those who make constant efforts to be neat and clean. The Holy Prophet [S.A.W.] has observed: "Purity and neatness are half of faith." In other words, Faith partly consists in cleaning one's soul and partly in keeping physically clean and pure.

The purity and neatness of soul implies cleansing the soul of all impurities such as infidelity, polytheism, sin and vice, and embellishing it with righteous beliefs and pure morals. The purity and neatness of the body denotes keeping it clear of all external filth and adorning it with neatness and good manners.

1. On waking up, clean your hand before putting it in a pot of water. You can never tell where your hands lay during sleep.
2. Do not discharge urine on the floor of bathroom/toilet.
3. When passing stool or urine, do not sit facing the direction of Qiblah, nor with your back to Qiblah. Having relieved yourself, use a clod or water to clean the private parts or purify yourself with water only. Do not use the dung, bone or charcoal for cleaning purpose. When the private parts have been cleaned, scrub your hands with soap or earth and wash them.
4. Do not sit down to eat when your bowels are under pressure. Relieve yourself of urine or stool before eating.
5. Use your right hand for eating and drinking. For cleaning the private parts of the body or for cleaning the nose, use your left hand only.
6. Discharge urine on soft ground, so that its drops do not splash around. Always pass the urine in a sitting posture. However, if the condition of the ground or some real hardship prevents from sitting down, you may urinate in a standing posture. Otherwise, in normal circumstances, it is a very dirty habit and should be strictly avoided.
7. Do not sit down to answer the call of nature on the riverside, the quay, on the thoroughfares or in shaded places. Such a practice causes inconvenience to others and is derogatory to rules of propriety and good manners.
8. Put on shoes and cover your head with a cap etc. before going to the lavatory and read the following prayer on your way:

*"Allah! I seek Thy protection against the devils of the masculine as well as the feminine species."*

*(Bukhari, Muslim)*

*On emerging from the lavatory, read this prayer:*

*"I thank Allah who relieved me of the burden and granted me ease."* *(Nasai, Ibn-e-Majah)*

9. Discharge your nose or phlegm with care in a spittoon, or do so in a place out of the sight of people

10. Avoid putting your finger in the nostrils and clearing the wax of your nose too often. Clear the nose and clean it well out of the sight of people, whenever the need arises.
11. Strictly avoid the practice of spitting phlegm into the folds of a handkerchief and rubbing them together. This is a despicable habit and must be avoided except when it cannot be helped.
12. While chewing betel leaf, do not talk in such a manner as to splash saliva on the person you are talking to, thus causing discomfort to him. If you chew tobacco or betel leaf frequently, you should take great care in observing the rules of oral hygiene. Beware also, lest you should talk with your mouth too close to the person addressed.
13. Perform ablution with great care and try to keep in a state of ablution most of the time, if not at all hours. Where water is not available, you may perform Tayammum. Recite:

*'In the name of Allah, the Most Beneficent, the Most Merciful' at the commencement of ablution and say the following prayer in the course of its performance:*

*"I bear witness that there is no god save Allah and He has no partner. And I testify that Muhammad is the servant of Allah and His Messenger. Allah! Join me with those people who repent most and take great care in keeping themselves pure and clean." (Tirmidhi)*

*When the ablution is over, say the following prayer:*

*"Allah! Thou art Pure and Supreme in Thy Praiseworthiness. I testify that there is no deity beside Thee. I seek Thy for giveness and I appeal to Thee." (Nasai)*

The Holy Prophet [S.A.W.] observed:

*The hallmark of my Ummah on the Day of Judgement will be that their foreheads and other parts of the body on which ablution is performed will be radiant with light. Hence whosoever wishes to enhance his light is free to do so." (Bukhari, Muslim)*

14. Brush your teeth with miswak (twig) regularly. The Holy Prophet [S.A.W.] has affirmed:

*"I would have decreed the brushing of teeth with a miswak (twig) during all ablutions but for the inconvenience it would have caused to the Ummah."*

*On one occasion, some people arrived to see the Holy Prophet [S.A.W.]. Their teeth were stained with yellow grease. On observing their teeth the Holy Prophet [S.A.W.] urged them to form the habit of using miswak.*

15. You must bathe at least once a week. Make it a point to bathe on Friday and join the Friday congregation in clean and neat dress. The Holy Prophet [S.A.W.] said:

*"Discharging of trust leads to Paradise." The Companions [R.A.A.] submitted: O Apostle of Allah! What is meant by Trust?"*

The Apostle of Allah observed:

*"Allah has appointed no greater trust than cleansing oneself of impurity by taking bath." Hence a person must take bath when he needs one.*

16. Do not go into or pass through the mosque in a state of impurity. If no alternative is available, perform the Tayammum before entering the mosque or passing through it.
17. Dress your hair with oil and comb. Trim the overgrown. hair of your beard with scissors; apply collyrium to your eyes; clip your nails and keep fingernails clean. Adorn yourself with propriety, simplicity and moderation.
18. Cover your face with a handkerchief on sneezing, so that the excretion is not splashed on anyone else. After sneezing say:

*"Praise be to Allah"!*

*The listener should say:*

*"May Allah show you Mercy"!*

*In response to this, you should recite:*

*"May Allah guide you."*

19. The Holy Prophet [S.A.W.] was very fond of perfume. After finishing the toilet on arising from sleep, the Holy Prophet [S.A.W.] invariably used perfume.

**HYGIENE AND HEALTH**

1. Health is not only a great blessing of Allah but also a valuable trust from the Almighty. Regard your health as of great value and take every care to safeguard it. Health once lost is hard to recover. As the whiteant eats into the books and destroys great libraries, similarly a little negligence or an ordinary sickness ruins the life. To neglect the rules of hygiene and to be indifferent towards proper maintenance of health is callous, even it is an act of ingratitude to the Almighty. The essence of human life is reason, morality, faith and knowledge. It is only the physical health which ensures the proper functioning of human faculties of reason, morality, faith and knowledge. In fact, physical health is the basic factor in the development of mind and the growth of reason. It is also a prerequisite for the performance of sublime acts of morality and the discharge of religious obligations. A weak and sick body has a feeble mind whose faculty of reason cannot but be unsound. When life is devoid of longing and ardour; when there is no courage and the will is weak; when the urges are exhausted-such spiritless existence is a drag on the infirm body. The true believers have to perform lofty deeds in life and discharge heavy responsibilities of state. It is imperative, therefore, that they should have robust physique, sturdy intellect and sound mind, firm will, high morale and a life full of spirit, enthusiasm and sublime passions. Healthy and spirited individuals make dynamic nations and such nations by offering supreme sacrifices in the struggle for existence achieve preeminent position and are a living symbol of the value and dignity of life.
2. You should always be cheerful, glad, alert and active. Made your life well-ordered, elegant, and healthy by means of good living, cheerful manners, joyful smiles and lively disposition. Avoid sorrow, anger, grudge or

anxiety, envy, jealousy, slander, narrowmindedness; don't lose your spirits and keep your mind clear of all complexities. These moral ills have an adverse effect on the digestive system and a defective digestive system is the major cause of poor health. Allah's Apostle observed:

*"Lead a simple life, adopt moderate habits and keep yourself cheerful."* *(Mishkat)*

*The Holy Prophet [S.A.W.] once saw an old man who was dragging on support on either side by two of his sons. The Holy Prophet [S.A.W.] inquired: "What has happened to this old man." The people told him: "This man had vowed to travel to the House of Allah on foot." The Holy Prophet [S.A.W.] observed: "It is not the will of Allah that this old man should torment himself" and then urged the old man to ride towards his destination.*

*Hadrat 'Umar [R.A.A.] once saw a youth walking along slowly like a sick man. 'Umar stopped the youth and inquired: "What sickness afflicts you?" He replied: "I am not ailing." Thereupon 'Umar took hold of a whip and threatening him with it said to the young fellow: "Walk on the way energetically with firm foot."*

*The Holy Prophet [S.A.W.] used to walk with a firm foot and stepped on the ground as if he were descending a slope.*

*Hadrat 'Abdullah bin Harith reports: "I never met a man who smiled more often than the Prophet of Allah [S.A.W.]."*

*The Holy Prophet [S.A.W.] taught the following prayer to his people and you should say this prayer more often:*

*"O Allah! I seek refuge in Thee from the anxiety and grief, from inability and sloth, from the burden of indebtedness and the domination of men."*

*(Bukhari, Muslim)*

3. Do not lift more burden than your strength can bear. Do not waste your physical energy. It is obligatory that you should save and protect your physical strength and use it with moderation according to your capability.

*Hadrat 'Aishah [R.A.A.] reports that the Holy Prophet [S.A.W.] observed:*

*"Act as much as is within your strength, for the Lord will not feel wearied but you will get weary."*

*(Bukhari)*

*Hadrat Abu Qais [R.A.A.] reports that he went to see the Holy Prophet [S.A.W.] when the Prophet [S.A.W.] was delivering a sermon. Hadrat Abu Qais [R.A.A.] stood waiting in the sun. At the bidding of the Holy Prophet [S.A.W.] he stepped into the shade.*

*(Al-Adab Al-Mufrad)*

The Holy Prophet [S.A.W.] forbade that a person should stand in a position where a part of his body is under the shade and the other part in the sun.

A lady of the Bahla tribe, Hadrat Mujiba [R.A.A.] relates: *"Once my father called on the Holy Prophet [S.A.W.] to seek religious knowledge. Having learnt some important matters about religion, my father returned home. A year later, he again went to see the Holy Prophet [S.A.W.]. The Holy Prophet did not recognise his visitor. Upon this, my father submitted: "O Prophet of Allah! Don't you remember me." The Holy Prophet [S.A.W.] said: No, I do not recognise you. Introduce yourself." My father submitted: "I belong to the tribe of Bahla. I came to see you last year also." The Holy Prophet [S.A.W.] observed: "Why are you in such a bad shape. When you came here last year you were in a much better state and looked fine." My father replied: "Since our last meeting, I have been continuously observing fasts. I eat only at night." The Holy Prophet [S.A.W.] observed: "It was utterly needless for you to torment yourself and ruin your health." Then the Prophet [S.A.W.] urged my father, "You should keep fasts during the whole of the month of Ramadan and in addition observe fast for one day during each month." My father submitted: "O Prophet of Allah! Permit me to keep more fasts." The Holy Prophet [S.A.W.] enjoined: "You should observe two fasts during each month." My father asked permission for more. The Holy Prophet [S.A.W.] said: "You can keep three fasts during each month." My father entreated for a further addition in the number of fasts. The Holy Prophet [S.A.W.] replied: "Well then, you may observe fasts during sacred months each year and then leave a gap. You may follow this course every year." While observing this, the Holy Prophet [S.A.W.] made a sign with three fingers, joined them and moved them apart.*

The point that the Holy Prophet [S.A.W.) wanted to bring home to his visitor was that he should observe fasts during the months of Rajab, Dhiqadah and Dhulhijah and leave a gap in fasting during the intervening years. The Prophet [S.A.W.] has affirmed:

*"It does not behove a believer to degrade himself." The people inquired: "In what manner does a believer degrade himself." The Holy Prophet [S.A.W.] observed: "He subjects himself to intolerable sufferings and thus degrades himself."* *(Tirmidhi)*

4. You should always be industrious, energetic, hard-working, painstaking and bold in your daily life. You should form the habit of facing all forms of hardship and tackling with the most difficult situations. Prepare yourself to lead the hard and simple life of a Mujahid (a fighter in the service of True Faith). Don't be ease-loving, careless, indolent, voluptuous, timid and a materialist. While dispatching Hadrat Muadh bin Jabal [R.A.A.] as Governor of Yemen, the Holy Prophet [S.A.W.] gave him the following instruction:

*"Muadh Deny yourself the love of pleasure for the servants of Allah are not pleasure-seekers." (Mishkat)*

*Hadrat Abu Umama [R.A.A.] reports the Holy Prophet [S.A.W.] as having said: "Simple living symbolises true Faith."* *(Abu Daud)*

The life of the Holy Prophet [S.A.W.] was ever a simple and hard one, like a Mujahid. The Holy Prophet [S.A.W.] took care to preserve his physical energy and strive to enhance it. The Prophet [S.A.W.] also liked to swim, for this sport provides the best physical exercise. Once the Holy Prophet [S.A.W.] and some Companions [R.A.A.] were swimming in a pool. The Holy

Prophet [S.A.W.] arranged the Companions in pairs of two and desired that each man should swim towards his partner. Hadrat Abu Bakr [R.A.A.] was paired with the Prophet, [S.A.W.]. The Holy Prophet [S.A.W.] swam towards Abu Bakr [R.A.A.] caught him and held him by the neck.

Horse was the Prophet's favourite riding animal. The Holy Prophet [S.A.W.] himself tended his horse. He used to rub and clean the mouth of his horse with his own sleeve. He would tie the hair of its mane into knots and used to say:

*"Goodness remains attached to its forehead till Doomsday."*

*Hadrat 'Uqba [R.A.A.] reports that the Prophet of Allah observed:*

*"Learn archery and horse-riding. I like the archers more than the horse-riders. He who learns the art of shooting arrows and then gives it up has paid scant regard to a Divine blessing."* *(Abu Daud)*

*Hadrat 'Abdullah bin 'Umar [R.A.A.] reports that the Holy Prophet [S.A.W.] stated:*

*"He who guards the soldiers of Islam against danger in the night passes a night better than Shab-e-Qadr."*

*In an address to his Companions, the Holy Prophet [S.A.W.] observed: "A time will come when the other nations will fall upon my followers as diners scramble over food."*

*Someone inquired: "O Prophet of Allah [S.A.W.]! Will our numbers so dwindle that other people will join forces in order to annihilate us?"*

*The Holy Prophet [S.A.W.] answered: "Not that your numbers will be small. In fact you will be much larger in number, but then your number will carry no weight, just as so many straws floating in flood-tide are weightless. Your enemies will no longer fear you, cowardice will creep into your hearts."*

*At this point a man enquired: "O Prophet of Allah [S.A.W.]! what will be the cause of this cowardice?"*

*The Holy Prophet (S.A.W.] observed: "The cause will be that you will grow to love the worldly life and hate death."*

*Hadrat Abu Hurrayrah [R.A.A.] reports that the Holy Prophet [S.A.W.] observed:*

*"He who holds the reins of his horse firmly and rides to serve the cause of Islam, lives the best life. From whichever spot the news of threat to the cause of Islam reaches him, he mounts his horse and rushes thither. He is so fearless of death as if he is after it." (Muslim)*

5. Women should also lead hard and strenuous life. They should perform all household chores with their own hands. They should form the habit of being active and train themselves to bear hardships. They should abstain from being work-shy, indolent or voluptuous. They should raise their children so that they learn to be sturdy, energetic and tough from the very beginning of their lives. Even when there are servants in home, do not encourage your children to depend on them for odd jobs. Teach children to cultivate the habit of self-help. The ladies of the Companions of the Holy Prophet used to perform house-hold tasks with their own hands. They would work in the kitchen; they would grind at the millstone; they fetched water for use in the home, washed clothes, sewed and led a strenuous life. In the hour of need, they took the responsibility of rendering medical aid to the wounded in the battle-field and supplied water to the fighting forces. Hard work keeps women fit; it ensures the purity of their morals and the good example of the mothers being as a model for character building of their children. From the Islamic point of view, a good wife is the one who keeps herself busy in housekeeping tasks. She should be so engrossed in household activities that signs of exhaustion due to hard work, the blackness of the kitchen and the soot of fire-smoke should be evident from her face. The Holy Prophet [S.A.W.] has stated:

"I and the woman whose cheeks are besmeared with kitchen smoke will be close together on the Day of Resurrection." (While saying this, the Prophet made a sign by joining his index finger with the middle finger).

6. Be an early riser. Keep your sleeping hours within limits of propriety. Don't sleep little, for in that case your body will not get proper rest and your limbs will feel exhausted and weary. On the other hand, do not sleep for long hours, for in that case you will become lazy and inactive. Follow the maxim: "Early to bed and early to rise, is the way to be healthy, wealthy and wise."

Get up early in the morning and offer prayers. Go for a stroll into the field or garden and relax there. The fresh air of the morning has a salutary effect on health. Make it a point to do some light exercise daily according to your physical strength and endurance. The Holy Prophet [S.A.W.] liked to divert himself by visits to the gardens. He used to go for a stroll in the garden once in a while. The Prophet [S.A.W.] forbade to remain awake and engage in conversation after 'Isha' (night prayer) and observed:

*"Only that person is permitted to remain awake after 'Isha' who is either engaged in talk concerning religion or has to discuss some important matter with the members of his household."*

7. Learn self-control. Keep your passions, fancies, desires and lusts under control. Guard against your ideas getting distracted or your eyes going astray. Peace of mind and contentment of the heart evaporate when the passions are given free rein and eyes begin to wander astray and the faces of such people lose all the beauty, grace and attractiveness. Having lost these attributes, these persons prove to be timid, weak-minded and cowards in every sphere of life.

The Holy Prophet [S.A.W.] has stated:

*"To cast a lascivious eye is the adultery of eyes and shameless talk is the adultery of tongue. Your lust presses a demand on you and your genitals either affirm or contradict this demand."*

A sage observes:

*"O Muslims! Keep away from sin. Sin entails six evils: three evils relate to this world and the other three are concerned with the eternal world. Those evils that relate to this world are:*

* Beauty and grace vanish from the face of man.
* The man is seized by the torment of poverty and destitution.
* It shortens the life of man.

8. Save yourself from intoxicants. They affect the brain as well as the stomach. Liquor, of course, is forbidden, but you should refrain from using all other things having an intoxicating effect.
9. Observe the rules of simplicity and moderation in all your activities. In physical labour, mental exertion, marital relations, eating, drinking, sleep and rest, anxiety, merriment, recreation, worship, walking and conversation-in short, in all your activities always follow a middle course, and regard it as the main source of virtue and well-being.

The Holy Prophet [S.A.W.] has said:

*"How wonderful it is to be moderate in the midst of plenty! And what a fine thing it is to follow a middle course in deprivation, and what a better course it is to be moderate in offering prayers."*

*(Musnad Bazaz/Kanz al Amal)*

10. Eat at the proper time. Abstain from overeating. Don't munch all the time. Take food only when you feel the appetite and stop eating before your stomach is filled, so that you should still feel slightly hungry when the meal is over. You must never indulge in overeating. The Holy Prophet [S.A.W.] observed:

*"The believer fills only one intestine while the non-believer eats to fill seven intestines."* *(Tirmidhi)*

*Good health depends on proper functioning of the stomach. Overeating makes the stomach sick. The Holy Prophet [S.A.W.] has explained this point in an allegory as follows:*

*"The stomach serves as a cistern. The veins receive their life-blood from this reservoir. Hence if the stomach is healthy, the veins will be irrigated with the juices of health, and in case the stomach is ill, the veins will only suck the juice of sickness."* *(Baihaqi)*

*Persuading the people to be abstemious in taking food the Prophet [S.A.W.] observed:*

*"One man's dinner is sufficient for two."*

11. Always eat simple food. Eat whole wheat bread. Do not eat while the food is piping hot. Avoid spiced and pungent foods and have no unnecessary craving for tasty delicacies.

Make it a point to eat simple, easily digestible, nourishing and healthful diet. Do not crave for delicious foods or foods that leave a pungent taste on the tongue.

The Holy Prophet [S.A.W.] preferred whole-wheat bread. He did not like bread made of soft flour or thin. He never ate while the food was piping hot, but waited till it cooled. Referring to the eating of food while it is piping hot, the Prophet [S.A.W.] some times observed: 'Allah has not ordained us to eat fire'; and some other time he would say: "There is no virtue in eating piping hot food."

Meat (especially joints of leg, pieces of neck and flesh of the backside) was the Prophet's [S.A.W.] favourite food. In point of fact, meat is an important and essential food for the nourishment of body and for forging a bold attitude of mind; and the believers should always be bold and sturdy.

The Holy Prophet [S.A.W.] has affirmed:

*"One who died without fighting in the cause of Allah and had no desire for such a fight has in a way died in the state of hypocrisy."* *(Muslim)*

12. Eat with perfect peace of mind and in a relaxed mood and chew the food well. Avoid eating in a mood of sorrow, anger, anxiety or perplexity. The food that is eaten in a cheerful and peaceful state of mind nourishes the body, whereas food that is gulped down in a state of anxiety or grief has an adverse effect on the stomach and affords no strength to the body. Don't be silent, sad

or woe-begone while taking meals nor show undue mirth by raising loud guffaws. Laughter during meals proves fatal sometimes.

Talk and laugh with moderation while taking meals. Eat in a pleasant and cheerful mood and offer thanks to the Almighty and when ill, take every precaution with regard to your meals.

Umme Mundhir [R.A.A.] relates:

*"The Holy Prophet [S.A.W.] once visited me. Bunches of date-fruit were hanging in the home. The Holy Prophet [S.A.W.) plucked the fruit and started eating it. Hadrat 'Ali [R.A.A.] did the same. The Holy Prophet [S.A.W.] however, forbade 'Ali [R.A.A.] and said: "You have just recovered from illness; you should not eat this fruit." So 'Ali [R.A.A.] stopped. Meanwhile, the Prophet [S.A.W.] continued to eat the fruit." Umme Mundhir [R.A.A.] further relates: "Later, I cooked some barley and beet-root. The Holy Prophet [S.A.W.] said to 'Ali [R.A.A.] "'Ali, take this. This food will do you good."*

*(Shamail Tirmidhi)*

"When he [S.A.W.] had a guest at meals, he used to prompt the guest repeatedly to eat more and until he had eaten to his fill and insisted on taking more, the Holy Prophet [S.A.W.] then stopped to prompt him."

During meals, the Holy Prophet [S.A.W.] used to be engaged in amiable talk and maintained an atmosphere of joy and cordiality.

13. Take a nap after the mid-day meal and go for a stroll after dinner. Avoid strenuous physical and mental exertion immediately after the meals. There is a well-known maxim in Arabic which runs thus:

    "Stretch out after the midday meal and take a stroll after taking dinner."

14. Take good care of your eyes. Don't expose your eyes to glaring light. Don't set your gage upon the sun. Don't read in either faint or intense light. Always study under a clear and soothing light. Avoid keeping yourself awake for too long. Protect your eyes from filth and dust. Apply collyrium to your eyes and always try to keep your eyes

clean. Go for a walk in the fields, gardens and green pastures and amuse yourself. The sight of greenery has a pleasant effect on eyes. Guard against casting evil glances, for this practice will dim the sparkle of your eyes and your general health will decline. The Holy Prophet [S.A.W.] has said:

"Your eyes have a right on you."

It is, therefore, incumbent upon a believer to value this Divine blessing. He should use this blessing according to the will of the Almighty. He should be particular about the protection of his eyes and keeping them clean. He should use all means which may be of benefit to his eyes and avoid everything that may cause injury to them. Similarly, a true believer should take care to preserve the strength of other limbs and organs of his body. The Holy Prophet [S.A.W.] observed:

*"O people! You should apply collyrium to your eyes. It clears away all wax from your eyes and helps in the growth of hair."* *(Tirmidhi)*

15. Be careful about dental hygiene and protect your teeth. Clean teeth keep you fresh, produce a good effect on digestion and cleanliness makes the teeth firm too. Form the habit of cleaning your teeth with a miswak (twig); use dental powder also. Don't spoil your teeth by too frequent chewing of betel leaf or using tobacco. Clean your teeth well after every meal.

*Unclean teeth cause various diseases. It was customary with the Holy Prophet (S.A.W.] that on getting up from sleep, he used to clean his teeth with a miswak (twig).* *(Agreed upon)*

Hadrat Aishah [R.A.A.] states:

*"We used to keep the water for ablution and the miswak (twig) ready for the use of the Holy Prophet [S.A.W.]. By the will of Allah when the Prophet [S.A.W.] got up from sleep he used to clean his teeth with the miswak (twig). Later, he performed ablution and then offered prayers."* *(Muslim)*

*Hadrat Anas [R.A.A.] has reported that the Holy Prophet [S.A.W.] observed:*

*"I have already laid much stress upon the need to clean your teeth with miswak (twig)."* *(Bukhari)*

*Hadrat Aishah [R.A.A.] relates that the Holy Prophet [S.A.W.] stated:*

*"The miswak (twig) cleans the mouth and the Lord is pleased by this act of cleanliness."*

The Prophet [S.A.W.] is reported to have said:

*"Had I not considered it a great inconvenience for my Ummah, I would have enjoined upon people to brush their teeth with a miswa k(twig) before each prayer."*

*(Abu Daud)*

*Some Muslims once came to see the Holy Prophet [S.A.W.]. Their teeth were unclean and were encrusted with yellow grease. Noticing this, the Holy Prophet [S.A.W.] said to them: "Your teeth look so yellow! You should clean them with a miswak."(Musnad Ahmad)*

16. When the need arises to answer the call of nature fulfil it promptly. Delay in answering the call of nature affects the brain and the stomach badly.
17. Pay full attention to keeping yourself pure, clean and tidy. The Holy Quran says:

*"Allah's favourites are those who take great care in keeping themselves pure and clean."* *(At-Tauba)*

The Holy Prophet [S.A.W.] has said:

*"Cleanliness and purity are the half of Iman (Faith)."*

In view of the great importance of cleanliness and purity, the Holy Prophet [S.A.W.] has given detailed injunctions about neatness and has stressed the need for observing purity and cleanliness in every matter. Keep all articles of food under cover. Protect them from being soiled and keep the flies away. You should have clean utensils. Keep your dress and bed-covers tidy and spotlessly clean. Keep your body clean by performing ablution and taking a bath. Cleanliness of body, neatness of dress and tidiness of all articles of use is refreshing and pleasant for the soul. The body also feels delightfully fresh. On the whole, purity and neatness have a salutary effect on human health.

Hadrat Adi bin Hatim [R.A.A.] stated: "I always remain in a state of ablution for each Salat (prayer) since I embraced Islam."

The Holy Prophet [S.A.W.] once asked Hadrat Bilal [R.A.A.]: "How did you manage to reach Paradise before me yesterday?" Hadrat Bilal [R.A.A.] submitted: "Whenever I proclaim the call for prayer, I invariably offer two Rakats of Salat (prayer) and as soon as I am out of the state of ablution, I perform ablution afresh and try to remain in this state always."

Hadrat Abu Hurrayrah [R.A.A.] reports the Prophet [S.A.W.] as having said:

> *"It is Allah's right upon every Muslim that he should take bath once a week and wash his head and body."*
> *(Bukhari)*

## THE ROBES

1. You should wear a dress which covers and protects your body and meets the requirements of modesty, honour and virtue. Your dress should also be an expression of culture, elegance and beauty. In respect of this blessing, Allah says in the Holy Quran:

> *"O children of Adam! We have sent unto you raiments to conceal your shame and to serve as protection and adornment."* *(7: 26)*

As a matter of fact, the word 'Rish' in the verse, literally means the wings of the bird. The wings of a bird lend beauty and grace to it and also seen as a means of protection for its body. The word, however, is commonly used when referring to beauty, elegance and fine dress. Of course the purpose of dress is to lend beauty and grace and to serve as protection against climatic effects. But the foremost use of dress is to cover private parts of the body.

Allah has inculcated modesty and diffidence in the nature of man. It was for this reason that when Hadrat Adam and Hadrat Hawwa (Eve) [A.S.] were deprived of the elegant robes of Paradise, they began to use leaves of trees to cover their bodies. Hence consider this as the principal use of dress and choose a dress which conforms to the requirements of modesty.

You should also make sure that your dress, besides affording adequate protection against climatic conditions, should also be such that it should lend an aura of grace, elegance and culture to your personality. Do not wear such dress which should make you an object of ridicule or provoke satirical comments from the people.

2. You should keep in mind while putting on clothes that dress is a blessing which Allah has conferred on man only. It has been denied to all other living creatures. Offer thanks to Allah for this special favour and blessing. Endowed as you are with this distinctive bounty, you should never act contrary to the decrees of Allah or show ingratitude. Dress is a remarkable favour from the Lord. While putting on dress, rekindle this feeling in your heart and express your sense of gratitude in the words which the Holy Prophet [S.A.W.] had taught to the believers.

3. Piety is the best apparel. Piety signifies purity of soul as well as righteous physical appearance. In other words you should wear dress of the kind which the Shariah has prescribed for the believers, which does not display arrogance or pride, which does not lend a feminine air to men nor a masculine appearance to women. The dress should be an emblem of your righteousness and devotion to Allah. The women should strictly conform to the rules set by Shariahin respect of female dress and men must observe the laws of Shariah with regard to their dress.

4. Put on a new dress with feelings of joy. Give some name to it when you don a new apparel and acknowledge the munificence and blessing of Allah. Inspired by a sense of gratitude to the Lord, recite the prayer which the Holy Prophet [S.A.W.] used to offer while putting on a new dress.

Hadrat Abu Said Khudri [R.A.A.] reports: "Whenever the Holy Prophet [S.A.W.] put on a new dress, head dress, shirt or a sheet covering, he used to recite the following prayer and insert the name of the garment in the recitation:

*Allah! Unto Thee belongeth all praise. Even as Thou hast clothed me in this (garment), I ask of Thee the good thereof and I seek refuge in Thee from the evil thereof, and the evil of that wherefor it hath been made."*

*(Abu Daud)*

The prayer bears the following meaning: Allah! Make me use this dress which You have bestowed on me for the purposes which You deem righteous. Enable me to cover my modesty with this dress and to protect my soul and body against immodesty and shamelessness; to make it a means of adornment and grace for my body; to eschew displaying ostentation, pride or arrogance and let me not transgress the bounds set by you for men and women in the use of dress.

Hadrat 'Umar [R.A.A.] stated: "The Holy Prophet [S.A.W.] observed: "Whosoever puts on a new dress and has means, should give away his old dress to the poor. On wearing a new dress, a person should recite the following prayer:

*"Praise be to Allah Who clad me with that wherewith I cover my shame, and where with I adorn myself in my life."*

*Whosoever reads the above prayer at the time of putting on a new dress, Allah will keep him under His care and protection in this life and in the life Hereinafter."*

*(Tirmidhi)*

5. Take care to put on the dress with the right side first. While putting on the shirt, Kurta, shervani or coat, wear the right sleeve first. Similarly while putting on a pyjama enter the right foot first. The Holy Prophet [S.A.W.] while putting on the shirt used to wear the right sleeve first and then put the left arm into the left sleeve. Similarly, the Holy Prophet [S.A.W.] used to put the shoe on his right foot first and then wore the left shoe. On taking off his shoes, the Holy Prophet [S.A.W.] first took off from his left foot and then from the right one.
6. You must shake the garments before putting them on, lest there be deadly insect hidden in them which might cause you harm. The Holy Prophet [S.A.W.] was once wearing socks in a jungle. He put on a sock and was

intending to put on the second one when a crow dived and carried off the sock. The crow soared to a great height and dropped the sock on the ground. The shock of landing threw out of the sock a snake which fell at some distance. On seeing this, the Holy Prophet [S.A.W.] offered thanks to Allah and observed: "It is the duty of every Muslim that on intending to wear socks, he should shake them first." (Tibrani)

7. Wear white dress. White dress is ideal for men, especially. The Holy Prophet [S.A.W.] observed: "Wear white dress. It is the best. You ought to wear white clothes in life and bury your dead in a shroud made of white cloth." (Tirmidhi)

On another occasion, the Holy Prophet [S.A.W.] observed: "You should wear white clothes, for the white clothes stays cleaner and put your dead in white coffins."

The phrase 'white cloth stays cleaner' implies that white cloth shows off the slightest stain instantly, which a person may clean immediately. If the cloth is dyed, the stains will not be seen instantly. Hence a person will not pay immediate attention to wash a dyed garment.

It is recorded in Sahih Bukhari that the Holy Prophet [S.A.W.] used to wear white clothes. In other words he [S.A.W.] not only liked to put on white dress himself, but also enjoined upon the male members of his Ummah to wear white clothes.

8. The length of your pyjama, or lungi should fall above the ankles. The Holy Prophet [S.A.W.] holds such people as the doomed ones and deserving of severe torment who out of pride and haughtiness let their pyjamas or lungis fall below their ankles. The Holy Prophet [S.A.W.] has affirmed: "There are three types of people with whom Allah shall not speak on the Doomsday, nor look at them, nor will He admit them to Paradise after purifying them; rather He shall ordain a painful torment for them." Hadrat Abu dhar Ghifari [R.A.A.] submitted: "O Apostle of Allah who are these unfortunate people?" The Holy Prophet [S.A.W.] observed:

"Firstly, he who out of pride and haughtiness lets his lower garments fall below his ankles.

Secondly, the man who reminds others of the favours he has done to them.

And thirdly, the one who wishes to promote his business by misrepresentation on oath." (Muslim)

Relating a personal anecdote, Hadrat 'Ubaid ibn Khalid [R.A.A.] says: "I was once walking in the holy city of Medina when a voice said from behind: Lift up your lower garment-by so doing a man not only guards himself from physical filth but also from the impurity of soul." Looking over my shoulder, I saw the Allah's Apostle [S.A.W.]. I submitted: "O Apostle of Allah [S.A.W.]! It is a simple sheet of cloth that I am wearing. How can it show haughtiness and pride?" The Holy Prophet [S.A.W.] observed: "Is it not obligatory for you to follow my example?" On hearing these words of the Holy Prophet [S.A.W.] my eyes at once fell towards his lower garment and I saw that it came to the middle of his calf."

The Holy Prophet's [S.A.W.] observation that by keeping the length of his pyjama or lower garment above the ankles the man is guarded against not only physical dirt but also impurity of soul, is highly significant. It implies that when the length of a garment falls below the ankles, it gathers filth from the ground and becomes dirty. Soiled clothes are always offensive to a person of neat and clean taste. Moreover, the habit of wearing garments whose length falls below the ankles betrays arrogance and pride and these two evils are symptoms of the impurity of soul. These considerations apart, the Quranic injunction 'The life of the Prophet is the best model for you to follow' should suffice for a pious believer.

According to a Tradition reported by Abu Daud, the Holy Prophet [S.A.W.] has given warning of terrible punishment for this offence. The Holy Prophet [S.A.W.] observed: "The pious believer should wear the length of his 'lower garment' up to the middle of his calf; there is no harm if the length falls to the ankles; but any part of the length which falls below the ankles shall burn in the fire. And on the Doomsday, Allah shall not even look at the man who out of pride and arrogance wears an apparel whose length falls below his ankles."

9. Do not wear silk. Garments of silk are befitting for females only. The Holy Prophet [S.A.W.] has strictly

forbidden men to wear female dress or to put on effeminate airs.

Hadrat 'Umar [R.A.A.] reports that the Holy Prophet [S.A.W.] observed: "Do not wear silk garments, for he who wears them in this world shall not wear them in the next." (Bukhari, Muslim) The Holy Prophet [S.A.W.] once observed to Hadrat 'Ali [R.A.A.]:

*"Cut this silk cloth into scarves and distribute them among the Fatimas."* *(Muslim)*

This also shows that silk dress is desirable for women. It was for this reason that the Holy Prophet [S.A.W.] urged Hadrat 'Ali [R.A.A.] to cut the silk cloth into scarves for the ladies, otherwise the cloth could have been used for some other purpose.

10. Women should not wear thin dress which should make their forms visible, nor should they put on a tightly fitting dress which might make their figures prominent and alluring. In this way, they would be exposing their bodies, despite having worn garments. The Holy Prophet [S.A.W.] has warned such immodest women of dire punishment.

*"Woman who are nude in spite of having garments on them, who allure others and are allured by others shall be consigned to Hell. Their heads are coquettishly inclined on one side like the humps of the Bakht camels. These women shall not enter Paradise, nor shall enjoy the sweet odour of Paradise, although the sweet odour of Paradise can be savoured from a long distance off."* *(Riyad-us-Salihin)*

On one occasion Hadrat Asma [R.A.A.] came to the Holy Prophet [S.A.W.] wearing thin clothes. On seeing her, the Holy Prophet [S.A.W.] turned his face at once and observed:

*"Asma, when a woman comes of age it is not lawful for her to expose any part of her body except face and hands."*

11. When wearing a Tehbund or pyjama do not lie down or sit in such a posture as to make prominent or lay bare any part of your body. The Holy Prophet [S.A.W.] has observed: "Do not walk with one shoe on. Do not squat

with one knee raised while you are wearing a Tehbund. Do not eat with your left hand. Do not wrap up your whole body in a sheet in such a manner as to make it impossible for you to move your hands freely for performing your work or for offering prayers. Do not lie flat and put one leg over the other lest it should uncover your body.

12. Men and women should not adopt the same fashions in dress. The Holy Prophet [S.A.W.] affirmed: "Allah sends curses on those men who adopt feminine fashions and on such women who adopt a masculine style." (Bukhari)

*Hadrat Abu Hurrayrah [R.A.A.] states: "The Holy Prophet [S.A.W.] pronounced a curse upon a male who puts on female dress and has cursed a female who dresses herself in masculine fashion." (Abu Daud)*

*Someone once mentioned to Hadrat 'Aishah' that there was a certain woman who wore masculine shoes, whereupon Hadrat Aishah observed: "The Holy Prophet [S.A.W.] has pronounced a curse upon such women who adopt masculine habits."*

13. The women must cover themselves with a scarf and keep their head and bosom veiled. They should not wear scarf of such transparent stuff as to reveal their hair. The scarf is meant to veil the beauty of the person. Allah ordains in the Holy Quran:

*"And draw their veils over their bosoms." (24: 31)*

*The Holy Prophet [S.A.W.] once received fine Egyptian veil. He cut out a piece and handing it to Hadrat Yahya Kalbi [R.A.A.] observed: "Cut a piece and make a shirt for yourself and give the other piece to your wife to use as a scarf, but tell her to stitch another layer of cloth under it so that her form may not be exposed to view." (Abu Daud)*

*Bearing this clear injunction of the Holy Book and Sunnah in mind, you should scrupulously follow the purport of Divine Command. Do not make a mockery of the Ordinance of Allah and His Messenger by wearing only a small strip of cloth around your neck.*

*Hadrat 'Aishah' [R.A.A.] states: "When this injunction was revealed, the women discarded thin garments. They started making their scarves out of coarse cloth."*

*(Abu Daud)*

14. Dress yourself in keeping with your means and status. Do not dress up to show off vanity and to display an attitude of haughtiness towards others or to make an indecent show of your affluence. On the other hand, your dress should not cost more than your means permit, for thus you will be guilty of the sin of extravagance. Do not look shabby and crest-fallen so as to make an impression of penury and helplessness upon others. Do not make a show of destitution, despite having everything. Put on proper, suitable and neat garments in keeping with your means and position. Some people appear destitute by wearing rags or patched garments and consider it an act of piety or virtue. Moreover, they view those who put on clean and neat dress as worldly-minded and irreligious. This conception of religion is wholly fallacious. Hadrat Abu Hasan 'Ali Shazli [R.A.A.] was once clad in very fine clothes. A destitute Sufi took exception to this and remarked: "What need have the servants of Allah to put on such elegant dress?" Hadrat Shazli [R.A.A.] answered: "Brother, I have put on this elegant dress to express my gratitude and homage to the Grand and Magnificent Allah. Your shabby appearance is a show of misery. You appear as if you were begging alms from the people." In reality, virtue does not consist in wearing rags, patched garments or clothes of inferior quality, nor does it require wearing luxurious apparel. The ingredients of virtue are the pious intentions and right thinking of the man. The truth is that every man should adopt a moderate and balanced attitude in all matters in consonance with his means and position. He should not let his soul grow dull by putting on destitute airs, nor should he display vanity and pride by wearing resplendent garments.

*Hadrat Abul Ahwas [R.A.A.] reports a Tradition from his father, "Once I went to the Holy Prophet [S.A.W.]. I was then clad in very poor and mean dress. The Holy*

*Prophet [S.A.W.] asked me: "Do you possess wealth and means?" I submitted: "Yes, I do." The Holy Prophet [S.A.W.] then enquired: "What kind of goods do you possess." I submitted: "Allah has blessed me with all kinds of goods-camels, cows, goats, horses besides slaves." The Holy Prophet [S.A.W.] observed: "When Allah has blessed you with wealth and means, your person should manifest His Bounty and Favour."* *(Mishkat)*

*The implication, is that when Allah has conferred ample means to you, why do you put on the garb of a beggar and destitute person? This is an act of ingratitude to Him.*

*Hadrat Jabir [R.A.A.] reports: "Once the Holy Prophet [S.A.W.] visited our house to see us. He chanced to see a man who was covered all over with dust and his hair was dishevelled. The Holy Prophet [S.A.W.] observed: "Does this man possess no comb with which to set his hair." The Holy Prophet [S.A.W.] then happened to see a man who was clad in a dirty dress whereupon the Holy Prophet [S.A.W.] observed: "Does this man not possess even that (soap etc.) with which to wash his clothes clean."* *(Mishkat)*

*A man submitted to the Holy Prophet [S.A.W.] "O Messenger of Allah! I like to have fine clothes and I like to dress my hair with oil, and wear nice shoes. In this manner, he named several niceties he was fond of and even mentioned that he wished that his lash should also be of the best quality. The Holy Prophet [S.A.W.] listened to him and then observed: "All these things are desirable and Allah views this fine taste with favour."*

*(Mustadrak Hakim)*

*Hadrat 'Abdullah bin 'Umar [R.A.A.] states: "I submitted to the Holy Apostle of Allah: "O Apostle of Allah! Would I be guilty of vanity and haughtiness if I wore fine and nice clothes." The Holy Prophet [S.A.W.] observed: "No, it is elegant to wear nice dress and elegance of dress pleases Allah."* *(Ibn Majah)*

*The following Tradition has also been reported by Hadrat 'Abdullah bin 'Umar [R.A.A.] "The Holy Prophet [S.A.W.]*

*observed: Put on both garments when saying prayers (in other words, dress yourself in full suit). Man owes it to Allah more than to any one else that he should go into His presence in his best apparel and in the neatest state." (Mishkat)*

*Hadrat 'Abdullah bin Masud [R.A.A.] states: "The Holy Prophet [S.A.W.], observed: "He who has even a little bit of pride in his heart shall not enter Paradise." A man submitted: "Every man wishes that he should put on fine clothes and wear nice shoes." The Holy Prophet [S.A.W.] observed: "Allah Himself is Graceful and elegance pleases Him. In other words, elegant dress does not connote haughtiness. Haughtiness consists in ignoring the rights of others and looking down upon others as mean and base." (Muslim)*

15. Observe good taste and propriety in dress and make-up. It is improper and offensive to good taste to go about with shirt unbuttoned at the chest, to wear buttons without proper arrangement, to roll up one leg of the trousers and keep the other down, to walk with one shoe on or to keep the hair dishevelled.

*One day, the Holy Prophet [S.A.W.] was seated in the mosque when a man with dishevelled hair, and unkempt beard came into his presence. The Holy Prophet [S.A.W.] made a gesture with his hand towards the man signifying that he should go and set the hair of his head and beard. The man went away and returned having put his hair in better shape. Whereupon the Holy Prophet [S.A.W.] remarked: 'Isn't it better to look elegant and fine than to wear unkempt hair. A man with dishevelled hair wears the look of the devil." (Mishkat)*

*Hadrat Abu Hurrayrah [R.A.A.] states: "The Holy Prophet [S.A.W.] observed: No one should walk with one shoe on; either wear both shoes or take off both." (Tirmidhi)*

*It is in the light of this Tradition that the* Ulama *have forbidden the wearing of only one sleeve and only one sock.*

16. Avoid wearing red, gaudy or resplendent dress or showy black or yellow apparel. Red, gaudy and resplendent dress is suited only to women and even women should observe proper rules about wearing such dress. As regards assuming superior airs by donning flowing robes and yellow garments, for the sake of displaying one's distinction, it is a sure sign of pride and haughtiness. Similarly, do not put on strange and funny clothes which may lend you an outlandish appearance and you may become an object of public ridicule.

17. Always put on simple, dignified, civilised dress and spend moderately on your clothes. Avoid luxury and extravagant finance in matters of dress. The Holy Prophet [S.A.W.) has observed:

*"Keep away from luxury, for the favourites of Allah are no lovers of ease and luxury." (Mishkat)*

*The Holy Prophet [S.A.W.] also affirmed: "Allah will adorn that man with the dress of honour and nobility who, in spite of possessing means and power, observes simplicity in dress out of humility and obedience to Allah." (Abu Daud)*

*The illustrious Companions were one day sitting together discussing worldly matters. The Holy Prophet [S.A.W.] remarked: "Simplicity of dress is one of the signs of Faith." (Abu Daud)*

*Once the Holy Prophet [S.A.W.] observed: "There are many a servant of Allah in the world whose outward appearance is humble; their hair are dishevelled and dusty and their dress is ordinary and simple, yet in the sight of Allah their stature is very high. Should they take a vow to do something, Allah fulfils their oath. Bra' bin. Malik [R.A.A.] is one among this type of people." (Tirmidhi)*

18. Give clothes to the destitute by way of expressing thanks to the Lord for having conferred the bounty of dress on you. The Holy Prophet [S.A.W.] has observed: "Whosoever gives clothes to a Muslim to cover his body, Allah shall clothe that man on the Day of Judgement in the green dress of Paradise." (Abu Daud)

*The Holy Prophet [S.A.W.] also affirmed: "A Muslim who gives clothes to another Muslim shall be afforded protection and safety by Allah as long as those clothes serve as a covering for the beneficiary."* *(Tirmidhi)*

19. Give fine clothes according to your means to your servants who serve you day and night.

The Holy Prophet [S.A.W.] observed:

*"The slaves, male and female, are your brothers and sisters. Allah has given them under your charge. Hence to whomsoever Allah has given power and control over some one, he should give him the same to eat as he eats himself and the same kind of dress to wear as he wears himself and he should not give him work to do which is beyond his capacity, and if the slave be unable to cope with the load of work, the master should share his burden."*

*(Bukhari, Muslim)*

## FOOD AND EATABLES

1. Wash your hands before taking your meals. It is in keeping with the rules of cleanliness and neatness that your mind should be satisfied about the cleanliness of your hands before starting the meal.
2. Say, Bismillah ir rahman ir rahim 'In the Name of Allah, the Most Beneficent, the Most Merciful', while starting the meal. If you forget this, then say as soon as you realise the oversight during the meal. Remember, the meal which is not consecrated by the Name of Allah is made lawful by the devil for himself.
3. Do not lean against anything when sitting down for a meal. Sit in a humble position with your knees raised or joint on the floor or with one knee prostrate and the other one raised. The Holy Prophet [S.A.W.] used to sit for meals in this posture.
4. Always eat with your right hand. However, the left hand may be used simultaneously with the right hand, if needed.
5. Use three fingers while eating. If required, use four fingers except the little finger. Do not put your fingers in the food up to their roots.

6. Do not take a big morsel, nor a small one. Put the second morsel into your mouth only after swallowing the first one.
7. Do not wipe your fingers with bread. This is a filthy habit.
8. Avoid brushing off the loaves and refrain from knocking them about also.
9. Eat out of the plate from the side nearest to you. Do not put your hand in the middle of the plate nor extend your hand to eat from that edge of the plate which is nearer to other diners.
10. If the morsel drops from your hands pick it up and eat it after cleaning or washing it.
11. Eat in company. Dining in company promotes cordiality and love and is a source of blessing.
12. Do not find fault with the food. Leave it if you don't like it.
13. Do not eat while the food is piping hot or simmering.
14. Avoid breaking into guffaws or indulging in too much conversation during taking food.
15. Do not sniff the food needlessly, it is a bad habit. Do not often open your mouth so wide during dinner that the other people may see the food you are munching between your teeth, nor should you pick your teeth repeatedly in the course of eating. The other diners will find this habit disgusting.
16. Sit down to eat and sit down also while taking a drink of water. However, if needed, you may eat fruit or drink water while standing.
17. If some soup is left over in the plate, drink it; otherwise clear the sediments from the plate with a finger and lick the finger.
18. Do not blow on the articles of food. The breath that we exhale is polluted and poisonous.
19. Take three breathing pauses while drinking water. By this method you can drink according to your need and get full satisfaction. Beware, drinking all the water in one breath may be harmful.

20. While eating in company pay due regard to the needs of the slow diners as well as those who eat at a rapid pace and rise only when all others have finished eating.
21. When you have finished eating, lick your fingers and then wash your hands.
22. Do not pick up two pieces or slices at once while eating fruit.
23. Do not drink water from the spout of a water pot or a goblet etc. Drink from such a container that you may clearly see the water that you are pouring into your mouth in order that no filth or harmful substance goes into your stomach.
24. Say this prayer at the end of the meal:

    "Praise be to Allah Who fed us and gave us drink and made us Muslims."

**EARLY TO BED, EARLY TO RISE**

1. When the dusk falls, call your children inside and do not permit them to play outside the home. It is safe not to let the children go out at night except in the case of an urgent need. The Holy Prophet [S.A.W.] has observed:

*"When the night falls make your children stay at home, for at this hour evil spirits stalk the earth. However, after an hour has passed you may permit the children to move out."*

2. At the hour of nightfall, say the following prayer. The Holy Apostle [S.A.W.] used to instruct his Companions [R.A.A.] to say the same.

*"O Allah! with Thy help do we enter upon the morning and with Thy help do we enter upon the evening. With Thy help do we live and with Thy help do we die. And unto Thee shall be the Resurrection." (Tirmidhi)*

*At the hour of the call for Magrib (evening) prayer, say this prayer:*

*"Allah, this is the hour of the approach of Thy night and the departure of Thy day and this is the time of Thy Muaddhin's call. Hence grant me salvation."*

*(Tirmidhi, Abu Daud)*

3. Do not go to bed before saying 'Isha prayers. Often the 'Isha prayer may be missed if you take a nap before prayer for who knows Allah will return life to man after this sleep (akin to death) or He forfeits his life for ever while he slumbers in deathlike sleep. The Holy Prophet [S.A.W.] did not like to sleep in a house which was not lit up at night.
4. Soon after the fall of night, light up your homes. The Holy Prophet [S.A.W.] abstained from sleeping in a house which was not lit up at night.
5. Do not keep awake till late hours in the night. Adopt the habit of going to bed early at night and rising early at dawn. The Holy Apostle [S.A.W.] observed in this regard: "After the time of 'Isha prayers, you may either keep awake for the purpose of remembering Allah or to talk over necessary matters with the members of household."
6. Abstain from keeping awake at night and making up for sleep during the day. Allah has appointed the night a time for peace and rest. He has made the day a time for keeping awake and a time for labour to earn one's living. Surah al-Furqan affirms:

*"And He it is Who created night a covering for you and sleep for repose and made the day (a time for) waking up."*

*And Surah-an-Naba affirms:*

*"And We made your sleep for repose and We made the night a covering and We appointed the day for livelihood."*

*And in Surah al-Namal (86) Allah says:*

*"Have they not observed how We have made the night that they may rest therein and the day bright (so that they may strive during its course). No doubt, there are signs in it for a people who believe."*

*The implication of making the night dark so as to serve as a time of peace and rest and making the day bright so that man may labour and strive is that one should keep a strict schedule of sleeping at night and working hard for earning one's livelihood during the day. In the light of day devote yourself energetically to work and make strenuous efforts to earn your living till your faculties and limbs begin to feel tired. Then in the night when an atmosphere of peace and privacy reigns, repose in bed in a calm and comfortable state. As soon as dawn breaks, arise and invoking the blessings of Allah enter into the field of practical endeavour with renewed vigour. People who due to indolence and lethargy drone in day time or keep awake throughout night enjoying sensuous pleasures and making merry are guilty of violating the law of nature. They ruin their health and undermine their lives. Those who sleep long during the hours of the day not only neglect their daily work but also deprive their body and soul of necessary repose and rest; for sleep during the day cannot serve as an alternative for repose at night in providing rest and nourishment. The Apostle of Allah [S.A.W.] even disapproved of the idea that a man should remain awake all night for offering worship to Allah and thus suffer an unbearable hardship.*

*The Apostle of Allah [S.A.W.] once said to Hadrat 'Abdullah bin 'Umar [R.A.A.]: "Is 't true what I have heard that you regularly keep fast during the day and pass all night in offering prayers?" Hadrat 'Abdullah [R.A.A.] submitted: "I confess this to be true." The Holy Prophet [S.A.W.] observed: "No, don't go on like that. Keep fast sometimes and eat and drink at other times. Similarly get some sleep and then rise and say prayers. You owe a duty to your eye."* *(Bukhari)*

7. Do not sleep on a very soft bed. The true believers should for bear love of ease, indolence and luxurious living in the world. Life is a Jihad (straggle) for the true believers. The true believers should, therefore, follow an energetic, strenuous and a hard-working pattern of life. Hadrat '*Aishah* [R.A.A.] related: The Holy Prophet [S.A.W.] slept on a bed made of a hide-skin filled with the bark of a palm tree." (Shamail Tirmidhi)

*Someone asked Hadrat Hafsa [R.A.A.]: "What kind of a bed did you make for the Holy Prophet [S.A.W.] in your house?" She replied: "There was a canvas cloth which we used to fold up and spread under the Holy Prophet [S.A.W.]. One day, I thought that if I folded the cloth into four layers it would make a softer bed. So 1 folded up the canvas into four layers and spread it for the Prophet [S.A.W.] to sleep on. Next morning the Apostle [S.A.W.] enquired: "What was it that you spread beneath me last night?" I submitted: "It was the same canvas cloth. However, I had folded it up into four layers to make a softer bed." The Holy Prophet [S.A.W.] observed: "No, keep it folded in two layers. The softness of the bed proved a hindrance in arising up for midnight prayers last night.* *(Shamail Tirmidhi)*

*Hadrat* Aishah *[R.A.A.] reports: "One day a lady from the Ansar visited our house and saw the bed of the Holy Prophet [S.A.W.]. She returned home and prepared a bedding and heavily padded it with wool to make it extra soft. She sent it as a gift for the Holy Apostle [S.A.W.]. When the Holy Apostle [S.A.W.] returned home, he saw the bedding and enquired: "What is it?" I submitted: "O Prophet so and so lady from the Ansar came and saw your bed. She went back and has sent this bedding as a gift for you." The Holy Prophet [S.A.W.] said: "No, return it to her." I liked that bedding so much that I did not really want to return but the Holy Prophet [S.A.W.] insisted so hard that I had to return it back to the lady."* *(Shamail Tirmidhi)*

*The Holy Prophet [S.A.W.] was one day sleeping on a mat. The mat left some marks on his august body. Hadrat 'Abdullah bin. Masud [R.A.A.] relates: "On seeing the marks of mat on his body I broke into tears." The Holy Prophet [S.A.W.] looked at me and enquired: "Why do you weep?" I submitted: "O Prophet of Allah [S.A.W.]! The Emperors of Rome and Persia rest on silk and velvet cushions and you go to sleep on such a rough mat." The Holy Prophet [S.A.W.] observed: "There is no point in weeping for it. They love the world and we crave for the Hereafter."*

*On one occasion, the Holy Prophet [S.A.W.] observed: "How can I lead a luxurious, easy and carefree life while the angel Israfil with a trumpet to his lips, with ears open, head bowed, stands waiting for the Lord's Command to blow the trumpet to usher in the Day of Doom."* *(Tirmidhi)*

The precedent of the Holy Prophet [S.A.W.] requires the true believers to lead a strenuous life in the world and to abstain from luxurious, carefree living.

8. Perform ablution before going to bed and sleep in a clean and pure state. If your hands are greasy wash them well before going to bed. The Holy Prophet [S.A.W.] has said: "The person whose hands are greased and goes to sleep without washing his hands has only himself to blame if he comes to harm (if he is bitten by some insect)."

The Holy Prophet [S.A.W.] used to perform ablution before going to sleep. On occasions when he wanted to sleep while in a state when a bath is obligatory, then he used to wash the unclean part and go to bed after performing ablution.

9. When going to bed, close the doors of your house, extinguish the wick lamp or lantern, and put out the burning fire. Once fire broke out in the home of a person in Medina at night. On that occasion, the Holy Prophet [S.A.W.] enjoined upon the people: "Fire is your enemy. Be careful to put it out before going to bed."

The Apostle of Allah [S.A.W.] further observed: "Do not permit your little children to go out at the hour of evening, for at that hour evil spirits stalk the earth. When an hour or so of the night has passed, let them go out if need be. Close your doors at night reciting (Bismillah) the name of Allah and extinguish the light after reciting (Bismillah) Allah's name, and tie the mouth of the waterskin with the recital of Allah's name and again recite (Bismillah) the name of Allah and cover the vessels in which you eat and dank. If there is no cloth cover available for this purpose, cover the puts and pans with something else.

10. Take care to keep the following things within reach of your bed at the time of going to sleep. Drinking water and a glass, a jug, a stick, a box of matches or torch for lighting purposes, a miswak (twig for cleaning the teeth),

a towel etc. If you are staying as a guest in a home, ask the host for directions to toilet rooms etc. You may thus save unnecessary inconvenience if a sudden need arises during the night. Seven things were always kept ready near the bed when the Holy Prophet [S.A.W.] was in repose:

*l A bottle of oil. 1 A comb. l Collyrium container. l Scissors. l A twig for cleaning the teeth (miswak). l A Mirror. l And a small wooden needle used for scratching the head etc.*

11. Keep your shoes and clothes near at hand while going to bed. This will save you from the trouble of looking for them on arising. Do not put on shoes at once after leaving the bed. Similarly, do not put on clothes without shaking them briskly. It is possible that some deadly insect may have crept into your shoes or clothes and, Allah forbid, may cause you harm.
12. Clean and give a brisk shake to your bed covers before lying down for sleep. If you get up from sleep and leave your bed for any reason, then shake the bed covers once again when you return to the bed. The Holy Prophet [S.A.W.] observed: "When a person leaves the bed at night and returns to it again, he should dust it thrice with the edge of his wrapping cloth, for he does not know what creature may have crept on to the bed in his absence." (Tirmidhi)
13. Say the following prayer, when you get into bed. The Prophet's [S.A.W.] close attendant Hadrat Anas [R.A.A.] reports that on going to bed, the Holy Prophet [S.A.W.] used to recite the following prayer:

*"Praise be to Allah Who gave us food and drink, provided us sufficiently, and gave us (a place for) shelter! How many there are who have neither a provider nor shelterer."* *(Tirmidhi)*

14. Recite some portion of the Holy Quran at the time of going to bed. The Holy Prophet [S.A.W.] invariably used to recite a portion of the Holy Quran before going to sleep. He has observed: "Allah sends an angel to a man who recites a portion of the Book of Allah before going

to sleep to protect him from all harm till the time of his rising." (Ahmad)

*The Holy Prophet [S.A.W.] has further observed: "When a man lies down on the bed, an angel and the devil call on him. The angel says to him: "Close thy deeds of the day with a virtuous act." And the devil says: "Close thy deeds of the day with an evil act." If that man then recites the name of Allah before going to sleep, the angel stands guard over him all night."*

*Hadrat* 'Aishah *[R.A.A.] has reported: "When the holy Prophet [S.A.W.] went to bed, he used to join his arms in the style of prayer and having recited the* Surahs *(last three Surahs of the Quran) used to blow upon his hands and then starting from his head, face and the front he passed his hands over his body as far as it could go. The Holy Prophet [S.A.W.] repeated this act three times."*

*(Tirmidhi)*

15. While going to sleep put your right hand under the right cheek and turn on the right side. Hadrat Bra [R.A.A.] relates: "The Holy Prophet [S.A.W.] used to rest his right hand under his right cheek. While retiring to sleep, the Prophet [S.A.W.] used to say the following prayer:

*"O Allah! Save me from Thy doom on the day Thou wilt raise Thy bondmen."*

*It is recorded in Hisn-e-Hasin that the Holy Prophet [S.A.W.] used to recite this prayer three times.*

16. Do not lie down on your belly nor take a turn to the left side of your body when going to sleep. The father of Hadrat Muish Tafkhat-al-Ghifari [R.A.A.], relates: "I was lying on my belly in the mosque. Presently a person startled me with a touch of his foot and observed: "Allah disapproves of this posture." When I looked up I saw he was the Holy Prophet [S.A.W.]. (A b u Daud)

17. Sleep in place where fresh air is accessible. Do not sleep in closed rooms where there is no opening for letting in fresh air.

18. Do not keep your face covered when asleep. This habit is harmful for health. Sleep with your face uncovered so that you may inhale fresh air.
19. Take care not to sleep on roofs which are not surrounded with a ridge of the wall or railing. Put on light before stepping down the stairs as a little oversight often causes grave consequences.
20. Even in the freezing cold, do not keep the stove burning while you are asleep, nor keep the lantern on in a closed room. The gases produced by fire are deeply injurious to health; sometimes they may even prove fatal."
21. Say the following prayer before falling asleep. Hadrat Abu Hurrayrah [R.A.A.] has reported: "The Apostle of Allah [S.A.W.] used to say this prayer before going to sleep.

*"In Thy name, my Lord! I lay my side (on the bed) and in Thy name I raise it. If Thou withhold my soul, then have mercy thereon. If Thou send it back, then guard it even as Thou dost guard Thy righteous bondmen."*
*(Bukhari, Muslim)*

*In case memory does not retain this prayer, here is a short prayer:*

*"O Allah! In Thy name do I live and die."*
*(Bukhari, Muslim)*

22. Form the habit of waking up in the small hours of the night. It is essential to rise in the last quarter of the night and remember Allah to master your desires and physical demands and to establish communion with Allah. The distinctive trait of the favourites of Allah, as Allah has Himself affirmed, is that they wake up in the night and bow in humility to Him and make prostrations and seek His forgiveness for their sins. It was the practice of the Holy Prophet [S.A.W.] that he reposed in the early part of the night and got up in the small hours and engaged himself in devotion to Allah.
23. Say this prayer on arising from sleep:

*"Praise be to Allah Who restored us unto life, having caused us to die and unto Him shall be the Resurrection."*
*(Bukhari, Muslim)*

24. Offer thanks to the Lord on seeing a happy dream and take it as a good omen. The Holy Prophet [S.A.W.] observed: "Prophethood now bears glad tidings and nothing besides." The people enquired: "What do the glad tidings signify?" The Apostle of Allah observed: "A happy dream" (Bukhari). The Holy Prophet. [S.A.W.] further remarked: "Whoever is more truthful among ye will see a more truthful dream." The Prophet [S.A.W.] instructed the people, "Offer thanks to the Lord and praise Him whenever you see a happy dream. And relate your happy dreams and relate them to your friends only." Whenever the Holy Prophet [S.A.W.] saw a happy dream, he related it to his Companions and he used to say to his friends. "Recount your dreams to me and I shall tell you their interpretation."
(Bukhari)
25. Invoke blessings frequently upon the Holy Prophet [S.A.W.]. Perchance Allah may bless you with a visit of His Apostle [S.A.W.].

Hadrat Maulana Muhammad 'Ali Mongiri once asked Hadrat Fazal Rahman Ganj Muradabadi, "Teach me some special Darood (prayer of Benediction) by which I may be blessed with the vision of the Holy Prophet [S.A.W.]." Hadrat Fazal replied: "There is no special prayer of Benediction. You need to cultivate deep devotion only." Later, after some deliberation he observed: "However, with the following Benediction Hadrat Syed Hassan [R.A.A.] had the vision of the Prophet:

*"Allah! shower Thy Grace upon Muhammad and his family to the ultimate extent of numbers which are in Thy Knowledge."*

*The Holy Prophet [S.A.W.] observed:*

*"He who sees me in dream does actually sees me, for the devil cannot appear in my form." (Shamail Tirmidhi)*

*Hadrat Yazid Farsi [R.A.A.] used to calligraph the Holy Quran. Once he was blessed with the vision of the Holy Prophet [S.A.W.] in a dream. Hadrat Ibn 'Abbas [R.A.A.] was alive at that time. Hadrat Yazid mentioned his dream to him. Thereupon Hadrat Ibn 'Abbas related this Tradition to him, "Whoever sees my vision in a dream actually sees me, for the devil can never appear in my form." Then 'Abbas asked Yazid: "Can you describe the person you saw in your dream?" Hadrat Yazid recounted: "His frame and height were of fine proportions. He had a brown complexion inclined towards fairness. He had dark eyes and a smiling, handsome, round face. He had a thick beard covering his whole visage and flowing down to and spreading over his bosom." Hadrat Ibn 'Abbas affirmed: "Yes, if you had seen the Holy Prophet [S.A.W.] in his life you could not have given a better description of him" (i.e., the description given by you fits the actual appearance of the Apostle) [S.A.W.] (Shamail Tirmidhi)*

26. When, Allah forbid, you see an unhappy or terrifying dream, never relate it to any one. Beseech Allah to protect you from the menace of the dream. If it pleases Him, you will be safe from any evil. Hadrat Abu Salma relates: "I often used to fall ill on seeing unhappy dreams. One day, I told of it to Hadrat Abu Qatada [R.A.A.] who related to me the following Tradition of the Holy Prophet [S.A.W.] "A happy dream is a blessing from Allah. If any of you sees a happy dream, he should not relate it to any one other than his sincere friend. If any of you sees a bad dream, he should not mention it to any one. On the other hand, as soon as he wakes from sleep he should recite." (Aaudhu billahi minashshaita nirrajim) three times and breathe a 'tut-tut' towards his left side and then take a turn over to the other side. In this manner, he will remain safe from the evil effects of the dream" (Riyad-us-Salehin, Muslim)

27. Do not relate false dreams conceived by your own imagination. Hadrat 'Abdullah bin 'Abbas [R.A.A.] states that the Holy Prophet [S.A.W.] observed: "The person who relates concocted dreams shall be awarded a punishment to bind two grains of bar ley in a knot and he will never be able to do it." (Muslim)

*And the Holy Prophet [S.A.W.] observed: "It is a great calumny that a man should relate what he has not seen with his own eyes." (Bukhari)*

28. When a friend relates his dream to you, give him a favourable interpretation and say a prayer to invoke the blessing of Allah upon him. A man once related his dream to the Holy Prophet [S.A.W.]. He observed: "You have seen a good dream and it shall have a happy outcome."

After the dawn prayers the Holy Prophet [S.A.W.] used to sit cross-legged and asked the people to relate to him if anyone had seen a dream and before listening to anyone's dream, the Holy Prophet [S.A.W.] used to say:

"May the goodness of this dream be bestowed on you and may you be protected from its evil effects. May this dream prove favourable to us and may it bring curse upon our enemies. Praise and thanksgiving is due to Allah alone Who is the Lord of all worlds."

29. If a dream strikes feelings of terror into you or an awkward dream perplexes you, you should recite the following prayer to get rid of fear or perplexity and ask your grown-up children also to learn it by heart.

Hadrat 'Abdullah bin 'As [R.A.A.] related that whenever a person saw a terrible or awkward dream, the Holy Prophet [S.A.W.] used to instruct him to say the following prayer:

*"I seek the protection of the perfect words of Allah against His wrath and anger and punishment; against the evil-doings of His creatures; against the fears of evil spirits and against the possibility that these evil spirits or their fears should assail me."* *(Abu Daud, Tirmidhi)*

## OTHER MANNERS

1. Walk with a medium pace. Do not rush to become an object of ridicule for the onlookers, nor drag your feet so wearily that people might think you are ill and start making anxious enquiries after your health. The Holy Prophet [S.A.W.] used to take long steps when walking and placed his feet firmly on the ground; he never dragged his feet while walking.
2. Walk with poise and dignity with eyes cast down. Do not continue to look sideways at everything along the path. It is childish and improper. The Holy Prophet

[S.A.W.] used to walk with his holy self inclined forward as if he were descending a slope. He [S.A.W.] used to move with dignity at a rather quick pace and kept an alert but self-possessed posture of body. He [S.A.W.] seldom looked sideways, right or left, on the road.

3. Walk humbly with even steps. Do not walk arrogantly and proudly. You can't split the earth with a kick nor are you going to scale the heights of mountains. What is the sense then, for striking arrogant and haughty postures in walking?
4. Walk with shoes on. Do not walk bare foot. Shoes protect the feet from injury by thorns, pebbles or other harmful bits and pieces lying on the way, as well as from the bites of deadly insects. The Holy Prophet [S.A.W.] observed: "Keep your shoes on most of the time. A person who keeps his shoes on is a kind of rider."
5. Be mindful of good taste, propriety and dignity when walking along the road. Walk with both shoes on, or with both feet bare. It is ridiculous to walk with a shoe on one foot and the other foot bare. Observe utmost care not to display such bad' taste or improper behaviour unless it is inevitable. The Holy Prophet [S.A.W.] observed: "No one should walk with one shoe on. Walk with both shoes on or with both feet bare."
(Shamail Tirmidhi)
6. Keep the ends of your dress folded in the course of walking to avoid the danger of entanglements. The Holy Prophet [S.A.W.] used to roll up his attire a bit while walking.
7. Walk shoulder to shoulder with your companions. Do not walk ahead of your companions to show off your higher rank. Sometimes walk hand in hand with your fellows in a spirit of close friendship. The Holy Prophet [S.A.W.] never displayed his distinguished rank while walking with his Companions [R.A.A.]. Often the Prophet [S.A.W.] would walk behind his Companions [R.A.A.] and sometimes took the hand of a Companion into his own sacred hand as a mark of intimate companionship.

8. Observe the following etiquettes strictly while walking along the road. Do not stop or sit on the way with the object of staring at the passersby. If on occasions you must stop or sit on the way, you should follow the following six rules: (i) Keep your eyes downcast. (ii) Remove harmful bits and pieces out of the way. (iii) Respond to the salutation of others. (iv) Persuade the people to do good and prevent them from doing evil. (v) Show the way to travellers who have lost direction. (vi) Help those who are in trouble or are facing hardship.
9. In the course of a journey, seek the companionship of the good and avoid travelling with the wicked.
10. Men and women should not walk in a mixed company on the road. The women should avoid the middle path and walk along the edge of the road. The men should walk apart from the women. The Holy Prophet [S.A.W.] affirmed: "Collision with a mud-stained swine drenched in stinking slush is tolerable, but it is undesirable that a stranger should rub shoulders with a female."
11. Whenever righteous women have to pass along the road they should cover their bodies, garments and all pieces of adornment carefully with a 'burqa' or a sheet and cover their faces with a veil.
12. Do not wear a piece of ornament which gives out a tinkling sound while you walk, or otherwise, walk with sod steps so that the tinkle of your ornaments may not invite the attention of those unrelated to you.
13. Women should not use strong perfumes if they intend to go out on the road. The Holy Prophet [S.A.W.] has disapproved of such women in strong terms.
14. When you emerge from your home, look up to the sky and say the following prayers:

    "In the name of Allah, I rely upon Allah. O Allah! We seek refuge in Thee lest we slip, or go astray or wrong or be wronged, or act foolishly or any one should act foolishly with us." (Musnad Ahmad)
15. On going to the bazar, say this prayer:

*"In the name of Allah. O Allah! I ask of Thee good of this market and the good of that which is therein and*

*I seek refuge in Thee from the evil thereof and the evil of that which is therein. O Allah! Behold I seek refuge in Thee lest I take a false oath or strike a bargain incurring loss."*

*Hadrat 'Umar bin Khattab [R.A.A.] stated that the Holy Prophet [S.A.W.] had observed: "The man who says this prayer on entering the bazar, Allah adds ten lakh virtues to his account and forgives his ten lakh sins and raises his merits by ten lakh degrees"*

*"There is no deity save Allah. He is One. No partner hath He. His is the Sovereignty and His is the praise. He giveth life and He giveth death. He is the Ever Living that never dieth. In His hand is all the good and He hath power to do all things."* *(Tirmidhi)*

1. You should set out on a journey at a suitable hour so that the journey may be completed in the shortest possible time and prayer times may also be properly observed. The Holy Prophet [S.A.W.] generally held Thursday to be a propitious day to start on a journey himself or for sending someone else on a journey.

2. Do not go on a journey alone. If possible, travel in the company of three persons. This ensures proper care of baggage and needs are easily met by mutual cooperation. Companionship during a journey also ensures safety from several dangers and mishaps. The Holy Prophet [S.A.W.] once observed: "If the disadvantages of travelling alone that I am aware of are made known to the people, no rider would go on a journey alone during the night." (Bukhari). On one occasion, a man having made a long journey came to the Holy Prophet [S.A.W.]. The Prophet [S.A.W.] enquired from the traveller, "Who is thy companion?" The traveller submitted: " O Prophet of Allah [S.A.W.] I have no companion. I have come alone." Thereupon the Holy Prophet [S.A.W.] observed: "A lone rider is a devil; two riders are devils, too; but three riders are riders all right." (Tirmidhi)

3. A woman must go on a journey in the company of her spouse or lawful kith and kin. In the case of ordinary travelling for a day or half, she may go alone, but it is

always discreet for a woman not to move out alone. The Holy Prophet [S.A.W.] has observed: "It is not permissible for a woman who believes in Allah and the Day of Judgement to go on a journey lasting for three or more days alone. She may, however, undertake such a long journey if she is accompanied by her father, brother, husband, her own son or any other lawful kith or kin." (Bukhari). The Holy Prophet [S.A.W.] is reported to have remarked on one occasion: "A woman should not go alone even on a journey of one day and one night." (Bukhari, Muslim)

4. Setting out on a journey when you get on to the vehicle of transport and it begins to move, say this prayer:

*"Glory be unto Allah Who hath subjugated this (beast) unto us, though we were unable to subdue it. Behold we are assuredly to return unto our Lord. O Allah! Behold, we beg of Thee in this journey of ours righteousness and piety and a conduct wherewith Thou wilt be well pleased. O Allah! Make this journey of ours easy for us, and roll up for us the distance thereof. O Allah! Thou art (our) companion in this journey, and representative in (our) household. O Allah! Behold, I seek refuge in Thee from the toil of this journey, from holding a sad sight and a bad reverse in my wealth and household and from deficiency after plenty, and from the curse of the oppressed. (Muslim, Abu-Daud, Tirmidhi)*

5. Pay due regard to the comfort and convenience of others on the way. Your fellow-travellers have a right on you. The Holy Quran affirms: *Was-sahibil-jahanbi.* ("Be nice to the companion beside you"). The term `companion beside you' includes all such persons who happen to be your fellow travellers any time, anywhere. The brief fellowship in the course of a journey imposes a duty on you to show the best conduct towards your fellow-traveller and take the utmost care not to cause him any physical or mental distress by word or deed. The Holy Prophet [S.A.W.] affirmed: "The chief of the nation is the servant of the people. The person who excels others in rendering good service to his fellow men can be

surpassed in piety by no one, save those who attain martyrdom in the way of Allah." (Mishkat)

6. Say two Rakats of Thanksgiving on leaving for a journey and on returning from it. Such was the practice of the Holy Prophet
7. When your train or bus ascends a slope or your aeroplane takes off and is air-borne, say this prayer:

*"O Allah, Thou art supreme over all heights and elevations. Praise and Thanks giving under all circumstances is due to Thee alone."*

8. If you have to halt in your journey at night, stay at a safe place where your life and goods are sufficiently safeguarded against thieves and brigands as well as from the menace of deadly animals or insects.
9. Having achieved the purpose of your journey, make haste to return home. Do not linger about aimlessly.
10. On return from a journey, do not enter your house suddenly without sending in advance information of your arrival. Offer two Rakats of prayers in the mosque, thus affording time to the members of your household during which they may make preparations to accord you a befitting welcome.
11. Take care of the comfort of the animals accompanying you during the journey and look after the needs and protections of the rider who accompanies you.
12. In the cold weather, carry your bedding with you. Do not cause unnecessary trouble to your host.
13. Carry a tumbler and a prayer mat during the journey to avoid inconveniences at times of need like purification, ablution, prayer and taking a drink of water.
14. When some persons are travelling together they should appoint one person from among themselves to act as their "Ameer" (leader). But each one should keep his ticket, money for necessary expenses and other baggage in his own custody.
15. When night falls in the course of a journey, you should say this prayer:

*"O earth! My Lord and Thy Lord is Allah. I seek refuge in Allah from three evil, and evil of that which is in thee, from the evil of that which bath been created in thee, and from the evil of that which moveth over thee. I also seek refuge in Allah from the lion and the Aswad, from the serpent and the scorpion, from the evil of the dweller in the land, from the begetter, and that which (the begetter) begetteth."* *(Abu-Daud)*

16. At the time of returning home from a journey, say this prayer:

*"We are returnees, penitents before our Lord, penitence that may not let any effect of our misdeeds remain on us."* *(Hisn Hasien)*

17. On sending off someone on a journey, accompany him for some distance. On taking leave, ask him to say a prayer and say this prayer for him when the traveller departs:

*"Unto Allah' I commend your faith, your trust, and the corgi elusion of your deeds."* *(Hisn Hasien)*

18. Extend a warm welcome to the traveller when he returns from the journey. Make affectionate remarks and shake hands with him or embrace him as need be or as the occasion demands.

## PARTICULAR MANNERS

1. Endure calamities with fortitude and calmness. Do not lose heart and never let your grief and sorrow exceed moderate proportions. No person in the world can remain safe and unaffected by sorrow, grief, calamity, hardship, affliction, failure or loss. The response of the believers and unbelievers is, however, different in this respect. The non-believer loses his sense under the burden of pains and sorrows and is completely immobilised by feelings of hopelessness and dismay. Sometimes he succumbs to grief and commits suicide. In contrast, the believer remains undaunted in the face of the greatest calamity and never loses his patience. At such times he becomes a symbol of patience and fortitude and remains firm like a rock. He takes the view that whatever has

occurred was decreed by Allah and no command of Allah is without wisdom or purpose. Hence whatever Allah commands is for the ultimate good of man and surely there is always an aspect of mercy in all the dealings of Allah with man. This reasoning produces a state of spiritual calm and the bitter taste of sorrow turns into sweetness. This faith in the predetermined destiny makes the burden of hardship light and calamity becomes easy to bear. Allah has affirmed:

*"Naught of disaster befalleth in the earth or in yourselves but it is in a Book before We bring it into being. Lo! that is easy for Allah that ye grieve not for the sake of that which hath escaped you."* *(Al Hadeed 22, 23)*

In other words one of the merits of putting faith in a divinely-appointed destiny is that the believer finds solace even amidst the greatest suffering deeming it to be the decree of the Providence. He remains unshaken and in all matters looks towards the Merciful Allah and thinks only of His Grace and endeavours to seek good out of every evil by employing the virtues of patience and contentment under all circumstances. The Holy Prophet [S.A.W.] has observed:

*"How excellent is the state of the true believers! He wins Grace under all conditions. If he is afflicted with grief, sickness or poverty, he bears them with fortitude and such trials bring good to him. If he is rewarded with happiness and prosperity it becomes the cause of goodness for him."* *(Muslim)*

2. On hearing a tragic or painful news or if you suffer loss or sustain grief or injury or are beset with a sudden misfortune, recite at once:

*"Lo! We are Allah's and Lo! unto Him are we to return."* *(al-Baqarah)*

The implication is that all our possessions belong to Allah; Allah has given us everything and He is the One Who will take away everything. We are his creatures and we must return to Him. We submit to the Will of God in all matters and are content with His Dispensation. All acts of Allah contain certain purpose, wisdom and justice. He acts with greater good in view.

It is the duty of His faithful servant never to resent the actions of the Lord. Allah has said:

*"And surely We shall by you with something of fear and hunger and loss of wealth and lives and crops; but give glad tidings to the steadfast who say, when a misfortune striketh them: Lo! we are Allah's and lo! unto Him we are to return. Such are they on whom are blessings from their Lord and Mercy. Such are the rightly-guided."*

*(al-Baqarah: 155-157)*

The Holy Prophet [S.A.W.] has affirmed: "When a man is afflicted with hardship and says this Allah removes his affliction and blesses him with a happy outcome and bestows on him what his heart desires in reward for it."

On one occasion when his lamp went off, the Holy Prophet [S.A.W.] said: *inna lillahi wa inna ilaihai rajiun* someone enquired: "O Holy Prophet [S.A.W.] Is it a calamity if the lamp goes off?" The Holy Prophet [S.A., W.] observed: "Yes, everything that causes hardship to a believer is a calamity." And the Holy Prophet [S.A.W.] has observed:

*"Allah forgives all the sins of those Muslims who suffer a torment of the soul or physical pain, illness, sorrow, grief or affliction, even the injury on account of the piercing of a thorn (and bear all these trials with patience)."* *(Bukhari, Muslim)*

*Hadrat Anas [R.A.A.] reports:*

*The Holy Prophet [S.A.W.] observed: "The more severe the trial and hardship, the greater its reward. When Allah cherishes love for a group of people, He puts them to trial to cleanse them more and to make them pure. Hence those who submit to the Will of Allah win His pleasure. And those who harbour resentment against Allah in the hour of trial, Allah also is displeased with them."*

*(Tirmidhi)*

*Hadrat Abu Musa Ashari [R.A.A.] relates that the Holy Prophet [S.A.W.] observed: "When the child of a person dies, Allah enquires from His angels: "Did you extract the soul of the child of one of my Creatures?" They submit: "Yes." Allah again asks them: "Did you extract the soul of the most beloved of my creature?" They submit: "Yes." Allah then enquires from them: "What did my creature say?" They submit: "In his hour of affliction, he praised Thee. Allah commands the angels: 'Build a dwelling for this creature of Mine in the Paradise and call it 'Bait ul-Hamd' (The House of Thanksgiving)." (Tirmidhi)*

3. It is natural to show grief on suffering from pain or meeting an accident. However, care should be taken that even under the stress of extreme pain and grief the tongue should not utter an unbecoming remark, nor the virtues of patience and contentment be forsaken.

*The Holy Prophet [S.A.W.] had his son Hadrat Ibrahim [R.A.A.] in his lap when the child was about to depart from this earthly life. On seeing this piteous sight tears started trickling down the eyes of the Holy Prophet [S.A.W.] and the Prophet observed: "O Ibrahim! we grieve over thy separation, but our tongue shall utter only that which conforms to the Will of Allah."*

*(Muslim)*

4. Even in the throes of grief, do not commit an act which may smack of ingratitude or complaint or which transgresses the limits of Shariah. It is unlawful for a believer to give vent to loud weeping, tearing off clothes, slapping cheeks, crying and shouting or beating of head or the chest in mourning. The Holy Prophet [S.A.W.] has said: "The man who tears off his clothes, slaps his cheeks and raves and shouts like pagans and wails is not a member of my ummah." (Tirmidhi)

*When Hadrat Jafar Tayyar [R.A.A.], the cousin brother of the Holy Prophet [S.A.W.] attained martyrdom and the news reached his home, the women of his household began to shout and cry and started wailing loudly. The Holy Prophet [S.A.W.] sent word, "Stop wailing." But the women continued their lamentations. The Holy Prophet [S.A.W.] forbade them a second time, but the women would not comply. Thereupon the Holy Prophet [S.A.W.] observed: "Fill their mouths with dust."*

*(Bukhari)*

On one occasion, the Holy Prophet [S.A.W.] was accompanying a funeral procession. A woman came carrying a stove. The Holy Prophet [S.A.W.] reprimanded her so severely that she ran away at one. (Shat-un-Nabi Vol. VI)

The Holy Prophet [S.A.W.] observed:

*"No one should carry fire or funeral music behind a bier."*

*There was a custom in Arabia that people who walked behind a bier used to cast away their cloaks as a mark of grief and kept only their shirts on. On seeing people in this state once the Holy Prophet [S.A.W.] observed: Are you observing a pagan custom! I was thinking of invoking such a curse upon you that your appearances might be deformed." The people at once put on their cloaks and never acted in that fashion again.*

*(Ibn Majah)*

5. Do not curse your illness, nor utter any word of complaint. Exercise utmost restraint and self-control and pray for the reward in the Hereafter.

The sins, of the believers are washed away by suffering illness or enduring tortures. The soul of the believer is purged and he attains capital reward in the Eternal world. The Holy Prophet [S.A.W.] has affirmed:

*"All pain that the believer endures on account of physical torture, illness or some other cause is rewarded by Allah in such fashion that Allah purges the believer of all his sins even as a tree sheds its leaves."*

*(Bukhari, Muslim)*

*Once on seeing a lady shivering, the Holy Prophet [S.A.W.] enquired from her, "O Umm Saib (or Musayyib)! Why are you shivering so?" She replied: "I am seized with fever. May Allah curse it!" The Holy Prophet [S.A.W.] advised her, "No, don't curse the fever. Fever purges the progeny of Adam of sins even as fire melts the ore to extract pure iron."* *(Muslim)*

Hadrat 'Ata bin Rabah [R.A.A.] describes a first-hand account as follows: "On one occasion when we were near the Kaaba,. Hadrat 'Abbas said to me, "Would you like to see a woman who will go to Paradise?" "Yes, certainly." Hadrat 'Abbas [R.A.A.] said: "Look at that black woman. She once went to the Holy Prophet [S.A.W.] and submitted, "O Prophet of Allah [S.A.W.] I am seized with such deep fits of epilepsy that I lose all consciousness and in that state I become completely naked: O Prophet of Allah! Pray to Allah in my behalf." The Holy Prophet [S.A.W.] observed: "If you continue to endure this affliction with patience, Allah will send thee to Paradise or if you wish I shall pray to Allah to cure thee." On hearing this, the lady submitted; "O Prophet of Allah [S.A.W.]! I am willing to endure this affliction. However, please pray to Allah to save me from the humiliation of becoming naked when gripped with fits." The Holy Prophet [S.A.W.] thereupon prayed to Allah on behalf of this lady. Hadrat 'Ata [R.A.A.] reports that he saw this tall lady, Umm Rafz, on the steps of the Kaaba."

6. Do not observe mourning for more than three days on the death of any one. It is natural to be stricken with grief and to weep on the death of relations, yet the period of mourning should not exceed three days. The Holy Prophet [S.A.W.] observed: "It is not lawful for a believer to mourn the death of someone for a period of more than three days. However, the lawful mourning period for a widow is four months and ten days: During this period, she should not put on a colourful dress, nor use any perfume nor should bedeck herself." (Tirmidhi)

On the fourth day after the death of the brother of Hadrat Zainab bint Jahsh [R.A.A.], some ladies visited her to offer condolences. Hadrat Zainab [R.A.A.] applied perfume to her person in the presence of everyone and remarked: "I did not need to use perfume at this time. However, I have done so now because I have heard the Holy Prophet [S.A.W.] to say, "It is not lawful for a Muslim lady to observe mourning for more than three days for any relation except her husband."

7. Advise each other to bear sorrow, grief or calamity calmly and patiently. When the Holy Prophet [S.A.W.] returned from the battle of Uhud, the ladies came to his holy presence to enquire after their relations and kin. When Hadrat Hamna bint Jahsh [R.A.A.] appeared, the Holy Prophet [S.A.W.] instructed her to bear her grief calmly, and said: "Be patient over the martyrdom of

your brother 'Abdullah, [R.A.A.] and she recited: (It is from Allah and we have to return to Allah) and prayed for the salvation of her brother." Then the Holy Prophet [S.A.W.] instructed her, "Be patient over the martyrdom of your maternal uncle Hamza [R.A.A.]." Hadrat Hamna [R.A.A.] again recited and prayed for the salvation of her uncle.

The son of Hadrat Abu Talha [R.A.A.] was gravely ill. Leaving his son in this precarious state, Hadrat Talha [R.A.A.] had to go out to work. The child died in his absence. Abu Talha's wife [R.A.A.] instructed the people not to report the news to Abu Talha [R.A.A.]. When he returned home in the evening after work, he enquired from the wife: "How is the child?" She replied: "He is in a more restful state." Then she brought dinner for Abu Talha [R.A.A.]. He ate it in peace and went to bed. Next morning the pious wife conveyed the sad news to her husband in a very wise manner. She asked him: "If someone lends something to somebody and then demands it back, what right has the possessor to withhold the thing from the real owner?" Abu Talha [R.A.A.] replied: "It is improper for the borrower to claim such a right." Thereupon the patient wife observed: "Be patient over the loss of your son then." (Muslim)

8. Welcome all hardships in the way of righteousness in good cheer and feel joy rather than sorrow at whatever distress befalls you in this way. Offer thanks to the Lord that He thus accepted your sacrifice in His way. Hadrat Asma' [R.A.A.] the illustrious mother of Hadrat 'Abdullah-bin-Zubayr [R.A.A.] once fell gravely ill. Hadrat 'Abdullah [R.A.A.] came to enquire after her health. The mother said to him "Son! in the first place, I wish that Allah should keep me alive until I witness one of the two things that either you should attain martyrdom on the field of battle and I should obtain the Grace of being patient on hearing the report of your martyrdom or you should gain victory and seeing you a victor I should be happy. As Allah willed it so Hadrat 'Abdullah-bin-Zubayr [R.A.A.] attained martyrdom in the lifetime of his mother. Hajjaj ordered to keep his dead body hanging on the stake. Hadrat Asma' [R.A.A.] was at that time too old and weak yet in spite of her

old age and weakness she arrived to look at this piteous sight. Instead of crying and wailing on seeing the dead body of her dear son, she addressed Hajjaj and said to him: "Has not the time yet come for this rider to dismount the horse"?

9. Support one another in grief and pain. Share the sorrows and afflictions of your friends and lend all help you can to alleviate their suffering. The Holy Prophet [S.A.W.] observed: "All Muslims are like one human body. If the eye becomes sore, the entire body feels distress. If there is pain in the head, all organs of the body suffer the agony." (Muslim)

At the time when Hadrat Jafar Tayyar [R.A.A.] attained martyrdom, the Holy Prophet [S.A.W.] observed:

*"Let food be sent to Jafar's house, for the inmates of his house, in the abundance of their grief will not be able to cook food". (Abu Daud)*

*Hadrat Abu Hurrayrah [R.A.A.] reports that the Holy Prophet [S.A.W.] observed: "A man who offers condolences to a woman whose child is dead shall be admitted in Paradise and he shall be wrapped in the sheet of Paradise". (Tirmidhi)*

*And the Holy Prophet [S.A.W.] also observed: "The man who solaces an afflicted person shall be rewarded in the same degree as the afflicted one". (Tirmidhi)*

In the same connection the Holy Prophet [S.A.W.] enjoined upon the people to join the funerals. Hadrat Abu Hurrayrah (R.A.A.] has reported: "The Holy Prophet [S.A.W.] observed:

*"The person who joins the funeral and says the funeral prayer will get a reward equal to one Qirat (Carat) and the person who after the funeral prayers attends the burial also will get reward equal to two Qirats (Carats)." Someone asked: "What will be the mass of these two Qirats?" The Holy Prophet [S.A.W.] observed: "The mass of these two Qirats will be equal to two mountains". (Bukhari, Muslim)*

10. When you are pressed under the burden of calamities and afflicted with sorrows, turn to Allah; offer worship

and bow in humility to Him and say prayers to Him. The Holy Quran affirms:

*"O ye who believe! Seek help through perseverance and prayer."* *(al-Baqarah)*

It is natural to be sorrowful and shed tears in a grief stricken state. However, avoid weeping loudly. The Holy Prophet [S.A.W.] used to weep in a muffled voice. He [S.A.W.] used to heave a cold sigh; tears would stream down the eyes and the voice which came out of his holy bosom used to be similar to the sound of a bubbling kettle or the turning of a grinding wheel. The Holy Prophet [S.A.W.] has himself described the state of his grief and weeping:

*"The eye sheds tears; the heart is filled with sorrow; yet our tongue utters only those words which are pleasing to our Lord." Hadrat Abu Hurrayrah [R.A.A.] reports that whenever the Holy Prophet [S.A.W.] felt worried, he used to look up to the heavens and said repeatedly (Gloried by the Lord the Magnificent) and when the sorrow deepened the Holy Prophet [S.A.W.] devoted himself to prayer with greater fervour, and used to say: (The Alive, The Eternal)* *(Tirmidhi)*

11. Say these prayers in the moments of intense grief and sorrow, when calamities befall and you are under heavy stress of grief and unrest. Hadrat Saad-bin-Waqqas [R.A.A.] reports that the Holy Prophet [S.A.W.] affirmed: "The prayer which Dhun-nun offered to Allah from the belly of the fish was as follows:

*"There is no deity except Thee. Be Thou glorified! Lo I have been a wrong doer."* *(21: 87)*

Hence any Muslim who says this prayer to Allah in times of distress or hardship, Allah surely accepts his prayer. It is reported by Hadrat Ibn Abbas [R.A.A.] that in moments of sorrow or grief, the Holy Prophet [S.A.W.] used to say this prayer:

*"There is no deity except Allah. He is the Master of Great Heaven. There is no deity except Allah. He is the Master of Heaven and Earth and the Master of High Heaven."* *(Bukhari, Muslim)*

Hadrat Abu Musa [R.A.A.] states that the Prophet [S.A.W.] observed:

*"This prayer is a panacea for ninety-nine ills. The least benefit to be derived from saying this prayer is that he who says this prayer remains safe from grief and sorrow."*

Hadrat 'Abdullah b. Masud [R.A.A.] reported that the Holy Prophet [S.A.W.] affirmed: "Any one who is afflicted with pain or distress and says this prayer, Allah will surely turn his sorrow and grief into happiness and felicity:

*"Allah! I am Thy servant. My father is Thy servant and so is my brother. Thou hast power over my whole being. It is Thy Law which rules my life. All Thy Commands in my case are most just. I beseech Thee in the name of all Attributes which thou have mentioned. Thy own or those which Thou revealed inThy Book or revealed to some among Thy creatures or kept them hidden in Thy veiled Treasures, to make the Great Book, the Quran, the pleasure of my heart, the light of my eyes, the balm for my affliction and a cure for my anxiety."*

*(Ahmad, Ibn Habban Hisn Hasien)*

12. If, Allah forbid, matters come to such a pass that the calamities and hardships oppress you so hard that life becomes unbearable and distress assume such fearful proportions that the burden of life hangs heavy on you, even under such circumstances do never call for death nor should you ever think of the disgraceful act of taking your own life. The act of suicide is a symptom of cowardice; it is the worst form of breach of trust and the most heinous sin. Under such conditions of perplexity and unrest, pray constantly to Allah in these words:

*"Allah! Keep me alive as long as it is better for me to live and if there be goodness for me in death, send me death."* *(Bukhari, Muslim)*

13. Say this prayer when you find any one afflicted with hardship. Hadrat Abu Hurrayrah [R.A.A.] related: The Holy Prophet [S.A.W.] observed:

*"He who says the following prayer on seeing the other afflicted with trouble will, Allah willing, himself remain*

*safe from this trouble: "Praise be to Allah Who saved me from that where with He hath afflicted thee and made me to excel with a marked excellence most of those whom he created."* *(Tirmidhi)*

1. Assailed by the threat of slaughter, devastation, tyranny, barbarity, mischief and strife unleashed by the enemies of faith or panic-stricken by the catastrophic effects of natural calamities under all circumstances use the insight of a true believer and probe into the real causes of these visitations. Instead of wasting time on superficial remedies, focus all your energies on putting into effect the injunctions contained in the Book of Allah and the Sunnah. The Holy Quran affirms:

*"Whatever of misfortune striketh you it is what you have earned by your own deeds. And He forgiveth much."*
*(Ash-Shura: 30)*

And the Holy Quran itself reveals the remedy:

*"And all of you together should turn to Allah in repentance, O Believers, so that you may get salvation."*

'Tauba' *(Repentance) denotes: 'To return', 'To have recourse to'. Immersed in the fearful cesspool of sins and vices, when the Ummah (Muslim Nation) feels a sense of shame and turns to Allah in a spirit of devotion and having washed the stains of her vices by tears of repentance, renews her pledge of allegiance to Allah- this state is described in the Holy Quran by the term 'Tauba'. This 'repentance' and 'petition for mercy' is the most efficacious and genuine remedy against the fear and dread of all forms of evil and strife.*

2. Do not degrade the honour of your national life by adopting a cringing attitude before the tyranny, oppression and mischiefs of the enemies of faith; do not reduce yourself under their awe to the indignity of begging the cruel enemy for mercy. Gird up your loins; strengthen your faith and remove weakness which produces cowardice in you and encourages the enemies of faith to oppress and extinguish you. The Holy Prophet [S.A.W.] has identified two causes for this weakness: *Attachment to the world; *Fear of Death.

Make a resolve that you will not rest in peace until you have eliminated these two weaknesses from your own self as well as from the general body of the Muslims. The Holy Prophet [S.A.W.] observed:

> *"My Ummah will pass through a time when other nations, considering you an easy prey, will fall upon you just as the hungry rush towards food. Someone asked: "O Prophet [S.A.W.]: Will our number diminish encouraging other nations to make an assault to devour us?" The Holy Prophet [S.A.W.] observed: "No, you will not then be less in number but will render yourself weightless like straws that float helplessly in the flood water. Your enemies will no longer fear you and your hearts will be stricken with cowardice." At this stage, a man enquired: "O Prophet [S.A.W.]! What will be the cause of such cowardice?" The Holy Prophet [S.A.W.] observed: "There will be two causes: (a) You will start loving the world and; (b) You will feel allergic to death and hate the very idea of it."* *(Abu Daud)*

3. Purge your society of sensuality, frivolity, rule of women, and wickedness. Make your collective strength impregnable and use it to eradicate evil and mischief. Make a determined effort to inculcate and promote bravery, zest and courage in each and every individual of your fraternity. The Holy Prophet [S.A.W.] has affirmed:

> *"When your rulers are righteous, and the rich among you are generous and large-hearted and when your collective affairs are decided by mutual consultation, then the surface of the earth is better for you than its belly (life is worth living). But when your rulers are persons of wicked character and the rich in your society are lovers of wealth (miserly), and when your affairs are determined by your women, then the belly of the earth is better for you than its surface.* *(Tirmidhi)*

4. Never fail to support the right even under the most adverse circumstances. To give away one's life in support of right is far better than to lead a godless and ignominious existence. Do not shrink from upholding

the truth in the severest of trials and in the face of the greatest threat. Respond to the threat of death with a smile and welcome the chance of attaining martyrdom with zest and eagerness. The Holy Prophet [S.A.W.] has said:

*"The wheel of Islam is on the move, beware you must turn towards the direction given by the Holy Quran. Be vigilant! The Quran and the political power will shortly part company. Beware lest you should forsake the Quran. In the times to come there will be rulers who will impose their will on you. If you obey them, they will lead you astray from the path of righteousness. And if you rebel against them, they will put you to death." A Companion [R.A.A.] submitted: "What should we do then, O Prophet [S.A.W.]!" The Holy Prophet [S.A.W.] replied: "Do what the companions of Jesus [A.S.] did. They were cut through with saws and hanged on the cross. It is far better to give one's life obeying the commandments of Allah than to live a life of disobedience to the Almighty."*

5. Strive constantly against those evils of the society which produce an atmosphere of fear and panic in the people and lead to poverty, famine and violence reducing the whole nation to a miserable and helpless lot suffering the oppressions and tyranny of their enemies.

*Hadrat Abdullah b. Abbas [R.A.A.] remarks: "Wherever dishonesty becomes the order of the day, the people lose heart and courage and are afraid of their enemies, and wherever adultery becomes common, the people are destined to perish. Whenever people start cheating in weights and measures, they certainly face famine and starvation and where justice is denied blood is inevitably to be shed there. And nation which commits breach of promise is doomed to become the slave of its enemy."*

*(Mishkat)*

6. When you are assailed by the dread of the foes, say this prayer:

*"O Allah! Behold, we place Thee in front of them and seek refuge in Thee from their mischiefs."*

*(Abu-Daud, Nasai, Hisn Hasien)*

7. When you are surrounded by the enemy, say this prayer: "Allah! Do safeguard our honour and respect, and bless us with peace in this state of fear and harassment." (Ahmad, Hisn Hasien)

8. On seeing the windstorm rising or a cloud overcasting the sky, you should feel apprehension and fear. Hadrat '*Aishah*' [R.A.A.] reports that "I never beheld the Holy Prophet [S.A.W.] breaking into laughter in such a manner as to make his sacred mouth wide open. In moments of joy, a thin smile used to play on his august face. When a windstorm arose or a cloud darkened the sky, he [S.A.W.] used to feel apprehension, he alternately stood up or sat down and this mood lasted until the clouds had burst into rain. I submitted: "O Prophet [S.A.W.]! I see that other people rejoice when they see a cloud and look forward to raining with joyous hope, yet I see that your holy face shows feelings of heaviness and anxiety on watching a cloud." Thereupon the Holy Prophet [S.A.W.] observed: "*Aishah*, how can I avoid the apprehension that this cloud will not bring down a calamity, when I have the precedent before me that the nation of 'Ad were visited with a calamitous windstorm. On beholding this cloud, the people of 'Ad had said: This cloud will pour rain over us." (Bukhari, Muslim). Say this prayer when you see a cloud or a windstorm rising.

If the windstorm fills the horizon with deep darkness say:

*I seek refuge with the Lord of the Dawn and I seek refuge with the Lord of Men* *(Surah 113: 114)*

Hadrat 'Aishah [R.A.A.] relates:

*"Whenever the Holy Prophet [S.A.W.] beheld the windstorm rising, he used to say the following prayer: "O Allah! Behold, I beg of Thee the good of this (wind) and the good of that which is therein, and the good of that which hath been sent therewith. And I seek refuge in Thee from the evil thereof and the evil of that which is therein and the evil of that which hath been sent therewith."* *(Muslim, Tirmidhi)*

9. When excessive rain threatens loss and destruction, say this prayer: "O Allah! let there be downpour in our

suburb; but not on us. Let the rain fall on hillocks, in the thickets on the mountains, rivers, and on the hot beds of plantations." (Bukhari, Muslim)

10. On hearing the roar of clouds and the thunderbolt, stop conversation and begin reciting the following verse of the Holy Quran:

*"And the thunder (of the clouds) hymneth His praise and (so do) the Angels for awe of Him." (Al-Rad: 13)*

*Hadrat 'Abdullah ibn Zubayr [R.A.A.] on hearing the thunderbolt used to stop talking and recited the same verse. (Al-Adab al-Mufrad)*

*Hadrat Kaab [R.A.A.] states that any one who recites this verse three times on hearing the thunderbolt will remain safe from its danger. (Tirmidhi)*

*The Holy Prophet [S.A.W.] on hearing the roar of the clouds and the thunderbolt used to say this prayer:*

*"O Allah! Slay us not with Thy wrath and destroy us not with Thy punishment but take us unto Thy protection." (Al-Adab-al-Mufrad)*

11. When fire breaks out, make energetic efforts to extinguish it and continue to say:

*(Allah is Great, Allah is Great). The Holy Prophet has observed: "When you see a fire blazing out say: "Allah-o-Akbar" (Allah is Great). 'Takbir' Glorification of Allah extinguishes the fire."*

12. When you are seized with fear and panic, say this prayer. God willing fear will vanish and you will attain peace of mind. Hadrat Bra' b. Azib reports: "A person once complained to the Holy Prophet [S.A.W.] "I suffer from panic all the time." The Holy Prophet [S.A.W.] enjoined upon him to say the following prayer. He recited this prayer frequently and Allah freed his heart from panic.

"Pure and Supreme is the Lord, the Real Sovereign, Faultless. Oh Creator of Angels and Jibbrail! Your Power and Awe reigns over the Heavens and Earth."

1. You must celebrate occasions of joy in a befitting manner. Rejoicing is a demand of human instincts and a natural

urge. Religion gives due importance to the satisfaction of natural instincts and permits their fulfilment subject to some useful restraints and conditions. Religion disapproves of marring the attractiveness of your personality by assuming artificial postures of dignity, unnecessary somberness, and constant moroseness. Religion allows you to be joyous on all lawful such occasions and enjoins upon you to keep your spirits high and live with zest. It is misunderstanding the religion if it is thought that giving expression to joy and to rejoice on lawful occasions does not conform with the dignity of religion.

If Allah grants you the favour of performing some religious duty; you or one of your relations attains high honour in learning and excellence; Allah blesses you with prosperity, wealth or some other bounty; you return safe from a long journey or any of your relations comes back from his travels to distant parts; you receive a visit from an honourable guest; a marriage comes off or the birth of a child takes place in your home; you receive report of the health and well-being of a near relative or the happy news of the victory or glorious achievement of the people of Islam; or on festivals-it is your natural right to celebrate these occasions with rejoicing.

Islam not only allows the holding of festivities, but regards this act as in perfect harmony with the spirit of religion.

*Hadrat Kaab ibn Malik [R.A.A.] relates: "When Allah had accepted my prayer for forgiveness and I received the glad tidings of it, I at once went to the Holy Prophet [S.A.W.] offered my salam. At that moment, the holy face of the Prophet [S.A.W.] was radiant with joy. Whenever the Holy Prophet [S.A.W.] attained some happiness, his face would glow like the radiance of moon and we used to take the brightness and radiance of his face as index of exceedingly joyous feelings in him, [S.A.W.].* *(Riyad-us Salihin)*

2. Feel free to do arrangements to celebrate a festival and join the festivities without inhibitions. On arrival at Medina, the Holy Prophet [S.A.W.] observed:

*"You used to celebrate festivities on two days during a year. Allah has now blessed you with two better days, i.e., 'Eid-ul-fitr' and 'Eid-ul-fitr." Therefore you should celebrate these two festivals of the year with great happiness and rejoicing and arrange reunions and indulge in recreation in joyous mood and give vent to your feelings of happiness in a natural manner. It is because of this injunction of the Holy Prophet [S.A.W.] that fasting is forbidden on the occasions of these two festivals.*

The Holy Prophet [S.A.W.] observed:

*"These two days are meant for feasting, celebration of joy in union with other people and to remember Allah."*
*(Sharah Maani-ul-Athar)*

On the day of 'Eid, be neat and clean and take a bath, put on the best dress according to your means, use perfume, eat good food and let the children enjoy themselves with proper means of recreation and games and permit to observe fun freely and without any hindrance.

Hadrat 'Aishah [R.A.A.] relates:

*"It was the 'Eid day and some slave girls were singing the verses which the Ansar had composed about the battle of Buath. While the girls were thus engaged in singing, Hadrat Abu Bakr [R.A.A.] came and exclaimed in astonishment: "How strange! Singing in the household of the Prophet [S.A.W.]!" The Holy Prophet [S.A.W.] answered: "Abu Bakr, never mind. Each nation has a festival day and today we celebrate our 'Eid."*

*Once on 'Eid day some negro acrobats were giving a demonstration of their skill. The Holy Prophet [S.A.W.] himself watched these exercises and let 'Aishah [R.A.A.] also see them from behind his back. The Holy Prophet [S.A.W.] cheered also. When 'Aishah [R.A.A.] grew weary, the Holy Prophet [S.A.W.] permitted her to depart.*
*(Bukhari)*

3. Observe the injunctions and mores of Islam in your rejoicings. Offer thanks to your Benefactor and prostrate before Him in gratitude. In the excitement of your joy,

do not perform any act nor adopt any attitude which does not conform to the spirit of Islam or is contrary to Islamic manners and injunctions. You must express your joyous sentiments, but observe the rule of moderation and do not let your expression of happiness take the better of the duty of obedience, devotion and humility and turn into a display of haughtiness and pride. The Holy Quran directs:

*"And exult not because of that which hath been given. Allah loveth not all prideful boasters."* *(57: 23)*

*Do not be so intoxicated by happiness as to forget Allah. The supreme happiness of the pious is to remember the Best of happiness all the more and offer prostration before Him in gratitude and acknowledge by action and speech the Benefactions, Greatness and the Glory of Allah.*

After observing fasts during the month of Ramadan and securing the blessings of reciting the Holy Quran and saying 'Tarawih' prayers during the month, when you sight the 'Eid-moon, your happiness knows no bounds. On realising that you have been successful in carrying out the injunctions of Allah by His Grace, you at once give away the share of your poor and needy brethren out of your wealth so as to make amends for any negligence in worship or error in discharging the duty of Devotion to Allah and also to enable the poor people to participate with others in the joys of the 'Eid. In acknowledgement of this favour of Allah, you express your befitting sentiments of joy by offering two prayers of thanksgiving to Allah and on the day of *'Eid-ul-Adha,* you commemorate the great and unique sacrifice of Hadrat Ibrahim and Hadrat Ismail [A.S.] and thus finding your own heart filled with the eagerness to make sacrifice when need arises you offer prostration to Allah in gratitude. And then the hymns of 'Praise be to Allah', '*Takbir* and 'Thanksgiving' resound through every community and are heard in all streets, lanes and roads. And when on 'Eid days you eat well and put on your best clothes and celebrate in lawful fashion according to the injunctions of the Shariah all these activities of yours are recorded as submission to and acknowledgement of the authority of Allah.

4. Invite others to join your celebrations and share your joy and similarly participate in the rejoicing of others to enhance their feelings of happiness. Exchange messages of felicitation on occasions of joy.

When the repentance of Hadrat Kaab-b-Malik [R.A.A.] was accepted by Allah and the Muslims got news of it they came in crowds to offer congratulations to Hadrat Kaab [R.A.A.]. They expressed their unbounded joy. Hadrat Kaab was so deeply moved by the felicitation and expressions of rejoicing displayed by Hadrat Talha [R.A.A.] that it remained fresh in his memory all through the rest of his life. In his old age Hadrat Kaab [R.A.A.] related the case of his trial and repentance to his son 'Abdullah and especially mentioned about Hadrat Talha's [R.A.A.] expressions of joy. He remarked: "I can never forget Talha's manner of congratulating me and his feelings of joy."

*The Holy Prophet [S.A.W.] on conveying to Kaab [R.A.A.] the glad tidings of the acceptance of his repentance expressed his personal feelings of great happiness and observed: "Kaab, this is the happiest day of the life!"*
*(Riyad-us-Salihin)*

*On occasions of marriage or birth of a child or on similar events of joy in the homes of other people, join in their celebrations and felicitate them on the happy occasion.*

*Hadrat Abu Hurrayrah [R.A.A.] reports that the Holy Prophet [S.A.W.] used to congratulate the newly-wedded in these words: May Allah keep you in prosperity and confer His blessings upon both of you and may He grant you the favour of living together in perfect harmony."*
*(Tirmidhi)*

*On one occasion Hadrat Hussain [R.A.A.] instructed someone to felicitate others on the birth of a child in the following manner: "May Allah grant you grace in this gift. May Allah grant you the favour of offering gratitude to Him. May Allah develop this child into a full-blended youth and raise him submissive to you."*

5. When a near relative or an acquaintance return from a long journey, go and welcome him and express your feelings of joy on his safe return and successful conclusion

of his mission. If he holds a function to celebrate the happy occasion of his safe return from the journey, go and join the party. On the other hand, when you return home safe from your travels and arrange a function to celebrate the occasion, invite your near relatives to the party. However, you must avoid unnecessary expense or ostentatious and lavish display. Do not incur expenditure which is beyond your means. When the Holy Prophet [S.A.W.] returned from the battle of Tabuk, the Muslim men and children had gone up to Thaniyyatul-Wada' to receive him [S.A.W.]. (Abu Daud)

When the Holy Prophet [S.A.W.] migrated from Mecca and reached Medina and prepared to enter the city from the southern side, the Muslim men, women, boys and girls came out of their homes to greet him [S.A.W.]. The small girls of the Ansar were singing this happy song:

*"Today, the moon arose upon us from the southern hill, Thaniyyatul Wada. It is our duty to offer thanks for the call and teaching of the Apostle who guided us towards Allah. O Prophet! You have been sent among us, you have brought a religion that we will bear allegiance to it." Once on his return to Medina from a journey, the Holy Prophet [S.A.W.] slaughtered a camel and a cow and arranged a feast for the people. (Abu Daud)*

6. Celebrate the occasions of marriage with joy and happiness and invite your relatives and friends to participate in the celebration of the happy event. The Holy Prophet [S.A.W.] permitted singing and playing of music on weddings. This injunction is meant to serve a two-fold purpose: the expression of the feelings of joy and the public announcement of the news of wedding.

*Hadrat 'Aishah [R.A.A.] married one of her female relations to a man from the Ansar. At the time of the departure of the bride, the Holy Prophet [S.A.W.] observed: "Why didn't these people send a slave-girl with her to play duff and sing some songs on the way." (Bukhari)*

*On the occasion of the wedding of Hadrat Rabi' bint Muawwadh [R.A.A.] some girls were sitting with her and playing on duff. They were singing some verses in praise of their fathers who had attained martyrdom in the battle of Badr. One of the girls recited this line: "And there is a prophet in our midst who knows what is to happen tomorrow." On hearing this, the Holy Prophet [S.A.W.] observed: "Leave this bit out and sing those verses which you were singing earlier."* *(Bukhari)*

7. On the happy occasions of wedding, arrange a feast for your relatives and friends according to your position and means. The Holy Prophet [S.A.W.] established the precedent of arranging 'Walima' feasts on his own marriages and enjoined upon others to follow the same practice. The Holy Prophet [S.A.W.] observed: "If nothing else, slaughter a goat and serve its meat to guests." (Bukhari)

If for some reason you cannot attend a wedding party, do send a message of congratulations. The practice of exchanging gifts on nuptials, weddings and on similar occasions of joy, renews and deepens the relationship and augments love and lends warmth to it. Nonetheless be careful to send gifts of the value which your means can afford and avoid ostentatious display.

## CLEANLINESS AND PURITY

One of the attributes symbolizing man's progress and demonstrating his humanity, as well as distinguishing him from the animals, is cleanliness.

***Impurities:*** It is demanded of a Muslim that he keeps away from impurities and purifies himself, his clothes, his place or immediate environment. These impurities are, for example, emetic, prostatic fluid, urine, intoxicants, human excrement, droppings of animals, blood, pus, and milk of animals forbidden as food. Whatever is severed from living animals is considered impure except parts of fish and locusts, and the wool of sheep, goat and camel. All animals are considered impure if they are not slaughtered according to the Islamic way.

If any such impurities have fallen onto a Muslim's body or clothes or 'place', then washing them off is an obligatory duty.

### *Bathing*

- Cleanliness of the human body is essential for various reasons. In addition to protecting the body against disease, it is an important factor when communicating with others in the society.
- Taking a bath from time to time is, therefore, the way to avoid smelling bad.

### *Where to Bathe*

- Men can bathe in a public bath, provided either they use a curtain or wear a lower garment.
- Urinating in a bathing place should be avoided if the ground is of earth, as this will accumulate impurities; if it is a tiled floor and has drainage, it is not forbidden.

### *When Washing is Obligatory*

Washing the whole body becomes necessary:

- After seminal emission this applies also to emission during sleep or a dream to remove sexual defilement.
- For a woman who has a sexual dream provided she sees signs of liquid; for a woman at the end of her menstrual period, and at the end of child-bed.

There are, in addition, special occasions when washing is recommended. These are the two Festivals in Islam, on embracing Islam, and every Friday before the congregational prayer.

### *Method of Washing*

A Muslim should observe the following:

- Before he starts to wash, he should be sure he has concealed himself from others.
- Place his clothes and towel in a clean place.
- As a first step, remove impurities before he begins washing.
- Wash his hands three times.
- Rinse his mouth and take water up into his nose.
- Wash his face and arms.
- Pour water on his body, beginning with the right side.

- Be sure that water has reached every part of his body and hair, and let the water run between his fingers and toes.
- When using soap, this must be followed by clean water so that none of the soap remains on his body. This is required when washing is obligatory.
- Bathing in a bath tub is permitted, provided that he follows this by taking a shower to guarantee that all impurities have been removed.

***Importance of Cleaning Certain Parts of the Body:*** Cleaning certain areas of the body where dirt mainly accumulates is necessary, such as:

- Shaving off pubic hairs, whenever necessary.
- Plucking out hairs under the armpits. If that is difficult then shaving can be substituted.
- Paring the nails: when paring the nails is necessary, a Muslim should start with his right hand, then his left hand, his right foot, and finally his left foot.

Keeping other parts of the body clean, in particular the face, head, hands and feet is of special importance. Doing so is especially refreshing to body and mind; moreover these are the parts most commonly in contact with other people. Special attention should also be given to cleaning the mouth, which is used in communicating with others. Two complementary ways of keeping the mouth clean and pleasant smelling are:

- Using a toothpick following meals.
- Using the miswak (tooth stick) or a toothbrush, starting from the right side of the mouth.

Any one of these methods is not a substitute for the others; they complement each other. It is difficult and impractical to carry a toothbrush everywhere; a miswak or a tooth stick, on the other hand, may be taken anywhere easily. In addition, a miswak can be readily used when meeting someone, when the smell of the mouth changes, and when returning home from work.

***Cosmetics and Adornment for Men:*** There are special rules for women, others for men, and still others common to both sexes.

### *Hair*

- Having a part of the head shaved and leaving a part unshaven is not an Islamic way of hair dressing. It should either be all shaved or all left.
- Attention to and care of hair-cleanliness and tidiness, i.e. combing it, using hair oil, keeping the comb clean, etc.-is Islamic conduct. However, this should not be exaggerated.
- There is no special Islamic hair style. However, the Prophet used to have three styles of hair: wafra (hair extending beyond the lobe of the ear), limma (hair descending below the lobe of the ear) and jumma (hair extending to the shoulder joints).

### *Beard*

- The beard is an element of beauty on a man's face, so it should be left unshaven.
- A beard should be kept clean and combed.
- A man should not be ashamed of grey hairs in his beard, and should not pluck them out.

### *Perfume*

- The best kind of perfume is musk oil. A man should perfume himself from time to time. If somebody offers him a perfume, it is better to accept it and not to reject it, as it is considered a good thing.

***Moustache:*** A moustache should not be allowed to grow too long. It should be clipped so that the upper lip is visible.

### *Signet Ring*

- Having a ring is permissible for a Muslim, even for those who are not married or engaged.
- It is forbidden for men to wear gold rings. In fact gold must not be used by men except for medical or dental purposes.
- The ring can be made of any metal except iron and gold. It should preferably be made of silver.
- The ring may be worn on the fingers of the left or the right hand.

### *Women's Make-Up and Adornment*

- There is nothing more fitting than for a woman to leave her beauty as it is, natural, without changes or additions.
- A woman is, however, allowed to beautify herself provided that she does so at home. A woman should make herself beautiful at home for her husband, by beautifying her face with cosmetics, by keeping herself clean and by having a pleasant fragrance.
- It is permissible for a woman to stain her hands with henna (a red plant-dye).
- It is permissible for a woman to use perfume in the presence of male relatives whom she is forbidden to marry.

### *Hair*

- A woman should try to keep her hair clean and tidy. In fact, hair for a woman is just like a beard for a man, i.e. a significant element of beauty.
- If a woman has short hair, she should not try to add false hair. If another lady asks her to help her fix false hair on her head, she should refuse.

### *Face and Hands*

- A woman should take special care to keep her face clean.
- If hairs have grown on a woman's face, she must neither be ashamed of it, nor try to remove them, nor pull out hairs for another woman. She must not be ashamed of her nature.
- A woman should never tattoo another woman or have herself tattooed.
- A woman should never pluck her eyebrows.
- Nails should not be allowed to grow long; they should be pared frequently.
- Make-up for ladies is forbidden outside the home, with the exception of black antimony on the eyes.
- Such things as sharpening the ends of the teeth and making spaces between them for the sake of beauty, are not allowed.
- A woman should keep her mouth clean and healthy.

### *Perfume*

- A woman is allowed to perfume herself only indoors and provided no stranger or non-mahram relative is there.
- A perfumed woman may not leave her home unless she has got rid of the smell of perfume. Any adornment that may be inviting to strange men is forbidden, as this is a step to corrupting the society.

### *General Guidelines for Both Sexes*

- Grey hair may be dyed any colour, except black. The preferable colours are blonde, red and henna.
- Antimony may be applied, from time to time, for it clears the sight, and gives the eyes beauty.

## PHYSICAL FUNCTIONS

***Sneezing:*** Sneezing is considered in Islam a blessing from God. The manners concerning it are these:

- A Muslim should not seek to restrain or prevent a sneeze; it is a healthy function. In any case, sneezing cannot be done at will, nor can it be easily suppressed.
- When about to sneeze, a Muslim should turn his face away or cover his mouth and nose with hand or handkerchief, thus lessening the noise and, at the same time, avoiding nuisance to those nearby.
- Since sneezing is considered a blessing from God, a Muslim should acknowledge this by saying: Al-hamdu lillah (Praise and thanks to God).
- When a Muslim sneezes and praises God, those who hear the praise should invoke a blessing on him by saying: Yarhamukallah (May God have mercy on you), to which the proper response is: Yahdikumullah wa yuslih balakum (May Allah guide you and grant you well-being).
- It is right to invoke a blessing on one who sneezes at the most three times. If he sneezes more often, this probably means he has a cold.

- If a Muslim sneezes and does not praise God, invoking a blessing on him is not required.
- If a Muslim sneezes and forgets to praise God, then it is the duty of Muslims near him to remind him kindly of his duty to thank God.
- Blessings for a non-Muslim who sneezes should be expressed in the words: Yahdikumullah (May God guide you on the Right Way).

***Yawning:*** Yawning is considered to be bad and as far as possible should be suppressed. A Muslim should:

- Try to refrain from yawning as much as possible.
- When yawning hold his hand over his mouth.
- Try not to make any sound when yawning.

### *Going to Bed: Necessary Preparation*

- A Muslim should be sure to relieve himself before going to bed.
- It is recommended to go to bed in a state of purity by performing 'wudu' (partial ablution).
- It is preferable, and hygienic, not to go to bed on a full stomach.

### *When to Sleep*

- Going to bed before 'isha' prayers is inadvisable lest the prayer be missed.
- Sleeping during a period of the day when a prayer time has begun should be avoided, unless the prayer be said first, again for fear that the prayer may be missed.
- For those who can afford it a brief siesta between the zuhr and 'asr' prayers is recommended. This helps to relax eyes and body and refreshes the person for the day's work that remains.
- Except to fulfil some necessary duty or to entertain a guest, a Muslim should retire to bed directly after 'isha.' In this way he will be refreshed and able to get up with the dawn and make full use of his day.

### *The Bed*

- The bed should be of simple design and construction. It should be neither too comfortable nor too uncomfortable; comfortable enough to provide the necessary relaxation without encouraging torpor or indolence.

- The bed should not be set too high off the ground this in the interest of humility.
- The bed should not be so placed that part of the body is in the sun and part in the shade.
- Security is important, therefore any roof area which lacks a protecting wall should be avoided. Likewise, lonely places where help cannot reach in the event of some emergency like sudden illness, attack from intruders, or fire.
- In the absence of a bathroom close by, as happens in rural areas, it is not forbidden to have a suitable vessel under the bed in which to pass water. This is obviously useful to the sick and elderly and those sleeping out of doors.

When Going to Sleep A Muslim should observe the following rules:

- Examine mattress and pillow to ensure that no harmful insects, etc. have hidden inside them.
- Pray with the words: Allahumma Bismika wa amutu wa ahya (In Your name, O God, I live and die).
- Sleep on his right side and avoid sleeping on his left side.
- Never sleep on his stomach.
- Should not try to force himself to sleep. Sleep should occur as naturally as possible, according to the body's needs.
- Make mention of God, and keep mentioning Him till sleep comes. This will help him relax and prevent thoughts of the day's difficulties and problems.
- Regulate his sleeping to conform to his body's real needs, neither more nor less.

### *When Awakening*

- Wake up with the dawn. The positive psychological effect on the whole day of doing so is clear and understood by those who experience it.

- Start the new day as he ended the previous day by mentioning God, praising and thanking Him.
- Clean his teeth with a toothbrush or tooth stick (miswak) when he gets up before performing 'wudu' for fajr, as also if he wakes up in the night for any length of time.
- If no running water is available, then, when he wakes, pour water over his hands first, before dipping his hand into a retaining vessel for water. This is because he does not know what his hand has touched during the night.

***When Having Dreams and Nightmares***

- To pretend to have had a dream which he did not is a sin: Islam rejects all forms of lying.
- If he sees in a dream what he likes, then he should recount it only to someone whom he likes. If he sees what he dislikes, then he should seek refuge in God from its evil and from the evil of the devil.
- Talk about dreams only to a friend or to someone of sound judgement.
- Dreams are for the individual who had them and not for others. If a Muslim feels he has seen the Prophet, upon him be peace, and/or received from him some kind of instruction or advice, he must keep it to himself and must not divulge it to others. Islam is complete and has never acknowledged dreams as a source of Islamic teachings.

***Relieving Oneself:*** The proper place is either one especially designed and built or a 'lavatory improvised out of doors. The following should be observed:

- A Muslim should enter the lavatory with his left foot first, saying: Bismillah Allahumma Inni audhu Bika min al-Khubthi wa al-Khabaith (In the name of Allah. Allah, in You I take refuge from all evils).
- One should not go to the lavatory in company, nor seek it there; nor should private parts be uncovered to others, as in men's rest rooms where men stand beside each other and urinate into fixtures placed for this purpose. A non-transparent screen between such fixtures is necessary.

- The lavatory must not be entered with unprotected feet. This is to avoid transfer to the body of impurities and dangerous micro-organisms.
- One should not begin to undress before entering the lavatory. Maximum privacy and decency is a necessity.
- Purification afterwards is necessary. This can be done by washing with water after urinating, and by using toilet paper and then washing with water in the case of a bowel movement.
- It is recommended that, when relieving oneself or washing afterwards, the right hand should not be used. This is in accordance with the Islamic way of devoting and confining the use of the right hand to good things such as eating, drinking, holding the Quran, etc. and confining the left hand to other things such as washing after relieving oneself, blowing one's nose, etc.
- Though taking care to avoid getting impurities on body or clothes, and washing afterwards, are necessary, exaggeration and obsessive squeamishness in either should be avoided.
- It is indecent for a Muslim to look at his private parts and his excretion.
- For a Muslim to urinate or relieve himself in the direction of the Qiblah is forbidden. Neither is facing nor turning his back to the Qiblah allowed, therefore turning towards the other two directions is required. This rule applies to all lavatory places indoors or out.
- Squatting is the best posture when passing water, though standing to do so is not forbidden if squatting causes physical difficulty (as in the case of the elderly).
- For a Muslim to talk while relieving himself is considered un-Islamic except in the case of real need. Likewise, reading while relieving himself.
- If someone greets a Muslim while he is relieving himself he should not respond till he leaves the lavatory; then he should apologize to him and return the greeting.
- A Muslim should leave the lavatory only after covering his body correctly.

- It is recommended that a Muslim does not pass water in the same place as he bathes.
- On coming out of the lavatory, a Muslim should say: Ghufranaka (O God, grant me forgiveness).

***Outdoors:*** There are certain rules for a Muslim when relieving himself outdoors, in places such as forests, deserts, camping sites:

- It is forbidden to do so in still water, in the shade, on the road or where people walk, in any cavity that may serve some animal or reptile as a dwelling, and in a windy place. This is in accordance with the Islamic principle, 'There should be neither harming nor reciprocating harm.'
- It is necessary for him to conceal himself and go where he will not be seen naked.
- It is wise to use such ground as avoids any risk of soiling himself or his clothes.

***Menstruation and Child-Bed:*** Menstruation and child-bed should be represented and treated as normal events that need not restrict a woman from leading a normal life. The few restrictions imposed upon women in these two states are as follows:

- Performing prayer, fasting, reading the Quran and staying at a mosque are forbidden.
- Circumambulation of the Kaaba is also forbidden, even for women performing pilgrimage who have become menstruous. They may perform all rituals of the pilgrimage except the circumambulation. The same restriction applies to men in a seminally defiled state.
- Sexual intercourse is also forbidden. A woman's husband may embrace and kiss her and touch her above the waist if he wishes.
- When her monthly period comes to an end, a woman may fast, but not pray until after she has taken a bath. After bathing she is required to make up for the fasting days missed during Ramadan, but not for prayers missed.
- It is the duty of every Muslim woman after menstruation or child-bed is ended to take a bath, washing the whole

body and hair; it is recommended that she applies musk (or other perfume if musk is unavailable) with a cloth to her private parts. After bathing she can make all observances forbidden during menstruation or childbed.

- A man should treat his menstruating wife in a normal way.
- Menstruous women are allowed to attend the Feast prayer though not to participate in it, provided the prayer is not held in the mosque.

***Man's Seminally Defiled State:*** A man who has become seminally defiled either during sleep, or love-making, or by any other means, is required to take a bath as soon as possible. While he is in a defiled state, before taking a bath, he may not pray, recite the Quran, or touch it, circumambulate the Kaaba or stay at a mosque.

The same rule applies to a woman who has become seminally defiled either during sleep or through sexual intercourse, including the case where her husband penetrates her but does not ejaculate.

# 3

## Respects and Regards

Offer devotions to Allah

Appoint no one His Partner

Be Good to:

• *Your Mother and Father,* • *Your Kith and Kin,* • *The Orphans,* • *The Needy,* • *The Neighbour — who is a relative, and* • *The Neighbour — who is not a relative,* • *The Companion — in whose fellowship you spend some time, however brief it may be, and* • *Be kind to the traveller,* • *The captives (slaves) who are under your charge. (4:36)*

### RESPECT TO PARENTS

1. Behave well towards your father and mother and consider this good conduct as a propitious act which will earn Allah's grace in this world as well as in the next. Next to Allah, man owes the greatest obligation to his parents. The greatness and value of this obligation towards one's parents may be realised from the fact that the Holy Quran at several points mentions the rights of parents and the rights of Allah simultaneously at one place. Furthermore, the Holy Quran has ordained the duty of offering thanks to the parents along with thanksgiving to Allah.

*"Thy Lord hath decreed that ye worship none save Him and (that ye show) kindness to parents." (17: 23)*

*Hadrat 'Abdullah ibn Masud [R.A.A.] relates: "I submitted to the Holy Prophet [S.A.W.] which deed will win the highest favour of Allah?" The Holy Prophet [S.A.W.] answered: "The prayer which is offered at the appointed hour." I submitted again: "Next to this which other deed will win the greatest favour of Allah?" The Holy Prophet [S.A.W.] affirmed: "Good conduct towards father and mother." I again submitted: "And next to this?" The Prophet of Allah [S.A.W.] observed: "Jihad (Fighting) in the way of Allah." (Bukhari, Muslim)*

*Hadrat 'Abdullah [R.A.A.] reports: "One day a person went to the Holy Prophet [S.A.W.] and submitted: "I give my hand into your hand and swear allegiance for performing Hijrat and Jihad and I beseech a reward from Allah in return for this." The Holy Prophet [S.A.W.] enquired: "Is one of your parents alive?" He submitted: "Yes, praise be to Allah, both my father and mother are alive." Thereupon the Prophet of Allah [S.A.W.] observed: "Well then do you really want to receive a reward from Allah for performing Hijrat and Jihad'?" The man replied: "Yes, indeed, I beseech reward from Allah in return for these acts.". The Holy Prophet [S.A.W.] observed: "Go then. Attend to your parents and serve them well." (Muslim)*

*Hadrat Abu Umama [R.A.A.] relates: "A man enquired from the Holy Prophet [S.A.W.]: "O Prophet of Allah [S.A.W.]! What are the rights of parents over their offspring?" The Holy Prophet [S.A.W.] affirmed: "Your entry into Paradise or Hell depends on your good or bad conduct towards your parents. " (Ibn Majah)*

In other words, if you treat them well, you will be sent to Paradise and if you violate the rights that your parents have over you, you will be consigned to serve as fuel for Hell-Fire.

2. Be grateful to your parents. Thanksgiving and an acknowledgement of debt and gratitude are the first duties which a beneficiary owes to the Benefactor. It is a fact that the parents are the palpable cause for our existence. Again, it is under their protection and upbringing that we grow up to an age of maturity. The extraordinary self-sacrifice, unparalleled devotion and deep affection with which they patronise us demand

that our hearts should be filled with sentiments of reverence, indebtedness, love and an acknowledgement of their magnanimity and every fibre of our heart should pulsate with feelings of gratitude to them. It is for this reason that Allah has ordained offering of gratitude to parents along with thanksgiving to Him.

"(We willed) that you should offer thanks to Me and remain grateful to your father and mother."

3. Always try to make your parents happy. Do not say anything in opposition to their will or temperament which may displease them, especially when they are advanced in age they acquire a peevish and irritable temperament. In old age the parents start making unexpected demands and begin proffering impossible claims. In this case also tolerate their behaviour in good cheer and do not say anything in anger in response to their demands which may cause them pain and may injure their feelings.

"If one or both of thy parents reach an advanced age with thee, say not 'fie' unto them nor repulse them."

As a matter of fact, the strength to tolerate unpleasant things is sapped during old age and weakness increases the sense of self-importance in old people. Hence they react sensitively to even the minor offensive matters. Keeping in view their delicate and sensitive nature, do not let your parents feel angry by any of your words or deeds.

*Hadrat 'Abdullah b. Amr [R.A.A.] relates that the Holy Prophet [S.A.W.] affirmed: "The pleasure of Allah is contained in the pleasure of the father even as His displeasure is contained in the displeasure of the father."*

*(Tirmidhi, Ibn Habban, Hakim)*

In other words, any one who wants to please Allah should seek the pleasure of his father, for if the father is angry, the favour of Allah cannot be earned. The one who makes his father angry provokes the wrath of Allah."

*Another statement of Hadrat 'Abdullah [R.A.A.] runs as follows: "A man left his parents weeping and came to the presence of the Holy Prophet [S.A.W.] for the purpose of offering allegiance to the Prophet [S.A.W.] for Hijrah. The Holy Prophet [S.A.W.] observed to him: "Go back to your parents and return after making them happy as you came after leaving them crying."* *(Abu Daud)*

4. Do service to your parents with heart and soul. If Allah has afforded you the opportunity to serve your parents, it is in fact a favourable opportunity for you to earn entitlement to Paradise and to win the Pleasure of Allah. Good service to parents secures blessings and grace in both worlds and man obtains salvation from the calamities of this world and the next. Hadrat Anas [R.A.A.] relates:

*"Any man who desires that his life should be prolonged and his subsistence may be increased ought to do good service to his parents and show kindness to them."*
*(Al-Targhib-wat-Tarhib)*

The Holy Prophet [S.A.W.] has observed:

*"Let that man be disgraced, and disgraced again and let him be disgraced even more." The people enquired: "O Prophet of Allah [S.A.W.]! who is that man?" The Prophet of Allah [S.A.W.] affirmed: "I refer to the man who finds his parents old in age both of them or one of them-and yet did not earn entitlement to Paradise by rendering good service to them."* *(Muslim)*

On one occasion, the Holy Prophet [S.A.W.] gave precedence to the obligation of looking after one's parents over one of the supreme forms of worship like Jihad.

The Holy Prophet [S.A.W.] forbade a companion [R.A.A.] to proceed on Jihad and urged him to look after his parents.

*Hadrat 'Abdullah ibn 'Amr [R.A.A.] relates that a person came to the presence of the Holy Prophet [S.A.W.] with the intention of participating in the Jihad. The Holy Prophet [S.A.W.] enquired from him: "Are your father and mother alive?" He submitted: "Yes, they are alive." The Holy Prophet [S.A.W.] thereupon observed: "Go and render good service to them. This is the Jihad."*
*(Bukhari, Muslim)*

5. Respect and adore your parents and do not show disrespect to them by a single word or action. The Holy Quran affirms:

*"But speak to them a gracious word."* *(17: 23)*

*On one occasion Hadrat 'Abdullah b. 'Umar [R.A.A.] enquired from Hadrat Ibn 'Abbas [R.A.A.]: "Do you wish to ward off Hell and gain entry into Paradise?" Ibn 'Abbas [R.A.A.] answered: "Yes, why not, I swear in the name of Allah I cherish this desire." Hadrat Ibn 'Umar then asked: "Are your parents alive?" Ibn 'Abbas [R.A.A.] replied: "Yes, my mother is alive." Ibn 'Umar [R.A.A.] remarked: "If you talk to them in a polite manner and look after their needs and feed them well, you will certainly be admitted to Paradise provided you abstain from capital evils."*

*(Al-Adab-ul Mufrad)*

*Hadrat Abu Hurrayrah [R.A.A.] once saw two men. He asked one of them: "What is your relationship with the other man?" The person replied: "He is my father." Hadrat Abu Hurrayrah [R.A.A.] thereupon advised him, "Look, never call him by his proper name, walk ahead of him nor sit before he takes his seat."*

*(Al-Adab-ul Mufrad)*

6. Be faithful and humble towards your parents.

*"And lower unto them the wing of submission through mercy."* *(17: 23)*

To offer humble obedience to parents implies to pay constant regard to their dignity. Do not assume a haughty attitude towards them, nor treat them with insolence.

7. Love your parents and consider this act as a privilege and a source of reward in the eternal world. Hadrat Ibn 'Abbas [R.A.A.] relates that the Holy Prophet [S.A.W.] observed:

*"The pious offspring who casts a single look of affection at his parents receives a reward from Allah equal to the reward of an accepted Hajj." The people submitted: "O Prophet of Allah [S.A.W.]: If someone casts a hundred such glances of love and affection at his parents, what*

*then?" The Holy Prophet [S.A.W.] observed: "Yes, indeed, even if one does so a hundred time a day, he will get a hundredfold reward. Allah is far greater than you imagine and is completely free from petty narrowmindedness.* *(Muslim)*

8. Obey your parents with full devotion. Even if they show some intransigence, obey their will cheerfully. Keeping in view the great favours which they have done to you, try to fulfil all their demands willingly which may be offensive to your own taste or temperament, provided, of course, they are not derogatory to the tenets of religion.

*Hadrat Abu Said Khudri [R.A.A.] narrates that a person came to the presence of the Holy Prophet [S.A.W.] from Yemen. The Prophet of Allah [S.A.W.] enquired from him: "Do you have any relations in Yemen?" He submitted: "Yes, my father and mother are there." The Holy Prophet [S.A.W.] then asked: "Did they give you permission to leave?" He submitted: "No, I did not take their permission." The Prophet of Allah [S.A.W.] thereupon observed: "Go back then and ask the permission of your father and mother. If they agree, come back and join the Jihad, otherwise, attend on them and render good service to them."* *(Abu Daud)*

Realise the value of rendering obedience to parents from the facts that a man came from miles intending to join the Holy Prophet [S.A.W.] in Holy war for the glory of religion, yet the Holy Prophet [S.A.W.] turned him back saying: "You can join the Holy War only if both your father and mother allow you to do so."

*Hadrat Ibn 'Abbas [R.A.A.] reports that the Holy Prophet [S.A.W.] observed: "The man who wakes up in the morning having previously discharged all the duties and obligations laid upon him by Allah concerning his parents, he will find the two gates of Paradise open for him on waking up in the morning; and in case there is only one parent, the person will find one door of Paradise open for him. And in contrast if a man wakes up in the morning having previously disregarded any obligations or duties laid upon him by Allah concerning his parents, then he will find two gates of Hell open for him on waking up in the morning; and in case one of the parents is alive, then the man will find one gate of Hell open for him." The man submitted: "O Prophet of Allah [S.A.W.], if the parents are treating him wrongly, what then?" The Holy Prophet [S.A.W.] affirmed: "Yes, even if they are treating him wrongly; yes, indeed even if they are treating him wrongly."* (Mishkat)

Consider your own goods as the property of your parents and spend your capital on them with an open hand. The Holy Quran affirms:

*"They ask thee, what they shall spend. Say what ye spend for good must go to parents."*

On one occasion a man came to the presence of the Holy Prophet [S.A.W.] and complained that his father took whatever goods he wanted from him. The Holy Prophet [S.A.W.] sent for that man's father. An old, infirm man came walking with the help of a stick. When the Holy Prophet [S.A.W.] interrogated him on the point, the old man submitted: "O Prophet of Allah [S.A.W.]! There was a time when I was strong and he was weak and helpless. I had money and he was empty-handed. I never forbade him then to lay his hands on anything that I possessed. Today, he is strong and healthy and I am old and infirm. He has money and I am empty-handed. He now denies me access to his goods." Upon hearing this tale of the old man, the Benefactor of the humanity [S.A.W.] burst into tears and addressing the son of the old man observed: "You and your goods are the property of your father."

10. Even if your father and mother are non-Muslims, treat them well. Continue to pay them respect and devotion and serve them faithfully. However, in case they command you to become a polytheist or indulge in a sinful act, refuse to obey them and sternly repulse their demand.

*"And if your (parents) pressurise you to associate some one with Me of which you have no knowledge, obey them not, yet continue to treat them well in the world."*

*Hadrat Asma' [R.A.A.] states: "In the sacred lifetime of the Holy Prophet [S.A.W.], my mother visited me on one occasion. She was a polytheist at that time. I submitted to the Holy Prophet [S.A.W.]: "My mother has come to pay me a visit and she is an unbeliever in Islam. How should I treat her?" The Holy Prophet [S.A.W.] observed: "Yes, you should continue to show kindness to your mother."* *(Bukhari)*

11. Offer prayers begging grace for your parents. Bring to mind their fervent appeals to the Allah and beg His mercy for them with a zealous and sincere heart. Allah ordains:

*"And say: My Allah! Have mercy on them both as they did care for me when I was little."*

*In other words, say: "O Creator, with mercy, devotion, affection and love my Allah they reared me in childhood and sacrificed their own pleasure and ease for my sake but, they, in their infirmity and helplessness of old age, are more deserving of kindness and love than I ever was. Allah! I can pay them no recompense. Do patronise them and show them mercy in their miserable state."*

12. Observe special care in looking after your mother. By nature, the mother is weak and more sensitive and needs your better treatment and devotion. Moreover, her favours and sacrifices are comparatively far greater than the father. Hence religion has conceded preferential rights to the mother and has enjoined upon the believers to treat their mothers with special consideration. The Holy Quran affirms:

*"And We have commanded unto man kindness towards parents. His mother beareth him with suffering, bringeth him forth with suffering, bearing of him and weaning of him is thirty months."* *(46: 15)*

*While enjoining upon the believers to show good behaviour towards both father and mother, the Holy Quran has drawn a poignant picture of constant suffering of pain and hardships by the mother and has excellently pointed out in a psychological manner the fact that the devoted mother deserves comparatively more of your service and kind behaviour than your father. The same fact has been elucidated in greater detail by the Prophet of Allah [S.A.W.].*

*Hadrat Abu Hurrayrah [R.A.A.] reports: "A man came to the presence of the Holy Prophet [S.A.W.] and submitted: "O Prophet of Allah [S.A.W.]! Who deserves the noblest treatment from me?" The Holy Prophet [S.A.W.] observed: "Your mother." He again submitted: "And next?" The Holy Prophet [S.A.W.] observed: "Your mother." When the man submitted for the fourth time: "And who next?" The Holy Prophet [S.A.W.] observed: "Your father." (Al-Adabul Mufrad)*

*Hadrat Jahma [R.A.A.] paid a call on the Holy Prophet [S.A.W.] and submitted: "O Prophet of Allah [S.A.W.]! I wish to join you in the Jihad and have come to solicit your guidance in this matter. I seek your command." The Holy Prophet [S.A.W.] enquired from him: "Is your mother alive?" Jahma [R.A.A.] submitted: "Yes, she is alive." Thereupon the Holy Prophet [S.A.W.], said "Return to her then and devote yourself to her service, for Paradise lies under her feet." (Ibn Majah, Nasai)*

Hadrat Awais [R.T.A.] was a contemporary of the Holy Prophet [S.A.W.], but he could never attain the privilege of calling on the Holy Prophet [S.A.W.]. He had an old mother to whose service he devoted himself day and night. He cherished a great desire to see the Holy Prophet [S.A.W.] and it was but natural for every Muslim to have a burning desire to catch a glimpse of the Prophet of Allah [S.A.W.]. Hadrat Awais [R.T.A.] indeed wanted to pay a call, yet the Holy Prophet [S.A.W.] forbade him to come. Similarly, Hadrat Awais [R.T.A.] cherished an ambition to discharge the obligation of Hajj, yet as long as his mother remained alive, Hadrat Awais [R.T.A.] never set out for the Hajj alone. He fulfilled the desire to perform Hajj after his mother's demise.

13. Treat your foster mother well. Do service to her and show her respect and adoration. Hadrat Abu Tufail [R.A.A.] states: "I once witnessed the Holy Prophet [S.A.W.] distributing meat at a place called 'Jarana'. Presently, a lady arrived and approached near the Holy Prophet [S.A.W.]. The Holy Prophet of Allah [S.A.W.]

spread out his sheet for her and the lady sat on it. I enquired from the people, "Who is this lady?" The people told me: "This lady is the foster mother of the Holy Prophet [S.A.W.]. (Abu Daud)

14. Remember your parents after they have passed away. Observe the following etiquettes to render good service to your deceased parents:

    (i) Offer prayers continuously invoking mercy of Allah upon your dead father and mother.

The Holy Quran enjoins upon the pious to say this prayer:

*"O our Allah! Grant forgiveness to me and my parents and pardon all the faithful on the day of Reckoning."*

*Hadrat Abu Hurrayrah [R.A.A.] states: "When the deceased is elevated to high degrees of favour, he enquires in astonishment: "How so?" He is informed by Allah, "Your offsprings have been offering prayers, begging mercy for you (and Allah has accepted those petitions of mercy)."*

Hadrat Abu Hurrayrah [R.A.A.] also states:

*"The Holy Prophet [S.A.W.] observed: The opportunity to do something ends with one's death yet there are three things which continue to afford benefit to him after death-a recurring charitable act; knowledge which he has imparted to others from which people derive benefit and thirdly, pious offsprings who continue to offer prayers invoking mercy of Allah upon him."*

   (ii) Fulfil all the contracts and promises made by your parents and carry out their will. Your parents must have made many agreements with some people, they might have made a covenant with Allah; they might have taken a vow; they might have promised to deliver goods to someone; they might have owed a debt to somebody but were unable to discharge it before death overtook them; they might have made a will at the time of their death. Fulfil all these obligations to the extent of your means.

   Hadrat 'Abdullah b. 'Abbas [R.A.A.] narrates: "Hadrat Sad b. Ubaba [R.A.A.] submitted to the

Holy Prophet [S.A.W.], "O Prophet of Allah [S.A.W.]! My mother had taken a vow, but she expired before discharging it. Can I carry out the vow on her behalf?" The Holy Prophet [S.A.W.] affirmed: "Why not! You must carry out the vow taken by her."

(iii) Show good conduct to the friends of your father and the female companions of your mother. Treat them with respect. Seek their advice just as you seek the advice of your elders and pay due regard to their opinions and advice. On one occasion, the Holy Prophet [S.A.W.] observed: There is no superior deed of piety than that man should do good service to the companions and friends of his father."

Once Hadrat Abu Darda [R.A.A.] fell ill and his condition continued to aggravate till they lost all hopes of his life. Hadrat Yusuf b. 'Abdullah [R.A.A.] made a long journey and came to enquire after his health. On seeing him, Hadrat Abu Darda asked in astonishment: "How are you here?" Yusuf b. 'Abdullah [R.A.A.] replied: "I have come here only to enquire after your health, for you were on terms of deep friendship with my late father."

*Hadrat Abu Darda [R.A.A.] relates: "When I arrived in Medina, 'Abdullah b. 'Umar [R.A.A.] paid me a visit and said: "Abu Darda, do you know why I have come to see you?" I replied: "No. I have no idea why you have come here." Thereupon Hadrat 'Abdullah b. 'Umar [R.A.A.] said: "I have heard the Prophet of Allah [S.A.W.] as affirming: "The man who wishes to render good service to his father, who is in the grave, ought to show good treatment to his father's companions and friends." Having related this saying of the Holy Prophet [S.A.W.] 'Abdullah b. Umar [R.A.A.] remarked: "Brother, my father 'Umar and your father [R.A.A.] were on terms of deep friendship. I wish to commemorate this friendship and fulfil its duties." (Ibn Habban)*

(iv) Show constant good treatment to the relations of your parents and entertain full respect and pay due regard to the sanctity of these connections. An indifferent and irresponsible conduct towards these relations is tantamount to treating your own parents with indifference and negligence. The Holy Prophet [S.A.W.] observed: "Do not observe indifference towards your forefathers. To show carelessness in your conduct towards your parents is to display ingratitude to Allah."

15. If, Allah forbid, you have been guilty of negligence in treating your parents well or discharging your full obligations towards them during their lifetime, do not despair of Allah's mercy. Offer prayers constantly invoking blessings of Allah upon your deceased parents. It is possible Allah may forgive your sin of negligence and admit you among the ranks of the pious people. Hadrat Anas [R.A.A.] relates: The Holy Prophet [S.A.W.] affirmed:

*"If a person does not observe filial devotion to his parents during their lifetime, and both parents or one of them passes away, the person ought to offer prayers for his deceased parents and beg His Mercy and beseech Him to grant salvation to them till Allah in His Mercy ordains their admission to the rolls of the pious people."*

## DOMESTIC LIFE

The sublime culture and civilisation which Islam envisages can only come into existence when we succeed in building up the structure of a righteous society. And a stable and well-organised family system is a prerequisite for the birth of a righteous society. Family life begins with the sacred matrimonial connection between husband and wife and the development of this connection into a permanently happy and pleasant matrimonial life chiefly depends on the full awareness of the etiquettes and duties of marital life in both husband and wife and their zeal, sincerity and devotion to observe those etiquettes and discharge obligations of married life. Let us in the first place deal with those etiquettes and obligations which concern the husband and then we shall proceed to discuss the etiquettes and duties to be observed by the wife.

1. Treat your wife well in life. Discharge your obligations towards her with a liberal heart and adopt a favourable

and self-sacrificing attitude in every matter concerning your wife. Allah ordains:

"And live with them in a good manner."

In a sermon to a mammoth congregation on the eve of Hajjatul-Widah (Last Hajj) of the Prophet [S.A.W.], the Holy Prophet [S.A.W.] enjoined upon the Muslims:

*"O people! Listen! Behave well towards women, for they are like captives with you. You have no right to give them harsh treatment save in the case when they show open disobedience. If they are guilty of disobedience, keep away from them in the bed room. In case you punish them, take care not to cause them severe injury. When they come round and obey your will, do not find pretexts to harass them. Listen carefully! you have some rights over your wives and your wives have some rights over you. They owe an obligation to you not to let your beds be trampled by anyone whom you dislike and not let anyone trespass into your house whose visit you do not like. And listen, you owe a duty to them to feed them well and provide good clothing to them."*

*(Riyad-us-Salihin)*

*In other words, make such provisions for their feeding and clothing as are befitting to a marital relationship of unique intimacy, union of hearts and a spirit of companionship.*

2. Entertain a good opinion about your wife as far as possible and adopt an attitude of politeness, toleration and magnanimity for the sake of amicable living with her. If she lacks beauty of face or person or is deficient in good manners, morality, good sense or skill in household affairs, bear these faults with patience. Look to her virtues and maintain a harmonious relationship by means of generosity, liberality of mind and self-sacrifice. Allah ordains:

*"And amity contains goodness."*

*And the believers are enjoined upon as follows:*

*"For if ye hate them it may happen that ye hate a thing wherein Allah hath placed much good."* *(4: 19)*

*The same subject has been elucidated by the Holy Prophet [S.A.W.] in the following Tradition: "No believer should hate his pious wife. If he dislikes one habit of his wife, it is possible he may like her for some other aspects of her character."*

As a matter of fact, each woman has some weakness of one sort or another and if the husband turns against her on account of her bearing a certain deficiency and conceives a hatred for her, a pleasant home life becomes impossible for the couple. Common-sense dictates that man should adopt a liberal attitude and reposing his trust in Allah should endeavour to live amicably with his wife. It is possible that Allah may vouchsafe to that man merely for the sake of this woman, such bounties which his limited mind cannot comprehend. For instance, this woman may possess excellent virtues of religion, faith, character and morality in reward for which Allah may shower blessings upon her own family or may be a pious soul is born of this woman who may prove beneficial for the whole mankind and may serve as a Sadaqa-e-Jariah (Continuing Charity) in favour of the father till the end of his life, or perhaps the woman may serve as a means of reforming the character of her man and thus may help him to gain proximity to Paradise or it may be that Allah may bless this man with large subsistence and prosperity because such a blessing of prosperity was destined for his wife. At any rate, do not ruin your married life impetuously on the grounds of an apparent defect in the woman. On the other hand, be wise and try to promote gradually an atmosphere of happiness and concord in the home.

3. Adopt an attitude of forgiveness and kindness. Forget all the faults of omission, stupid actions and disobedient attitude of your wife. The woman is deficient and weak in wisdom and Common-sense and bears an extremely passionate temperament. Hence try to bring her round with patience, calmness, kindness, affection and devotion. Try to get along with her with patience and restraint. Allah ordains:

*"O ye who believe! verily, among your wives and your children, there are enemies for you, therefore beware of them. And if ye efface and overlook and forgive, then Allah is Forgiving, Merciful."* *(Attaghabun: 14)*

*The Holy Prophet [S.A.W.] affirmed: "Be good to women. The woman has been created out of the rib and the uppermost part of the rib ends in a curve; so if you try to straighten out the curve, it will break, yet if you leave it alone, the curve will remain. Hence, be good to women."*
*(Bukhari, Muslim)*

4. Treat your wife politely and show love and affection to her. The Holy Prophet [S.A.W.] has affirmed:

*"The believers who possess perfect faith are those who display the best manners, and the best among you are those who treat their wives in the best possible manner."*
*(Tirmidhi)*

Politeness and tenderness of behaviour can best be judged in the home. People are constantly living amidst their family members and the real temper and moral conduct of man is completely revealed in the free and uninhibited atmosphere of the home. It is a fact that only such believers possess perfect faith who display civility, kindness, and affectionate behaviour towards their family members and who support, sympathises, love and adore inmates of their household.

*Hadrat 'Aishah [R.A.A.] reports: "I used to play with dolls along with my playmates in the house of the Holy Prophet [S.A.W.]. On the arrival of the Holy Prophet [S.A.W.] all of them used to hide themselves in the nooks and corners of the house. The Prophet [S.A.W.] used to search out each one of them and send them to join me in the play."* *(Bukhari, Muslim)*

Once on the occasion of Hajj, the camel of Hadrat Safiyah [R.A.A.] sat down on the ground and she was therefore left behind while the entire caravan passed on. The Holy Prophet [S.A.W.] came to her and found her weeping without restraint. The Holy Prophet [S.A.W.] stood there wiping off her tears with the edge of a sheet with his own holy hands. While the Prophet of Allah [S.A.W.] wiped off tears from her eyes, she [R.A.A.] continued to weep unrestrainedly for a long time."

5. Make liberal provisions for all the needs of your wife and do not stint in expenses. Feel a sense of pleasure and comfort in spending your lawful earnings on

members of your family. You owe an obligation to your wife to provide her with food and clothing and to struggle energetically, in order to earn enough money to discharge this obligation, is the most pleasant duty of a husband. The performance of this duty with an open and cheerful heart earns for the believer the reward of a happy marital life in this world and a favourable recompense and bounty in the world to come. The Holy Prophet [S.A.W.] has affirmed:

*"You spend a dinar in the way of Allah; you spend another dinar to ransom a slave; you give away one dinar as alms to a beggar; and there is one dinar which you spend on your family. Among all these, the dinar that will earn the best reward and blessings of Allah is the one which you have spent on your family."*

*(Muslim)*

6. Teach your wife the rules and manners enjoined by religion. Let her observe Islamic morality and make her life graceful. Make every possible effort to train and mould her according to the Islamic pattern of life so that she may prove to be a good wife, good mother and a pious devotee of Allah and may discharge her duties as a wife efficiently and faithfully. Allah affirms:

*"O ye who believe! Save yourselves and your family from the Fire of Hell."*

*As the Holy Prophet [S.A.W.] devoted himself to preaching and teaching the laws of religion outside the home, likewise he continued to perform the same function inside his home. Making an illusion to this fact, the Holy Quran addresses the wives of the Holy Prophet [S.A.W.] in these words: "And remember the verses of Allah and the matters of wisdom that are conveyed to you in your house."*

*The Quran has advised the believers through the ministry of the Holy Prophet [S.A.W.]: "And urge upon the inmates of your house to observe prayers and fully abide by this obligation yourself too."*

*The Prophet of Allah [S.A.W.] affirms: "When a man wakes up his wife during the night and they offer two*

*Rakats of Prayers together, Allah ordains that the man's name should be included in the rolls of the male remembers of Allah and the woman's name in the register of those females who offer praises to Allah and remember Him."* *(Abu Daud)*

The second Caliph Hadrat 'Umar [R.A.A.] used to stand all night offering devotions to Allah. Near the hour of dawn he used to wake his wife saying: "Rise, get up and say prayers," and later he [R.A.A.] used to recite this verse also:

*"And urge upon the inmates of your house to observe prayers and fully abide by this obligation yourself."*

7. If you possess several wives; show equal treatment to all of them. The Holy Prophet [S.A.W.] used to observe great care in dispensing equal treatment to his wives. On the eve of setting out for a journey the Prophet of Allah [S.A.W.] used to draw lots and took with him the wife whose name was decided by the toss. Hadrat Abu Hurrayrah [R.A.A.] states that the Holy Prophet [S.A.W.] observed:

*"If a man has two wives, but does not treat them with equality and even-handed justice, he shall be resurrected on the Day of Judgement in such a condition that half of his body is paralysed."* *(Tirmidhi)*

'Justice' and 'equality' imply to treat them equally in all matters and show the same kind of behaviour to each wife. As regards the fact that a man may be specially attracted towards one wife or may be drawn to her or cherish deeper feelings of love for her, Allah will award no punishment to the man for it.

8. Obey your husband with a willing heart and feel pleasure and satisfaction in being faithful to him. This is what Allah commands a wife to do and the believing woman. Who acts according to the will of Allah wins His Favour. The Holy Quran affirms:

*"The pious wives are those who show obedience to their husbands." The Holy Prophet [S.A.W.] observed: "No woman should keep fast without the permission of her husband."* *(Abu Daud)*

*Stressing the importance of rendering obedience and devotion to her husband, the Holy Prophet [S.A.W.] has warned the woman:*

*"There are two types of persons whose prayers do not rise above their heads-the prayer of a slave who deserts his master until he returns to his service and the prayer of a woman who shows disobedience to her husband until she recants from this behaviour."*

*(Al-Targhib-o-Al-Tarhib)*

9. Protect your honour and chastity. Keep away from all matters of activities which contain a possible threat to violate your honour or chastity. This is what Allah commands and it is also an essential prerequisite for making your marital life happy and pleasant. No amount of devotion and obedience of the wife can win the heart of her husband if the seeds of suspicion about her infidelity are once sown in his mind. Even an ordinary act of carelessness on the wife's part may prompt the devil to fill the heart of her husband with indelible doubts and suspicions. Hence keeping in view this human weakness, exercise utmost vigilance in such matters.

The Prophet of Allah has affirmed:

*"If the woman offers prayers five times a day, protects her honour and chastity, remains faithful to her husband, she may enter Paradise by whichever gate she likes."* *(Al-Targhib-o-Al-Tarhib)*

10. Do not go out of the house without leave or permission of your husband. Do not call at homes of which your husband disapproves, nor admit anyone into your house whom your husband dislikes.

Hadrat Muadh ibn Jabal [R.A.A.] narrates that the Prophet of Allah [S.A.W.] observed:

*"It is not lawful for a woman who believes in Allah to admit a man into her house whose visit is disapproved of by her husband or that she should go out of the house against her husband's will or she should obey the will of someone else in opposition to her husband's wishes."*

*(Al-Targhib-o-Al-Tarhib)*

In other words, obey the wishes of your husband, even watch and be mindful of the slightest indications of his approval or disapproval. Do not follow the counsels of others which are in opposition to the will of your husband.

11. It should be your permanent concern to make your husband happy by your words, actions, behaviour and manners. This is not only the real secret of a successful marriage, but a means to win the favour of Allah and admittance into Paradise. The Holy Prophet [S.A.W.] has affirmed:

*"The woman who dies in such a state that her husband was entirely satisfied and in concord with her, will certainly enter Paradise."* *(Tirmidhi)*

Furthermore, the Holy Prophet [S.A.W.] observed:

*"When a man calls his wife to fulfil the sexual urge and she declines and for this reason the husband remains angry with her all night, the angels send curses upon such a wife till dawn."* *(Bukhari, Muslim)*

12. Love your husband and value his companionship. He is the adornment of your life, your life's support and a great companion and helper in the course of your life. Give thanks to Allah for this great Bounty and value this Bounty too with all your heart and soul. The Holy Prophet [S.A.W.] observed on one occasion:

*"For the two who love one another there is no better thing than the 'Nikah' (matrimonial tie)."*

Hadrat Safiyah [R.A.A.] cherished deep love for the Holy Prophet [S.A.W.]. When illness overcame the Holy Prophet of Allah [S.A.W.], Hadrat Safiyah [R.A.A.] spoke with genuine concern: "Would Allah that I had fallen ill instead of you, O Holy Prophet of Allah [S.A.W.]!" At this expression of deep love by Hadrat Safiyah [R.A.A.], the other wives of the Holy Prophet [S.A.W.] looked towards her in astonishment. Thereupon the Holy Prophet [S.A.W.] observed:

*"She is not merely making show of her affection; she is expressing her genuine love."*

13. Acknowledge the debt of gratitude you owe to your husband and remain grateful to him. Your greatest

benefactor is your husband who is always concerned with making you happy, providing for your needs and feels satisfied when he has made all provisions for your comfort.

*Hadrat Asma [R.A.A.] narrates the Tradition: I was once with my neighbour friend when the Holy Prophet [S.A.W.] passed near me. He [S.A.W.] said 'Salam' [peace be on you] to us and observed: "Avoid being ungrateful to those whom you owe a debt of gratitude. One of you, for instance, lives with her parents in an unmarried state for a long period. Then Allah confers upon her a husband. Subsequently, Allah grants her offspring. Yet in spite of all these favours when she feels enraged with her husband on some matter, she utters, 'Never have I received anything good from you." (Al-Adabul Mufrad)*

*The Holy Prophet [S.A.W.] in a warning statement to an ungrateful and unthinking wife observed:*

*"On the Day of Judgement, Allah will not even look at a woman who is ungrateful to her husband, despite the fact that a wife can never get along without her husband."*
*(Nasai)*

14. Feel happy in doing service to your husband and afford maximum comfort to him at the expense of your own inconvenience. Devote yourself to his welfare in all matters and by means of this sincere service capture the deep affections of his heart. Hadrat 'Aishah [R.A.A.] used to wash the clothes of the Holy Prophet [S.A.W.] with her own hands, anointed his sacred head with oil, combed his hair, and rubbed perfume on his holy person. The other contemporary pious ladies [R.A.A.] served their husbands in the same manner.

On one occasion, the Holy Prophet [S.A.W.] observed:

*"It is unlawful for a human being to prostrate before another human. If it had been permissible, the wife would have been ordained by Allah to offer prostration to her husband. The husband has the supreme right over his wife, and such is the optimum degree of this right that in case a husband's whole body is covered with wounds and the wife licks them all with her tongue,*

*the obligation she owes to her husband is even then not discharged in full measure."* *(Musnad Ahmad)*

15. Safeguard the home, property and goods of your husband. After marriage consider the husband's home as your own and spend the wealth of your husband wisely and economically on the adornment of your home, on the enhancement of the prestige of your husband and on securing a better future for your children.

Consider the advancement and prosperity of your husband as your own personal achievements. Praising the virtues of the women of the tribe of Quraish, the Holy Prophet [S.A.W.] observed:

*"How excellent are the women of the tribe of Quraish! They are most affectionate towards children and most efficient guardians of their husband's homes."*

*(Bukhari)*

Describing the virtues of a pious wife, the Holy Prophet [S.A.W.] observed:

*"Next to the fear of Allah the most useful and the bountiful reward for a believer is a pious wife. When he asks her to do something, she does it cheerfully. When he looks at her, she pleases him to the core of his heart. When he swears upon her trust, she fulfils his oath. When he goes away, she protects her honour and chastity in his absence and finally in superintendence of her husband's goods and property she remains truly faithful and devoted to his interest."* *(Ibn Majah)*

16. Observe cleanliness, manage you household affairs wisely and look after the decoration and furnishing of your homes. Keep your house clean. Arrange everything tidily and use things with proper care and skill. A clean and tidy home, neatly furnished rooms, good management of household affairs and home economy and a beautifully dressed and adorned wife wearing a pleasant smile on her lips....all this charges the home atmosphere with currents of deep love and affection and the marital life is enriched with happiness and blessings. This is the only way for a wife to gain her personal salvation and to win the favour of Allah.

On one occasion during a meeting Hadrat 'Aishah [R.A.A.] saw that the wife of Uthman b. 'Mazun [R.A.A.] was dressed in plain clothes and wore no adornments. Hadrat 'Aishah [R.A.A.] was taken aback and enquired:

> *"My good lady! Has your husband 'Uthman gone out on a journey?"*

You can judge from the exclamation of Hadrat 'Aishah [R.A.A.] what a propitious act it is for a married woman to adorn and beautify herself for her husband.

Once a Muslim lady of Medina [R.A.A.] presented herself before the Holy Prophet [S.A.W.]. She was at that time wearing gold bangles. The Holy Prophet [S.A.W.] expressed his disapproval of her wearing the gold bangles. The lady submitted:

> *"O Prophet of Allah [S.A.W.]! If a woman does not adorn herself and make her person attractive for her husband, she would soon lose her value for him."*
>
> *(Nasai)*

## CARE FOR THE CHILDREN

1. Consider your children as a bounty of Allah. Celebrate the birth of a child with joy and exchange messages of congratulation on such occasion. Welcome the birth of children with prayers for grace and blessings of Allah. Offer thanks to Allah that He has conferred upon you the favour of rearing one of His creatures and that He has afforded you the opportunity of leaving behind an heir to represent you in spiritual as well as mundane life.

2. If you are childless, pray to Allah for favour of granting you pious offspring in the same manner as the venerable Prophet of Allah Hadrat Zakriya [A.S.] had prayed to Allah for the grant of pious offspring.

*"Allah! Bestow upon me by Thy bounty goodly offspring. Lo! Thou art the Hearer of prayer."* *(3: 38)*

3. Do not feel downcast on the birth of a child. Strictly guard against feeling remorse or considering the birth of a child as a burden on account of financial hardship, ill health or for any other reason.

4. Do not procure an abortion. Abortion or killing a child after birth are both acts of heinous barbarity, gruesome cruelty and extreme cowardice and entail ruination in this world and Hereinafter. Allah affirms:

*"Those who kill their children out of their foolishness are the great losers."* *(6: 140)*

In an impressive condemnation of human shortsightedness, Allah has clearly forbidden the genocide of children:

*"Slay not your children fearing poverty. We shall provide for them and for you. Lo! the slaying of them is great sin."* *(17: 31)*

On one occasion a companion [R.A.A.] enquired from the Holy Prophet [S.A.W.], "O Prophet of Allah [S.A.W.]! Which is the greatest sin?" The Holy Prophet [S.A.W.] observed: "Polytheism." The companion [R.A.A.] again asked: "And what next" The Holy Prophet [S.A.W.] observed: "Disobedience to parents." The companion [R.A.A.] enquired the third time: "And which sin is the greatest next to it?" In answer to this, the Holy Prophet of Allah [S.A.W.] observed: "To kill you children fearing that they will share your sustenance."

5. At the time of delivery, recite Ayat-ul-Kursi and the following two verses of Surah Al-Aaraf near the pregnant woman. Recite also Surah 'Al Falaq' and Surah 'An-Nas' repeatedly and after each recitation blow your breath over the woman awaiting delivery:

*"Allah! There is no Allah save Him, the Alive, the Eternal. Neither slumber nor sleep overtaketh Him, unto Him belongeth whatsoever is in the heavens and whatsoever is in the earth. Who is that interecedeth with Him save by His leave? He knoweth that which is in front of them and that which is behind them while they encompass nothing of His knowledge save that what He wills. His throne includeth the heavens and the earth and He is never weary of preserving them. He is the Sublime, the Tremendous."* *(2:255)*

The two verses of Surah Aaraf are as under:

*"Lo! your Lord is Allah Who created the heavens and the earth in six days, and then sat upon the throne of*

*His Kingdom. Who makes the night cover the day which is in haste to follow it and has made the sun and the moon and the stars subservient by His Command. His verily is all creation and commandment. Blessed be Allah the Lord of the worlds! (O mankind) Call upon your Lord humbly and in secret. Lo! He loveth not aggressors." (7: 54, 55)*

6. After birth, bathe the infant and say adaan in its right and Iqamat in its left ear. On the birth of Hadrat Hussain [R.A.A.], the Holy Prophet [S.A.W.] had said adaan and Iqamat in his ears." (Tibrani)

*The Holy Prophet [S.A.W.] is also reported to have affirmed: "Whenever someone begets a child and says Adaan in its right and Iqamai in its left ear, the child is immunised against the affliction of* Umm-ul-Sibiyan *by this act." (Abu Yala)*

There is great wisdom in conveying the names of Allah and His Messenger [S.A.W.] to the ears of a new-born infant.

In his work entitled 'Tuhfa-tul-Wadud', 'Allama Ibn Qayyim observes: "The significance of this act is that the proclamation of the Greatness and Glory of Allah should be the first to reach the ears of a human being. And the affirmation of belief which he will render in full consciousness later in order to enter the fold of Islam should be conveyed to him in the very first day of his life as a man is prompted to recite Kalima-e-Tauhid (Affirmation of belief in One God) at the time of his death. Another advantage of saying the Adaan and Iqamat in the ears of the child is that the devil, who lies in ambush planning to entrap the human being in trials, flees on hearing the sound of Adaan and before the devil can draw the soul of the child towards himself, the child is called towards Islam and worship of Allah."

7. After the Adaan and Iqamat get a date chewed by some pious man or woman and paste its pulp on the palate of the infant and ask that man or woman to offer a prayer invoking grace and blessings of Allah upon the child. Hadrat Asma [R.A.A.] reports: "When 'Abdullah ibn Zubayr [R.A.A.] was born I put him in the lap of the Holy Prophet [S.A.W.]. The Holy Prophet [S.A.W.] asked

for a date, chewed it and applied his sacred saliva inside the mouth and pasted the chewed pulp of date on the palate of 'Abdullah ibn Zubayr. Afterwards, the Holy Prophet [S.A.W.] offered a prayer invoking grace and blessings of Allah upon the child."

*Hadrat 'Aishah [R.A.A.] states: "Infants were brought to the presence of the Holy Prophet [S.A.W.]. The Holy Prophet [S.A.W.] used to* Tehnik *and pray for the favour and blessings of Allah upon him." (Muslim)*

When Hadrat Imam Ahmad ibn Hambal [R.A.A.] was blessed with a child, he asked for Meccan date which was available in the home and requested a pious lady Umm 'Ali [R.T.A.] to perform the Tehnik.

8. Give your child a fine name, preferably a name resembling that of the Prophets [peace be upon them] or put a prefix 'Abd with some attribute of Allah, just as 'Abd-Allah or 'Abd-Rahman, to make up a name for your child.

*The Holy Prophet [S.A.W.] has affirmed: "On the Day of Judgement, you shall be called by your names. So prescribe fine names for yourselves." (Abu Daud)*

Furthermore, the Holy Prophet [S.A.W.] observed: "Among all your names 'Abdullah and, 'Abdul Rahman are the favourites of Allah." In addition, the Prophet [S.A.W.] affirmed: "Prescribe those names which resemble the names of the Prophets [A.S.]."

It is recorded in Bukhari that the Holy Prophet [S.A.W.] also observed: "Name your children after my name, but do not give them my 'Kuniyyat'."

9. If you have prescribed a wrong name due to ignorance, change it and prescribe some good name. The Holy Prophet [S.A.W.] used to alter wrong names. The name of one of Hadrat 'Umar's [R.A.A.] daughter was 'Asia. The Holy Prophet [S.A.W.] changed it and named her Jamila [R.A.A.]. (Muslim)

*The original name of Hadrat Zainab [R.A.A.] the daughter of Abu Salama [R.A.A.] was 'Barrah' which means the pious one'. On hearing this name, the Holy Prophet [S.A.W.] observed: "Do you make a self proclamation of piety?" The people submitted, "What other name shall we prescribe then?" The Prophet [S.A.W.] observed: "Name her Zainab."* *(Abu Daud)*

10. Perform the Aqiqa ceremony on the seventh day of the birth of a child. Sacrifice two lambs for a boy and one if the baby is a girl. However, it is not obligatory to slaughter two lambs for a boy. You may sacrifice one animal also. Get the hair of the head of the baby shaved off and give away in charity gold or silver equal in weight to these hair. The Holy Prophet [S.A.W.] has observed:

*"Prescribe a name for the child on the seventh day after birth and perform 'Aquiqa ceremony after getting the baby's head shaved off."* *(Tirmidhi)*

11. Get the male child circumcised on the seventh day after birth. However, if for some reason the operation is put off, it is obligatory to get the circumcision performed before the male child reaches the age of seven. Circumcision is part of Islamic faith.
12. When the child learns to speak, teach him first of all to recite: *La Ilaha Illallahu.* (There is no god but Allah.) The Holy Prophet [S.A.W.] has observed:

*When your offspring starts speaking, teach him to recite:* La Ilaha Illallahu. *(There is no god but Allah) and never fear about his end. When the milk teeth are uprooted, order your child to observe prayers.*

The Tradition also records that whenever a child in the household of the Holy Prophet [S.A.W.] began to speak, the Prophet [S.A.W.] used to teach him the second verse of Surah al-Furqan in which the concept of the belief in One God has been beautifully expressed in a concise form.

"He unto Whom belongeth the sovereignty of the heavens and the earth, He hath chosen no son nor hath He any partner in the sovereignty. He hath created everything and hath meted out for it a role."

13. Feed the child on your breast-milk. The mother owes this obligation to the child. The Holy Quran has made repeated references to this favour of the mother to her

child and has enjoined the pious to treat their mothers with extraordinary devotion in return for their favour. It is the duty of the mother to inculcate in the soul of the child belief in One God, devotion to the Prophet [S.A.W.] and love of religion along with the drops of her milk which she feeds to the child. She should make sure that the heart and soul of her child completely assimilates the spirit of religion. Do not ease your burden by transferring the duty of rearing the child to a nurse. Perform this pleasant obligation of religion yourself and enjoy spiritual satisfaction and ecstasy.

14. Avoid frightening the children. The fright instilled in the mind of the child in the early years overshadows his mind and intellect for the remainder of his life and these children usually prove incapable of achieving extraordinary success in life.
15. Make it a point not to shout at, reproach or rebuke children on every trifling matter. Make an affectionate endeavour to train the children to form good habits with devotion and good sense instead of expressing annoyance or contempt on the faults of children. However, act in such a way that children must remain in fear that you will not tolerate any of their actions which do not conform to the dictates of religion.
16. Always treat your children with affection, love and tenderness. Keep them happy by providing for their needs and requirements according to you means. Promote sentiments of loyalty and devotion in your children.

Once Hadrat Muawiyyah [R.A.A.] asked Ahnaf ibn Qais [R.A.A.], "Say, in what manner the offspring should be treated?"

Ahnaf ibn Qais [R.A.A.] answered: *'Amir-ul-Mominin,* the offspring are the fruit of our hearts, a support for our backs; we are like the sky providing a protective shade over them; we are like a soft and harmless ground on which they recline. It is they who give us the incentive to perform great deeds. Hence if they demand anything from you, fulfil their demand with a generous heart. If they are stricken with sorrow, alleviate their grief. Consequently they will love you and appreciate your paternal concern. Do not be an intolerable burden on them to the extent that they should in annoyance wish that you were better dead than alive and hate to come near you."

Hadrat Muawiyyah [R.A.A.] was deeply moved on hearing this wise speech of Ahnaf ibn Qais [R.A.A.] and remarked: "Ahnaf, [R.A.A.] I swear in the name of Allah that when you came and sat beside me I was burning with rage against Yazid."

Later, when Hadrat Ahnaf [R.A.A.] departed Hadrat Muawiyyah's [R.A.A.] anger had cooled down and he felt reconciled to Yazid. He at once sent two hundred dirhams and two hundred dresses as a token of love to Yazid. On receiving these presents, Yazid divided them into two equal portions and despatched one hundred dirhams and a hundred dresses as a gift to Hadrat Ahnaf ibn Qais [R.A.A.].

17. Pat the heads of children with affection; take them up and seat them in your laps, fondle them and treat them in good humour. Do not rule over them as an irate tyrant. Such an attitude stunts the growth of affectionate sentiments towards parents in the hearts of children, destroys their self-confidence and adversely affects the development of their inborn faculties.

On one occasion Aqra' ibn Habith [R.A.A.] came to the presence of the Holy Prophet [S.A.W.]. The Holy Prophet [S.A.W.] was at that time engaged in fondling Hadrat Hassan [R.A.A.]. Aqra' [R.A.A.] felt rather surprised and submitted, "O Holy Prophet [S.A.W.] do you also fondle children. I have ten children and have never shown fondness to even one of them"— The Holy Prophet [S.A.W.] raised his eyes and taking a look at Aqra' observed: "If Allah has deprived your heart of kindness and affection, what can I do!"

Hadrat 'Amir [R.A.A.] held a high post in the government during the reign of Hadrat Umar [R.A.A.]. He once paid a call at the house of Hadrat 'Umar [R.A.A.] and was astounded to see that a few children had mounted the chest of the Caliph and were engaged in play. The Caliph realised the feelings of annoyance writ large on the face of 'Amir [R.A.A.] and enquired, "What manner of treatment do you show to your children?" 'Amir [R.A.A.] now got the opportunity to express his viewpoint on the matter. He said: 'Amir-ul-Mominin, as soon as I enter my house the people of my household are struck with terror and stand dumb with fear." On hearing this, Hadrat 'Umar [R.A.A.] said in a deep tone of sorrow:

*"Amir [R.A.A.], you are a follower of the Holy Prophet [S.A.W.] and yet are ignorant of the important injunction that a Muslim should behave towards his family members with extreme love and deep tenderness."*

18. Concentrate all your efforts to train and educate your children in piety and honesty and consider the greatest sacrifice too little to achieve this purpose. This is an obligation laid upon you by religion; it is a favour you owe to your children; and it is the greatest good that you can do to yourself. The Holy Quran affirms:

*"O Believers, protect yourself and the people of your household from the ire of Hell."*

The only means of obtaining salvation from Hell-Fire is that man should be aware of all the requisite knowledge about religion and his life should pass in loyalty and devotion to the commands of Allah and His Messenger [S.A.W.].

*The Holy Prophet [S.A.W.] has observed: "The best gift that a father can bestow upon his son is to arrange good education and training for him." (Mishkat)*

*In addition to this, the Apostle of Allah [S.A.W.] affirmed: "The actions of man cease with his death. But there are three deeds whose reward and blessing continue to reach him even after death: One that he should make a Sadaqa Jariah (Recurring Charity). Secondly, he should leave behind a legacy of knowledge from which people may continue to derive benefit; thirdly, pious offspring who continuously invoke mercy of Allah upon him."*

*(Muslim)*

In fact the pious offspring are the only means of keeping alive your cultural traditions, religious doctrines and the concept of faith in One God, after you have expired. The believer prays for pious offspring so that the younger generation may keep the message of the old generation ever green and alive.

19. When the children attain the age of seven years, teach the 'Namaz' and urge them to observe prayers. Take

them to the mosque with you to arouse their interest. If the children neglect to observe prayers when they have attained the age of ten, administer suitable punishment to them. By word and action make it absolutely clear to them that you will not tolerate their evasion of saying prayers.

20. When the children attain the age of 10 years, give them separate beds to sleep in. The Holy Prophet [S.A.W.] has observed:

*"When your children are seven years old, urge them to observe prayers. When they attain the age of ten and neglect saying prayers, punish them, and after this age provide separate bedding to them."*

21. Always keep your children neat and clean. Take care that they are clean, neat and bathed. Keep them dress pure and clean. However, avoid excessive adornment or ostentation in dressing up children. Keep the dress of a female child simple and clean. Do not spoil the nature of your children by dressing them up in gaudy and flamboyant clothes.

22. Do not point out the faults of your children in the presence of others and strictly abstain from degrading or hurting the self-respect of your children.

23. Do not express your dismay at reforming your children in their presence. Instead praise them generously even for their ordinary virtues in order to boost up their morale. Make constant endeavours to encourage them, and to foster self-confidence and boldness in them so that they may strive for the highest goals in the field of life.

24. Keep telling the children the stories of the Prophets [A.S.], tales of the pious people [R.A.A.] and episodes of the courageous feats of the illustrious companions of the Holy Prophet [S.A.W.]. This must be considered an essential means of training, civilising, character-building and arousing love for religion among the young and despite countless other preoccupations you must find some time to talk on these subjects with your children. Recite to them the Holy Quran in a sweet rhythmical

voice frequently and on occasions relate to them the stirring stories and traditions of the life and work of the Holy Prophet [S.A.W.]. In this manner, you should try to inculcate in the hearts of the young warm sentiments of true love and devotion to the Holy Prophet [S.A.W.].

25. Let the children distribute food or money to the poor with their own hands sometimes so that the virtues of liberality, generosity and charity to the poor may develop in their hearts. On occasions, let brothers and sisters distribute shares of food or other eatables among themselves without your aid. This will create in them an awareness of the rights of others and accustom them to fair-dealing.

26. Do not comply with each legitimate or non-genuine desire of the children. By means of patience and common-sense teach them to give up this habit. Be strict with them at times and do not turn them into obstinate and self-willed youngsters by showering excessive love upon them.

27. Avoid thundering and shouting at the highest pitch of your voice and urge the children to speak softly in a moderate tone and abstain from shouting or railing at each other.

28. Inculcate the habit of self-help in children. They should not look to the servants to do every little job for them. This habit makes the children lazy and crippled in some ways. Foster the habits of sturdiness, hard work and strenuous application among the children.

29. In the event of an altercation taking place among children, do not lend undue support to your own child. You must realise that the sentiments which you cherish in your heart for your child are exactly the same which other people have for their children. Keep in view the faults of your own child and in all untoward circumstances try to pinpoint the error and fault of your own child and then make an earnest endeavour to eliminate these childish shortcomings in a wise manner by exercising constant vigilance.

30. Show equal treatment to all your children and avoid going to extremes in the matter of behaving towards children. If you are naturally drawn towards a particular child then, of course, it can't be helped. Yet in behaviour and dispensation of requirements you must show equal treatment and evenhanded justice. Do not show distinctive favour to a child to the dismay of other children. This will foster inferiority complex, hatred and frustration and all this will finally erupt into rebellious conduct. These evil sentiments greatly retard the development of natural faculties of a child and leave an adverse effect on the moral and spiritual growth of child's personality.

*On one occasion Hadrat Bashir [R.A.A.] took his son Hadrat Noman [R.A.A.] to the presence of the Holy Prophet [S.A.W.] and submitted: "O Prophet of Allah [S.A.W.]! I possessed one slave and I have transferred that slave to the ownership of this son of mine." The Holy Prophet [S.A.W.] enquired: "Have you given a slave to each of your sons?" Hadrat Bashir [R.A.A.] submitted: "No." Thereupon the Holy Prophet [S.A.W.] commanded him: "Take the slave back from him. Fear Allah and show equal treatment to all of your children." Hadrat Bashir [R.A.A.] returned home and revoked the transfer of ownership of the slave to Noman. According to another tradition, the Holy Prophet [S.A.W.] had observed on that occasion: "Do not make me a witness of sin. I shall not be a witness to injustice." In yet another tradition it is reported that the Holy Prophet [S.A.W.] observed to Hadrat Bashir [R.A.A.]: "Do you wish that all your sons should behave equally well towards you?" Hadrat Bashir [R.A.A.] submitted: "O Prophet of Allah (S.A.W.]: Yes, why not!" The Holy Prophet [S.A.W.] observed: "Do not act in this manner then." (Bukhari, Muslim)*

31. Always present a good practical model before the children. Your own life style serves as a mute and permanent precept for your children. Children constantly lean and adopt lessons from your own conduct in life. Do not tell a lie even as a matter of fun before the children.

*Hadrat 'Abdullah b. 'Amir [R.A.A.] relates an episode from his own life as follows: "One day when the Holy Prophet [S.A.W.] was present in our house, my mother called for me and said: "Come here, I have something for you." The Holy Prophet [S.A.W.] was watching. He [S.A.W.] observed to my mother, "What is it that you want to give to the child?" My mother submitted: "I wish to give him a date." The Holy Prophet [S.A.W.] observed: "If you had called the boy on the pretext of giving him something and in fact did not give him anything on his arrival, surely this sin of falsehood would have been added to the scroll of your deeds."* *(Abu Daud)*

32. Celebrate the birth of a female child with as much rejoicing as you observe on the birth of a male child. Boy or girl, both are a gift from Allah and only He knows better whether a boy or a girl is propitious for you. It does not behove a faithful of Allah to demure or feel crest-fallen on the birth of a girl. Such behaviour is the height of ingratitude and an insolence towards the Omniscient and Merciful Allah.

*The Tradition records: "When a girl is born to someone Allah sends angels to his home who pronounce: "O inmates of this house! peace be on you." The angels take the baby girl under their wings and passing their hands on her head in a gesture of affection observe: "This is a weak creature born out of a weak creature. Whosoever protects and rears this infant girl, Allah shall sustain him till doomsday."* *(Tibrani)*

33. Train and bring up your girls with a sense of great pleasure, spiritual satisfaction and in the spirit of religion. In return for this pious service anticipate from Allah that He will admit you to the uppermost level of Paradise. The Holy Prophet [S.A.W.] has affirmed: "The man who patronises three daughters or three sisters, educates them and teaches them good manners and behaves kindly towards them till they become independent of his care by the will of Allah, is entitled by Allah to enter Paradise." Thereupon a person submitted: "If there be only two daughters or two sisters?" The Holy Prophet [S.A.W.] said: "The same reward will

be given for similar conduct towards two daughters or two sisters." Hadrat Ibn 'Abbas [R.A.A.] observes: "Had the people enquired about the reward for rearing one girl in this manner, the Holy Prophet [S.A.W.] would have given the same glad tidings." (Mishkat)

*Hadrat 'Aishah [R.A.A.] narrates, "One day a woman accompanied by two small girls came to visit me and begged me to give her something. I had only one date which I handed over to her. The woman divided the date into two halves and gave one half to each girl, leaving nothing to eat for herself. Afterwards she stood up and went out. The same moment the Holy Prophet [S.A.W.] entered the house. I related the whole matter to him [S.A.W.]. On hearing the case, the Holy Prophet [S.A.W.] observed: "Any man who is put to trial on account of daughters being born to him and he comes out of the trial successful by virtue of showing good treatment to his daughters, these girls will serve him as a shield against the fire of Hell on the Day of Judgement." (Mishkat)*

34. Do not look down upon the female child, nor show preference to the boy over the girl in any matter. Treat both with equal love and behave towards both in an equal manner. The Holy Prophet [S.A.W.] has affirmed: "Anyone who is blessed with the birth of a girl and does not bury her alive in the manner of the pagan days and does not look down upon her; neither shows preference to the boy over the girl nor considers the boy in any way superior to the girl, such a man will surely be admitted into Paradise by Allah." (Abu Daud)

35. Give the prescribed share to the girl out of your property will and with careful attention. This share is ordained by Allah and no one has the authority to increase or decreases the amount of this share. It does not behove a pious believer to make excuses in the matter of paying the share of the girl or to feel content by giving away some fraction of it according to his own personal views. Such an action is a breach of covenant with Allah as well as tantamount to offering an insult to the religion. (Allah forbid!)

36. Along with these practical measures, say prayers from the depths of your soul and with sincere devotion of heart for your offspring. We may trust the Munificent and Kind Allah that He will not let earnest prayers offered by the parents out of the depth of their soul go unanswered.

## MAKING FRIENDS

1. Love your friends and become the object of love of your friends. The man who is held in deep affection by his friends and who cherishes feelings of love for his friends is the most fortunate person. The person who avoids the company of other people and whom the people regard with feelings of disgust is the most deprived man. The man who has no wealth is not poor. In point of fact great poverty consists in being friendless. A friend makes life beautiful, acts as a supporter in the journey of life and is a gift of Allah. Make friends and become friends of others. The Holy Prophet [S.A.W.] has affirmed:

*"The believer is an embodiment of love and affection. And the man who neither loves other nor is loved by others has no good or virtue in him."*

*(Mishkat, Bab-ul-Shafqat)*

The Holy Quran has affirmed:

*"The believing men and believing women are protecting friends of one another." (9: 71)*

The Holy Prophet [S.A.W.] used to cherish deep feelings of affection for all his illustrious companions [R.A.A.] so each one of them entertained the happy thought that the Holy Prophet [S.A.W.] loved him more than any one else.

Hadrat 'Amr b. al-Aas [R.A.A.] reports: "The Holy Prophet [S.A.W.] used to converse with me with such deep attention and sincerity and lavished such great care on me that I came to believe myself to be the best person among my people. And one day I submitted to the Holy Prophet [S.A.W.]: "O Prophet of Allah [S.A.W.]: Who is better-Me or Abu Bakr?" The Holy Prophet [S.A.W.] observed: "Abu Bakr is the better one." I submitted again: "Who is better-Me or 'Umar [R.A.A.]?" The Holy Prophet [S.A.W.] affirmed: "Umar is better." I submitted once more: "O Prophet of Allah [S.A.W.]: Who is better-Me or 'Uthman [R.A.A.]?" The Prophet of Allah [S.A.W.] observed: "Uthman is better than you." I then requested the Holy Prophet [S.A.W.] to explain the real matter in detail whereupon the Holy Prophet [S.A.W.] told me the plain truth. I felt greatly ashamed of myself and wondered what impelled me to ask such questions!

2. Maintain amicable social relations with your friends and try to develop sincere links and continue to cement friendships. Avoid adopting an attitude of annoyance with your friends or keeping aloof from them. When a man lives in the society of other men and has to participate in social matters, it is inevitable that he should suffer different kinds of shocks. Sometimes his sentiments are hurt; at other times his reputation is tarnished; one times his peace is disturbed, other times his usual activities are interfered with. Sometimes things are done against his temper and desires; at other times his patience and endurance are severely tried and at times he has to suffer great financial loss. In other words, he has to face all kinds of trials and tribulations. But when a man suffers these hardships, his heart is strengthened and he gains in wisdom and experience. Good morals develop in his personality and passing through a natural process of training and purification he makes rapid spiritual and moral progress. He thus acquires the sublime virtues of patience, forbearance, selflessness, affection, sympathy, humanity, respect, loyalty, devotion and cooperation, sincerity and love, generosity and gallantry, kindness and favour to the highest degree and he becomes an instrument of goodness and blessing for the human society. Every man holds him in esteem and values his friendship; each man considers him a source of blessing in his favour. The Holy Prophet [S.A.W.] has observed:

*"The Muslim who participates in social matters with other men and shows forbearance if he suffers any pain from them is a far better person than the one who isolates himself from the people and is dismayed at the hardships caused by others."* *(Tirmidhi)*

3. Form friendships with the pure and righteous people. In the choice of friends do keep in mind the thought as to how far the people with whom you are forging bonds of amity and friendship can prove useful to you from the viewpoint of religion and morality. There is a famous maxim which says: If you wish to ascertain the moral state of a man, look at the moral condition of his friends." And the Holy Prophet [S.A.W.] has observed: "A man follows the beliefs of his friend. Hence each man should deeply consider the question as to what kind of a man is the person with whom he is striking a friendship." (Musnad Ahmad, Mishkat)

The observation that a man will follow the beliefs of his friend implies that when a man keeps the company of his friend he will be affected by the sentiments, thoughts, taste and the mental outlook of his friend. He will inevitably begin to judge things to the standard of likes and dislikes adopted by his friend. Hence a man should exercise utmost care in choosing a friend and should establish bonds of affection and friendship with a person whose taste, temperament and activities conform to the tenets of faith and religion. The Holy Prophet [S.A.W.] has enjoined: "Develop a relationship of love and friendship with a believer only and eat and drink in his company only." Furthermore the Holy Prophet [S.A.W.] affirmed:

> *"Keep company with the believer and only the righteous should eat from the Dastar Khwan of a believer."*

Eating together naturally stimulates sentiments of warm affection and love between friends and these links should only be developed with the believers who are Allah-fearing and righteous people always keep away from those who have forgotten Allah and are irresponsible and indifferent in carrying out the commands of religion and are immersed in immorality. The Holy Prophet [S.A.W.] has described the nature of relationship with a good and bad friend in a sublime allegory:

> *"The example of a good or a bad friend is like that of a dealer of musk-perfume and an ironsmith who stokes the furnace. In the company of the perfumer you will certainly derive some benefit i.e. you will buy musk perfume or at least its sweet odour will afford pleasure*

*to you. On the other hand, the furnace of the ironsmith will burn your house or set your clothes ablaze or the foul fumes emitted by the furnace will give you a headache."* *(Bukhari, Muslim)*

The Tradition is recorded by Abu Daud in the following words:

*"The example of a pious friend is like that of a muskperfumery shop-keeper. If nothing, at least the benefit of sweet smell can be derived from this friend. The example of an evil friend is like that of a furnace. Even if your clothes are not set ablaze, your dress will certainly be blackened by the fumes of the furnace."*

4. Love your friends for the sake of Allah. The favourites of Allah are those who join together on the basis of Allah's religion and struggle shoulder to shoulder with perfect unity of mind and soul to discharge their obligation of establishing the religion of Allah and stand like a solid wall in defence of their creed.

The Holy Quran affirms:

*"Lo! Allah loveth those who battle for His cause in ranks as if they were a solid structure."* *(61: 4)*

And the Holy Prophet [S.A.W.] has affirmed:

*Allah will ordain on the Day of Judgement: Where are those people who used to love their fellows for my sake only. I shall place them under My own shadow."* *(Muslim)*

The enviable state of dignity in which these people will find themselves on the Day of Judgement has been described by the Holy Prophet [S.A.W.] in these words:

*"There are some loyal servants of Allah who, though they are not Prophets or martyrs, yet they shall be elevated to such high status by Allah on the Day of Judgement that the Prophets and martyrs will envy their good fortune." The illustrious companions [R.A.A.] submitted: "O Prophet of Allah [S.A.W.]! Who will be these fortunate persons?" The Holy Prophet [S.A.W.] affirmed: "These will be the people who loved each other on the basis of the religion of Allah-they were not related*

*to one another by blood, nor had any commercial connection with each other. I swear by Allah, the faces of these people will be glowing with radiance nay they will be the emblems of pure light. When all the people shall be trembling with fear, they shall be free from fear. When all the people will be grief-stricken, they shall know no sorrow."*

Afterwards the Holy Prophet [S.A.W.] recited this verse of the Holy Quran:

*"Lo! verily the friends of Allah are (those on whom fear (cometh) not, nor do they grieve." (10: 62)*

*Hadrat Abu-Darda [R.A.A.] states that the Holy Prophet [S.A.W.] observed: "Some people shall be raised from their graves on the Day of Judgement in a state that their faces will be glowing with radiant light. They shall be seated on pulpits made of pearls. Other people shall envy their elevated state. These dignified people, however, will neither include Prophets nor martyrs." The companions submitted: "O Prophet of Allah [S.A.W.]! Who are these people? Tell us their distinguishing qualities." The Holy Prophet [S.A.W.] observed: "These are the people who love each other for the sake of Allah only." (Tibrani)*

5. Consider the love of pious people as a source of salvation in the eternal life and a means of winning the favour of Allah. Pray to Allah to bless you with the love of righteous people and beseech His favour to admit you to the ranks of the pious. Hadrat 'Abdullah ibn Masud [R.A.A.] narrates: "A person came to the presence of the Holy Prophet [S.A.W.] and submitted: "O Prophet of Allah [S.A.W.], a person loves a pious man for his piety, yet himself does not emulate the good deeds of this pious man, how shall he be treated in the next world?" The Prophet of Allah [S.A.W.] affirmed: "It does not matter at all. Man shall find himself in the company of that person whom he loves." (Bukhari)

One night the Holy Prophet [S.A.W.] was blessed with the vision of Allah. Allah said to the Holy Prophet [S.A.W.]: "Ask what thou wilt?" Thereupon the Holy Prophet [S.A.W.] said this prayer:

*"Allah! I beseech Thy favour to perform good deeds and avoid evil deeds and I seek the love of the poor and implore Thee to grant me forgiveness and show me Thy Mercy. When you wish to send a calamity over a people, lift me in a state in which I may enjoy Your protection from the calamity. I implore Thy love and I beseech Thee to grant me love of that person who loves Thee and grant me the favour to perform deeds which may serve as means of obtaining nearness to You."*

*Hadrat Muadh ibn Jabal [R.A.A.] states that the Holy Prophet [S.A.W.] affirmed: "Allah ordains that I owe love to those people who develop links of love and friendship among themselves for My sake and assemble at one place to recite My name and meet each other for the love of Me and show good treatment to each other in order to win My favour."* *(Ahmad, Tirmidhi)*

The Holy Prophet [S.A.W.] giving an inspiring description of the meeting of two friends, observed:

*"A man set out to call on his friend who lived in another habitation. Allah appointed an angel to await him on the way. The angel enquired of him: "Where are you going?" The man made the answer: "I am proceeding to that village to see my brother." The angel further enquired: "Does he owe you a debt of favour which you are now going to receive from him?" The man replied: "No, I am going to meet him only because I love him for the sake of Allah." The angel thereupon told him: "Listen then! God has sent me to convey to you the glad tiding that Allah loves you as much as you love your friend for Allah's sake."* *(Muslim)*

6. Make friendship with those who deserve to be your friends from the viewpoint of Islam and then by your utmost to maintain a loyal and devoted friendly relationship throughout your life. As the choice of pious people as friends is a matter of utmost importance, so equally is the continuous endeavour to maintain and strengthen these bonds of friendship.

The Holy Prophet [S.A.W.] has affirmed: "On the Day of Judgement when there will be no shade anywhere except under the heaven of Allah, only seven types of people will find place under the shade of Allah's heaven. Of the first type will be two persons who were friends of each other for no other purpose except for the sake of Allah. The love of Allah would have forged a common link of friendship between them and they would separate from each other in the same condition. In other words, their friendship would be based on their common love of Allah and they would endeavour to maintain and cement this bond of friendship throughout their lives. And when one of them would be near the end of his life, their friendship would be intact at that time and they would part in this world as friends.

Trust your friends. Behave cheerfully while you are in their company. Avoid being gloomy and making your friends gloomy. Be informal, frank and good natured amidst friends. Do not frown; nor stand on formality. Try to act as an informal companion, a good-natured mate and a cheerful comrade among your friends. Your friends should not feel bored with your presence; rather they should feel happy and alive in your company and should feel drawn towards you.

*Hadrat 'Abdullah ibn Harith [R.A.A.] relates: "I have never seen a person who smiled more often than the Holy Prophet of Allah [S.A.W.]." (Tirmidhi)*

*Hadrat Jabir b. Samrah [R.A.A.] narrates: "I was present in over hundred sittings with the Holy Prophet [S.A.W.]. In these sittings the illustrious companions [R.A.A.] used to recite verses and related stories and anecdotes dating back to pagan times. The Holy Prophet [S.A.W.] used to hear all this in silence and even joined in laughter himself at times." (Tirmidhi)*

*Hadrat Shuraid [R.A.A.] reports that "on one occasion I was sitting behind the Holy Prophet [S.A.W.] on the back of an animal. During the journey I recited a hundred verses of Umayyah ibn as-Salt to the Holy Prophet [S.A.W.]. After each verse the Holy Prophet [S.A.W.] asked me to recite some more verses and I complied." (Tirmidhi)*

*Similarly, the Holy Prophet [S.A.W.] sometimes himself used to relate stories in his company. Hadrat 'Aishah [R.A.A.] reports: "Once the Holy Prophet [S.A.W.] related a story to the members of his household. A lady submitted: "This strange tale resembles the stories of Khurafa." The Holy Prophet [S.A.W.] asked her: "Do you know the real story of Khurafa?" and then himself narrated the true story of Khurafa in great detail. Similarly, the Holy Prophet [S.A.W.] once related a very interesting story of eleven women to Hadrat 'Aishah [R.A.A.].*

*Describing the informal conduct and cheerful temper of the illustrious companions [R.A.A.] Hadrat Bakr ibn 'Abdullah [ R.A.A.] relates:*

*"The illustrious companions [R.A.A.] used to throw the peelings of melon at each other in playful fun, yet when the time came for attack or defence the valour of the companions [R.A.A.] outweighed others in this field also."* *(Al-Adab-ul-Mufrad )*

*Hadrat Muhammad b. Ziyad [R.A.A.] reports: "I have seen the times of the righteous forebears. Several families of them lived in a single mansion. On many occasions it so happened that a family received a visit from a guest. At that moment food would be cooking in a pot in the quarter of another family. So, the host who had received a guest would go to the quarter of his neighbour and bring over the food without informing the family. The owners of the pot would then go about searching for their pot of food and would ask the people: "Who has taken away my pot?" The host who had taken the pot would then confess to him. "Brother, I had received a visit from a guest so I took away your pot of food." The owner of the pot of food would thereupon say, "May Allah bless you by increasing the quantity of this food." Muhammad ibn Ziyad [R.A.A.] also states that when these people baked bread, the same thing happened.*

*(Al-Adab-ul-Mufrad)*

A saying of Hadrat 'Ali [R.A.A.] is as follows:

*"Let your heart be free at time. Let your mind conceive pleasant notions, for mind also gets weary even as the body is fatigued."*

8. Do not be dull and spiritless. Be of good cheer and keep your spirits high. Beware, however, that your cheerful temper and humour does not exceed proper limits. Along with a cheerful temper, fun and recreation, you should never forget to observe sanctity of religion, prestige and self respect, balance and moderation in your activities.

*The illustrious companion of the Holy Prophet [S.A.W.], Hadrat Abdul Rahman [R.A.A.] reports that the illustrious companions of the Holy Prophet [S.A.W.] neither were devoid of humour nor talked about in a lifeless manner. They used to recite verses and narrate tales and legends of pagan times in their sittings. But when in any matter something was demanded of them which did not conform to justice and truth, the pupils of their eyes were inflamed with such intense anger as if they were seized with a fit of madness."*

*(Al-Adab-ul-Mufrad)*

Somebody remarked to the renowned traditionist Hadrat Sufyan b. Uyaina [R.A.A.] that humour is a nuisance. He answered:

*"No, humour is a Sunnah, but only for the man who knows the suitable occasion on which to practise it and has the ability to indulge in good jokes."*

*(Sharh Shamail Tirmidhi)*

9. If you love someone, you must express your love to that person. Its psychological effect on that person will be that he will develop a sense of nearness to you. The exchange of feelings and passions on both sides will augment love and sincerity to an extraordinary extent. Love then will no longer be merely a feeling confined within the heart but will begin to play a potent role in practical life. Thus people will have an opportunity of taking deep interest in the individual lives of each other and coming nearer to each other.

*The Holy Prophet [S.A.W.] has affirmed: "Any person who cherishes in his heart sentiments of love and sincerity for his brother, he should express these sentiments to his brother and tell him clearly that he holds him in love and affection."* *(Abu Daud)*

*On one occasion a man passed in front of the Holy Prophet [S.A.W.]. Some people were at that time in attendance on the Prophet [S.A.W.]. One of them submitted; "O Prophet of Allah [S.A.W.]! I love this man for the sake of Allah alone." On hearing this the Holy Prophet [S.A.W.] enquired from him: "Have you told this to the man?" The man submitted: "No, I have not." Thereupon the Holy Prophet [S.A.W.] urged the man: "Go and tell the man that you love him for the sake of Allah." The man stood up at once and approaching the passer-by expressed to him his sentiments. The passer-by made the answer: "May Allah love thee for whose sake you entertain feelings of love for me."*

*(Tirmidhi, Abu Daud)*

In order to cement the bonds of friendship and to bring friends closer to each other for their mutual benefit, it is essential that you should take proper interest in the individual and private matters of your friends and express to them your special feelings of devotion and concern.

The Holy Prophet [S.A.W.] has observed:

*"When a man establishes ties of friendship and fraternity with another person he should ascertain from him his name, father's name and particulars about his family as this strengthens the roots of mutual friendship."*

*(Tirmidhi)*

10. Adopt a moderate course in expressing your love and in the conduct of mutual relationship. Do not display such unconcern that your love and connection may appear doubtful, nor permit yourself to go to such extremes of passion that your love and friendship may assume the form of craziness and perchance you may suffer a shock at times (Allah forbid!) Always observe moderation and keep your feelings at balance. Adopt a moderate attitude which may be enduring and long-lasting. Hadrat Aslam [R.A.A.] states that Hadrat 'Umar [R.A.A.] observed: "Your love should not assume the

form of madness, nor should enmity excite you to perpetrate torture on other." I submitted: Sir, how should we de so?" Hadrat 'Umar [R.A.A.] observed: "In this manner that if you love someone you start hugging him in a childlike fashion and display other forms of childish behaviour. And if you feel angry with someone, you resolve upon the destruction of his life and property and utter ruination." (Al-Adab-ul-Mufrad)

*Hadrat 'Ubaid Kindi [R.A.A.] reports: I heard Hadrat 'Ali [R.A.A.] observing: "Adopt a tender and moderate attitude towards your friend; he might turn your enemy tomorrow. Likewise, follow a tender and moderate course in your conduct towards the enemy; he might become your friend sometime later." (Al-Adab-ul-Mufrad)*

11. Be loyal and devoted to your friends. The best form of devotion to your friend is that you should increasingly try to elevate his morals. You should be more concerned with his salvation in the eternal world than his advancement in the material world. The Holy Prophet [S.A.W.] observed: "Religion wholly consists in seeking the welfare of others." The real test of a well-wisher is that one should wish for his friend the same thing that one wishes for his own self, for a man can never be his own illwisher.

The Holy Prophet [S.A.W.] has affirmed:

*"I swear by Him Who hath power over my life, no man can be truly pious unless he wishes for his brother the same thing that he wishes for himself."*

Laying down six obligations which each Muslim owes to the other, the Holy Prophet [S.A.W.] observed: "And the believer should act as a well-wisher of his brother both in his presence and absence."

Furthermore, the Holy Prophet [S.A.W.] affirmed:

*"Without doubt Allah has ordained the ordeal of fire for that man and He has forbidden his entry into Paradise who forfeits the right of a brother Muslim after having sworn to fulfil his obligation." Someone from among the illustrious companions [R.A.A.] submitted: "What if that*

*obligation relates to a very minor thing?" The Holy Prophet [S.A.W.] affirmed: "Yes, even if he owes an ordinary branch of the 'Pelu' tree to another Muslim."*

12. Share the grief and sorrow of your friends. Likewise, participate actively in their joyous occasions. The purpose of your sharing their grief should be to alleviate their suffering and the aim of your participation in their festivities ought to be to enhance their joy. Every friend rightly expects from his sincere associates that they will stand by him in times of trial and will never desert him in the hour of need. Similarly, he anticipates that his friends will add to his felicity by increasing the grace of his festive parties with their presence and active participation.

The Holy Prophet [S.A.W.] has observed:

*"The Muslim fraternity is like a mansion. Even as each brick supports and cements the other brick, so does a Muslim act as a supporter and a source of strength for the other Muslim." So saying the Holy Prophet [S.A.W.] interlocked the fingers of his both hands and thus explained the mutual link and close connection that ought to subsist among the Muslim community.*

*(Bukhari, Muslim)*

The Holy Prophet [S.A.W.] enjoined:

*"In their sense of mutual love and affection and perception of common distress, you will find Muslims as one body; if one organ of this body is afflicted, the whole body is affected by fever and sleeplessness."*

*(Bukhari, Muslim)*

13. Meet your friends in a cheerful, amicable, joyous and sincere manner. Greet them warmly and observe proper etiquettes in receiving them. Avoid showing an indifferent, cold and unconcerned behaviour. These evils create a rift in the hearts. Say words of praise and thanks and joy and satisfaction during meetings with your friends. Abstain from talk which reveals sorrow, grief and low spirits. Behave in such a manner during meetings with your friends that they should be thrilled with feelings of joy and liveliness. Do not greet them

with such a gloomy face that they may feel crestfallen and may come to regard your fellowship as intolerable nuisance.

The Holy Prophet. [S.A.W.] has affirmed:

*"Do not look upon any pious deed as insignificant, may it be greeting your brother with a cheerful heart."* *(Muslim)*

*On another occasion, the Holy Prophet [S.A.W.] observed: "Your smile on seeing a brother is also an act of sacrifice on your part."* *(Tirmidhi)*

Tenderness, politeness and civility generate feelings of affection and love in the heart and it is on the basis of these virtues that a good society can be formed.

The Holy Prophet [S.A.W.] observes:

*"I tell you the distinguishing marks of a person for whom the fire of Hell has been made unlawful and who is a forbidden person for the Hell Fire to consume: He is a man who bears a sweet temper, tender heart and is soft-spoken."* *(Tirmidhi)*

The illustrious companions [R.A.A.] relate that the Holy Prophet [S.A.W.] used to be attentive with his whole posture towards the person with whom he was talking and listened to the talk in rapt attention. Once the Holy Prophet [S.A.W.] was sitting in the mosque. A man paid a call and the Holy Prophet [S.A.W.] shifted his posture and shrank a little. The man submitted: "O Prophet of Allah [S.A.W.]! there is ample room here." The Holy Prophet [S.A.W.] observed:

*"A Muslim owes it to his brother that on seeing him, he should move for him a little."* *(Baihaqi)*

*Describing the virtues of the believers, the Holy Quran affirms: "They are always very gentle to the believers."*

The Holy Prophet [S.A.W.] has elucidated the same fact in the following words:

*"The believers are forbearing and soft-hearted like a camel who is tied with a nose band; the camel is drawn to whichever direction his nose-band is tugged and if he is made to sit on a stone, he complies."(Tirmidhi)*

14. Whenever you differ among yourselves on any matter resolve it at once. Always take the initiative to seek forgiveness and to admit your fault.

Hadrat Abu Darda [R.A.A.] reports: "Once there was an exchange of hot words between Hadrat Abu Bakr and Hadrat 'Umar [R.A.A.]. Hadrat Abu Bakr [R.A.A.] felt it hard and went to the Holy Prophet [S.A.W.] in a very sad and sorry mood and submitted: "O Prophet of Allah [S.A.W.]! A difference arose between 'Umar and myself whereupon I flew into rage and we exchanged some bitter words. Later, I felt greatly ashamed of myself and solicited 'Umar [R.A.A.] to forgive me. But, O Prophet of Allah [S.A.W.]! 'Umar was not reconciled and declined to forgive me. I am feeling very much upset and uneasy so have I come to you. The Holy Prophet [S.A.W.] observed: "Allah will grant you forgiveness and salvation". Meanwhile Hadrat 'Umar [R.A.A.] also realised his fault and rushed to Hadrat Abu Bakr's [R.A.A.] house. He was informed that Abu Bakr [R.A.A.] has gone to the presence of the Holy Prophet [S.A.W.]. Whereupon 'Umar [R.A.A.] also hurried to the presence of the Holy Prophet [S.A.W.]. Signs of anger and displeasure appeared on the countenance of the Holy Prophet [S.A.W.] on seeing Hadrat Umar. Noting the displeasure against Hadrat 'Umar, Hadrat Abu Bakr [R.A.A.] felt deeply perturbed. He fell on his knees and submitted to the Holy Prophet [S.A.W.] in great humility "O Prophet of Allah [S.A.W.]! 'Umar is not at fault. All blame rests on me. I committed the fault. It was I 'who spoke harshly to him." Thereupon the Holy Prophet [S.A.W.] observed: "Allah sent me as His Prophet among you and when in the early days you refuted me, it was Abu Bakr who affirmed his faith in me and stood by me at the cost of his life and property. Would you now aggrieve my companion?"

Do not lose time in making peace. The longer the delay in resolving quarrels, the deeper grow the roots of contention, and the wider grows the gulf of separation between the hearts. The following precept of Hadrat 'Isa [A.S.] contained in the Bible is intensely heart-warming:

> *"So if you are engaged in offering sacrifice at the altar and you suddenly recall to mind that your brother has some complaint against you, leave your offering at the altar and return at once to your brother to make peace*

*with him. Then go back to the altar and make your offering."*

The Holy Prophet [S.A.W.] has observed:

*"The deeds of the people are presented to Allah on every Monday and Thursday and every believer is granted pardon except the one who nurses a grudge against any of his believing brothers. Allah ordains: "Leave them so that they may resolve their quarrel."*

Who knows whether the next moment will bring death or life! Who knows whether he will witness the next Monday or Thursday! Why and on what hope do you delay in purifying your heart and settling the complaints of your friends? Is any sensible person who believes in the Day of Judgement ready to present himself with an impure, dark and gruesome heart before the Almighty Allah?

Beware also that if your friend admits his fault and requests pardon, you should accept his excuse and forgive him from the core of your heart. The Holy Prophet [S.A.W.] has affirmed:

*"The Muslim who declines to accept the confession of his fault and a request for forgiveness from his brother Muslim is held guilty of a sin as grave as the sin of cruelty and oppression committed by an Octroi man who extorts an illegal cess."*

15. Restrain your tongue even if friends talk or behave in a manner which is offensive to your temper or taste. Do not utter harsh or offensive speech in retaliation. Instead let the matter pass with tact and gentle conduct.

The Holy Prophet [S.A.W.] observed:

*"Hadrat Moosa [A.S.] submitted to Allah: My Allah: 'Which one is the dearest to you among your creatures?' Allah affirmed: 'That one who hath the power to take revenge' yet forgives."* *(Mishkat)*

In addition to this, the Holy Prophet [S.A.W.] observed:

*"The heaviest thing put in the balance of a believer on the Day of Judgement will be his politeness. Allah looks upon that person with intense wrath who utters indecent and foul speech."*

Hadrat 'Abdullah ibn Mubarak [R.A.A.] had defined the virtue of politeness in three ways:

ii(i) A person should meet others with a bright, smiling face.

i(ii) A man should spend his wealth on the destitute and needy persons.

(iii) A person should not cause harm to any one.

*Hadrat 'Aishah [R.A.A.] reports: "The Holy Prophet [S.A.W.] observed: "The worst man in the eyes of Allah on the Day of Judgement will be the one whom the people avoid on account of his indecent and foul speech."*
*(Bukhari, Muslim)*

16. Do not shirk your duty to reform your friends and train them in righteousness. Do not let vanity and pride take root in the character of your friends which is the greatest hurdle in their reformation and moral uplift. Always try to persuade your friends to realise their omissions and errors and develop moral courage to confess their faults. They should always be mindful of the fact that failure to realise one's shortcomings and insistence upon one's faultlessness mars one's spiritual development.

As a matter of fact it is very easy to show off false humility, to call oneself as insignificant and to display submissiveness in style and manners, but it is extremely difficult to sustain an injury to your feelings, to listen to and admit your shortcomings with a cool mind and to tolerate the criticism directed by your friends against your personal faults. Yet true friends are those who keep an enlightened eye on the conduct of their friends and are always alert and alive to the task of protecting each other from the evils of vanity and pride by sincere counsel and practical example.

The Holy Prophet [S.A.W.] affirms:

ii(i) The passion which is allowed to prevail upon one's good sense.

i(ii) The greed and lust which is allowed to become the guiding principle of one's life.

(iii) And vanity-the most dangerous of the three ills." (Baihaqi, Muslim)

Criticism and accountability are lancets which purge the moral existence of man from all undesirable elements. They augment moral strength and infuse new life into the individual and the society. To take offense, to get irritated and to consider oneself as above the criticism and accountability of friends is detrimental to one's moral being as well as to evade healthy and constructive criticism of one's friends to check and protect them from moral degradation. Do feel uneasy if you find hideous faults and shortcomings in your friends and take wise measures to eliminate those blemishes on the characters of your friends. Similarly, give a chance with genuine humility and urge to your friends that they should expose to you your own foibles and faults. When your friends discharge this unpleasant duty towards you, do not be vainglorious, but welcome their criticism with large heartedness, cheerfully and with a grateful heart. Express your gratitude to them for their sincerity and kindness. The Holy Prophet [S.A.W.] has described this exemplary friendship in a most eloquent allegory.

> *"Each one of you serves as a mirror to his brother. Hence if your see any fault in your brother, eliminate it."*
>
> *(Tirmidhi)*

There are five illuminating points in this allegory which can make your friendship exemplary in genuine terms:

(i) The mirror reflects the spots and stains on your person when you stand before it with the intention of locating these spots and stains. When you stand aside, the mirror ceases to reflect these blemishes. Similarly, you should expose the foibles of your friend only if he willingly presents himself before you for criticism and chastisement with an open mind. At the same time, make it sure that his mind is receptive to your criticism and that his heart is eager to accept suggestions for the correction of his faults. In the absence of these conditions, you should keep silent and put off the matter wisely for a later occasion. In the absence of your friend especially you should exercise the utmost care not to utter a single word pointing to any shortcoming of your friend, for this would be counted as back-biting and backbiting divides the hearts rather than uniting them.

(ii) The mirror reflects very honestly all such spots or stains which are really present on the face; it neither hides their number nor makes an addition to them. Furthermore, the mirror reflects only those deformities which are outwards and apparent; it does not expose the hidden blemishes, neither probes inward, nor presents an illusory picture of your demerits. Likewise, you should also present a genuine and true picture of the inadequacies and faults of your friends. Moved by sentiments of undue politeness and flattery you should neither suppress the exposure of a few foibles of your friends nor exaggerate their dimensions or add to their number in the heat of your passionate oratory and declamation. Moreover, point out only those faults of your friends which are exposed in the normal conduct of life. Do not display curiosity or an eagerness to spy into the secrets of others. To expose the secret faults of your friends is no moral service, in fact it is a perilous and immoral act on your part.

The Holy Prophet [S.A.W.] once ascended the pulpit and warned the congregation in a very high tone of his holy voice:

*"Do not pry into the vices of Muslims. Allah exposes the hidden vices of a person who seeks to expose the faults of his brother Muslims; and when Allah decides to expose the faults of someone, He inevitably reduces the man to disgrace, even if such a man hides himself in the inner recesses of his home."*
*(Tirmidhi)*

(iii) The mirror discharges its duty unaffected by any sort of motives. Any one who faces the mirror, the mirror shows him his true image without any reservations. The mirror nurses no grudge or vendetta against anyone, nor wreaks vengeance on anybody. You should also chastise your friends unaffected by personal motives, feelings of vendetta grudge, pique, or dishonesty. Your only motive in criticising your friends should be to enable him to reform himself, as a man adorns himself by eliminating spots and stains from his person by locating them through their reflection in the mirror.

(iv) No one feels annoyed at seeing his true image in the mirror, nor commits the blunder of breaking up the mirror in a fit of rage. Instead most people on looking into the mirror begin to adorn themselves by removing the apparent defects on their persons and in fact realising the valuable services of the mirror in this regard are thankful to it in their hearts. They are fully conscious of the fact that the mirror has proved extremely helpful to them in the task of embellishing their persons. They believe that the mirror has done its natural duty remarkably and they put it away carefully for use at another time. Similarly when someone presents your true picture before you in his own words, do not retaliate in annoyance. Instead express your gratitude to him for his sincere performance of the obligation of friendship. Feel grateful to him in your heart also, apart from offering him thanks in words and set about reforming yourself at once. Realising the value and greatness of your friends with an open mind and with a sense of extreme gratitude, request your friend to continue to show you the favour of his valuable suggestions.

(v) The final point is that "every Muslim selves as a mirror unto his brother Muslim." A brother is an emblem of sincerity and love for his brother. A brother is loyal, devoted, sympathetic a well-wisher and a helper in grief to his brother. He feels restless on seeing his brother in trouble and is overjoyed at his happiness. Hence the criticism of a brother and a friend if motivated by feelings of extreme sincerity, devotion, sympathy and love. It will be characterised by a desire for the welfare and extreme concern for the best interests of his friend. Every word of this friendly criticism will reflect the spirit of reformation. Such a form of criticism may be rightly expected to unite the hearts and correct the wrongs.

17. Exchange gifts in order to express your feelings of sincerity and love for your friends and to deepen the relationship of love and affection. Mutual exchange of

gifts unites the hearts and cements the bonds of love.

The Holy Prophet [S.A.W.] has observed:

*"Exchange gifts with each other. This will generate mutual feelings of love and eliminate feelings of animosity and estrangement from your hearts."*

*(Mishkat)*

The Holy Prophet [S.A.W.] himself often used to send gifts to his illustrious Companions [R.A.A.]. The Prophet's Companions [R.A.A.] also frequently exchange presents and gifts among themselves. In the matter of exchanging gifts always keep within your means. Whatever the status of the receiver, do not think that your gift should necessarily be a costly one. Give according to your means and whatever is easily available.

The real worth of your gift depends on your sincerity and the nature and depth of feelings with which you have presented the gift. It is the feelings of sincerity and deep passions of love and devotion which unite the hearts and the cost or value of the gift is insignificant in this regard. Do not regard the gift of your friend as insignificant, however cheap in cost it may be. Instead put a high value on the feelings of love and sincerity reflected by the gift of your friend.

The Holy Prophet [S.A.W.] observed:

*"Even if someone offers me the leg of a goat as a gift, I shall accept it and if someone invites me to a dinner consisting of a cooked leg of goat, I shall certainly join the feast."* *(Tirmidhi)*

You must answer a gift with a gift. The Holy Prophet [S.A.W.] used to observe this rule strictly. The Holy Prophet's [S.A.W.] favourite gift was perfume. You should also consider the present of a perfume as a propitious gift. In the present-day circumstances, the presentation of a book can also be regarded as a propitious gift.

In this connection, you should hold common feasts at times. Invite your friends to dinner at home. When friends invite you to functions at their homes, make it a point to join their parties. Mutual entertainment promotes feelings of love and affection, and bonds of fraternity are further cemented. However, on these occasions instead of observing excessive formalities and laying out lavish quantities of food and drink, you should put more emphasis on displaying and augmenting the feelings of love and sincerity.

18. Look after your friends. Stand by them in their hour of need, even at the cost of your own life and property. Asbahani relates in a tradition: "A person came to Hadrat 'Abdullah b. 'Umar [R.A.A.] and asked: Which one is the most favourite of Allah among the people?" Hadrat 'Abdullah b. 'Umar [R.A.A.] answered: "The most favourite person of Allah among the people is he who affords the greatest benefit to his fellow men. The deed which wins the greatest favour of Allah is that you should make a Muslim happy in such manner that you should alleviate his suffering or hardship or make a provision of food to satisfy his hunger. I would go out with a brother Muslim in order to help him in his need rather than sit in the mosque of the Holy Prophet [S.A.W.] and perform Itikaf. Allah shall fill the heart of that man with His favour on Doomsday who controlled his rage at a time when he could give vent to his fury, if he so wished. And the person who accompanied his brother in order to help satisfy his need and actually provided for his need shall be rewarded with the favour of Allah on Doomsday when the other people will be staggering, this person will walk with a firm gait."

The Holy Prophet [S.A.W.] has affirmed:

*"Any man who provides for the need of his brother, Allah shall always keep fulfilling the need of that man. And any person who alleviates some hardship of a Muslim, Allah on Doomsday shall remove one of his hardships out of the many hardships of that day."*

*(Bukhari, Muslim)*

The Holy Prophet [S.A.W.] also affirmed:

*"Allah continues to help a man as long as he continues to help his brother."* *(Tirmidhi)*

Hadrat 'Abdullah b. 'Abbas [R.A.A.] has reported that the Holy Prophet [S.A.W.] observed:

*"The reward and blessing for the act of providing for*

*the need of a brother Muslim exceeds the reward and blessing for performing an I'tikaf for a period of ten years."* (Tibrani)

Hadrat Anas [R.A.A.] states that the Holy Prophet of Allah [S.A.W.] observed:

*"A Muslim who conveys a message of felicity and happiness to a brother Muslim and thus affords him happiness, Allah shall, on Doomsday, make this messenger happy."* (Tibrani)

19. Be a trustworthy confident. If a friend, relying on your good faith, confides his secret to you, you should safeguard his secret. Do not betray the confidence of your friend. Make your heart an iron vault for the safe keeping of secrets, so that friends may take counsel with you without hesitation and also in order that you may proffer good advice to your friends and extend your full cooperation to them.

Hadrat 'Umar [R.A.A.] narrates:

*"When Hafsa [R.A.A.] was widowed, I called on 'Uthman [R.A.A.] and said to him: "If you are agreeable I should give Hafsa in marriage to your." 'Uthman [R.A.A.] answered: "I shall think over the matter." I waited for his message for many nights. Later 'Uthman [R.A.A.] met me and said: "I have no intention of marrying at the moment." I then went to see Abu Bakr [R.A.A.] and proposed: "If you wish you may take Hafsa [R.A.A.] as your wife." Abu Bakr [R.A.A.] kept silent and make no answer. I was offended at the silence of Abu Bakr. I was more deeply offended with him than even at the response of 'Uthman [R,A.A.]. Many days passed and one day the Holy Prophet [S.A.W.] sent me a proposal to marry Hafsa [R.A.A.]. I accepted the proposal and gave Hafsa [R.A.A.] in marriage to the Holy Prophet [S.A.W.]. Later one day Abu Bakr [R.A.A.] met me and said: "You talked to me concerning Hafsa [R.A.A.] and I kept silent. My response might have caused you some pain." I replied: "Yes, I did feel sore at your silence." Abu Bakr [R.A.A.] thereupon told me: "I knew that the Holy Prophet [S.A.W.] himself intended to send a proposal for marriage with*

*Hafsa [R.A.A.]. The Holy Prophet [S.A.W.] had confided this secret to me and I did not intend to reveal it. If the Holy Prophet [S.A.W.] had not expressed his intention concerning Hafsa [R.A.A.], I would certainly have accepted your proposal." (Bukhari)*

*Hadrat Anas [R.A.A.] relates: "One day I was playing with boys of my age when the Holy Prophet [S.A.W.] arrived and blessed us with 'salam' [peace be on you]. The Holy Prophet [S.A.W.] told me his need and sent me on some errand. The errand took rather a long while. When it was over and I reached home late my mother enquired: "Where have you been for so long?" I answered: "The Holy Prophet [S.A.W.] had sent me on an errand." She asked: "What for?" I said: "It is a secret matter." Thereupon my mother advised me: "Look, do not reveal the secret of the Holy Prophet [S.A.W.] to anyone." (Muslim)*

20. Your moral conduct towards the people should be characterised by a cosmopolitan, vast, comprehensive, and tolerant outlook, so that people of every taste and temper, thought and ideal may feel an uncommon sense of attraction towards you. Keeping in view the particular taste, viewpoint and temperament of every one, behave towards each person so wisely that no one's feelings are hurt. Do not adopt the unwise attitude of measuring everyone according to your own particular standard of propriety, nor make an absurd and unsuccessful attempt to mould every one according to your own taste and temperament. The variety of tastes and temperaments is a beauty of Nature. Do not deform the beauty. Keep your relations according to the nature of acquaintance and the temperament of your friends, give them respect and importance accordingly and keep them attached in bonds of friendship with you by means of your own liberal behaviour and good character.

An all-round genius as the Holy Prophet [S.A.W.] was, men of all tastes and temperaments found consolation and contentment in his august company. Nobody felt any uneasiness due to the magnanimous toleration and extraordinary charitable nature of the Holy Prophet [S.A.W.]. The august company of the Holy Prophet [S.A.W.] included embodiments of toleration and affection like Abu Bakr [R.A.A.] and men of iron nature and courage like 'Umar Farooq [R.A.A.], pacifists who trembled at the prospect of war like Hassan b. Thabit [R.A.A.] as well as the gallant victor of Khybar Hadrat 'Ali [R.A.A.].

There was Abu dhar Ghifari [R.A.A.] a saintly, gloomy figure as well as 'Abdul Rahman b. 'Auf [R.A.A.], sumptuously rich and elegant in person. It was by virtue of the cosmopolitan outlook, excellent conduct, deep love for humanity and the highest degree of statesmanship of the Holy Prophet [S.A.W.] that men of divergent personalities were extremely devoted to the person of the Holy Prophet [S.A.W.] and the Prophet of Allah [S.A.W.] himself treated everyone of them with such deep.consideration that every one thought himself the most favourite friend of the Holy Prophet [S.A.W.]. Again, it was owing to this cosmopolitan moral view-point, statesmanship, wisdom and unique selflessness that the Holy Prophet [S.A.W.] formed that matchless group of illustrious companions [R.A.A.], who despite their variegated natures and temperaments, were welded together in a unique combination characterised by uncommon unity, cooperation and enviably deep mutual love and affection. The mankind as a whole may rightly consider this era as the essence and substance of its long existence so far.

Your friendships, in fact, can only be successful and longlasting when your collective attitudes and behaviour reflect rationality, liberalism, patience and tolerance, forbearance and magnanimity, forgiveness and selflessness, mutual understanding and humility, submissiveness, mutual accommodation of each other's sentiments and due consideration of each other's interests in every day life. You may judge from the following few references from the life of the Holy Prophet [S.A.W.] how considerate, magnanimous, liberal, forbearing and tolerant was the Prophet of Allah [S.A.W.] towards the natural needs, feelings and frailties of human beings:

> *"I come to offer prayer and wish to prolong the prayers. But I hear some infant crying on the woman's side and I shorten my prayers, for I cannot afford to put the mother of the child to inconvenience by prolonging the prayers."* *(Bukhari)*

Hadrat Malik bin al Huwarith states:

> *"Some of us young men of the same age group paid a visit to the Holy Prophet [S.A.W.] in order to learn religion from him. We stayed with the Holy Prophet [S.A.W.] for twenty days. The Holy Prophet was very kind and tender in his dealings. At the end of our twenty days' stay, the Holy Prophet [S.A.W.] felt that we were anxious to return home. The Prophet of Allah [S.A.W.] enquired from us: "Tell me about the people you have left behind at home." we related to him [S.A.W.] the affairs of our households in detail. Whereupon the Holy Prophet [S.A.W.] commanded us: "Go back to your wives and children. While living among them teach them everything you have learnt here and urge them to observe piety. Tell them the proper timings for offering prayers. When the time for prayer comes, one of you should call the people for prayers by saying Adaan and he who excels in knowledge and good morals among all of you, should act as leader (Imam) in the prayer."*
>
> *(Bukhari, Muslim)*

Hadrat Muawiyyah b. Hakam Sulami [R.A.A.] relates one of his own experiences as follows:

> *"I was saying prayers behind the Holy Prophet [S.A.W.] when a man sneezed. Forgetting that I was saying my prayers I spontaneously replied* Yarhamukallah *whereupon the people started rebuking me. I said to them: "May Allah protect you, why do you stare at me?" I felt, however, that the people wanted me to observe silence, so I kept mum. When the Holy Prophet [S.A.W.] had finished the prayers-May my father and mother be sacrificed for him, for never had I seen nor saw afterwards anyone who was a better teacher and guide than the Holy Prophet [S.A.W.] he did not reproach me, neither beat me, nor rebuked me. He [S.A.W.] only observed: "This is worship and it is not proper to talk in the prayer. Prayer is meant to announce the purity of Allah, to acknowledge His Greatness and to recite the Quran."*
>
> *(Muslim)*

21. Be very much particular in prayers. Pray for your friends and request them to remember you in their prayers. Pray for your friends in their presence as well as in their absence. Think of your friends and pray for them by name in their absence. Hadrat 'Umar [R.A.A.] reports: "I requested leave of the Holy Prophet [S.A.W.] to perform 'Umrah. Granting the leave, the Holy Prophet [S.A.W.] observed: "O My brother, do not forget us in your prayers." Hadrat 'Umar [R.A.A.] said: "I felt so happy on hearing this observation of the Holy Prophet [S.A.W.] that I would not have felt happier had I been offered the whole world."

The Holy Prophet [S.A.W.] has affirmed:

*"When a Muslim says a prayer for his brother Muslim in absentia, Allah accepts his prayer and appoints one of his angels on the Muslim who is offering the prayer so that when this Muslim prays for his brother Muslim the angel says: "Amen, you shall receive from Allah for yourself too what you are asking for you brother."*

*(Muslim)*

Beseech Allah in your sincere prayers: "Allah, clear our hearts of all grudge, vendetta, enemity and misunderstanding and tie us with bonds of sincerity and love. Make our relationships pleasant by means of mutual cooperation and love." Say this prayer of the Holy Quran also:

*"Our Allah! Forgive us and our brethren who were before us in the faith, and place not in our hearts any rancour towards those who believe. Our Allah; Thou art full of pity, Merciful."* *(59.' 10)*

## MANNERS FOR THE HOST

1. Express your joy and love on the arrival of a guest. Greet him with a cheerful heart. Welcome him with open arms and show him every mark of respect and honour. Do not display stinginess, indifference, cold attitude or resentment.

The Holy Prophet [S.A.W.] has observed:

*"The people who believe in Allah and the Day of Judgement should show hospitality to their guests."*

*(Bukhari, Muslim)*

Hospitality includes all those matters which are essential for showing due respect and honour to the guest and to make provisions for his comfort, peace, happiness and fulfilment of his needs. Showing respect to your guest means treating your guest with politeness and in good cheer; to entertain him with pleasant conversation, to make provisions for his rest and relaxation; to introduce him to your other respectable friends; to look after his needs, to arrange provisions of food and drink for him with a liberal and generous mind and to give personal service and attention to all the requirements of your friend.

*"Whenever respectable guests paid a visit to him, the Holy Prophet [S.A.W.] used to attend to their hospitality himself."*

"Whenever the Holy Prophet [S.A.W.] served meals to his guest he [S.A.W.] used to prompt the guest repeatedly to partake more of the food. When the guest had taken to his fill and expressed inability to eat more, it was then that the Holy Prophet [S.A.W.] ceased urging him to take more.

2. When a guest arrives, say Salam [peace be on you] to him and pray for him. Then enquire about his health.

The Holy Quran affirms:

*"Hath the story of Ibrahim's honoured guests reached thee (O Muhammad) when they came in unto him and said: "Salam" Hadrat Ibrahim answered salam."*

*(51: 24-25)*

3. Show generous hospitality to your guests and offer them the best that is readily available. On arrival of his guests, Hadrat Ibrahim [A.S.] at once got busy in making arrangements for their dinner. He [A.S.] had a fat calf in his home, which he slaughtered and got it roasted for his guests.

*"Then he went apart unto his house folk and brought a fatted calf roasted for the guests; and presented it before them."* *(51: 26, 27)*

*Faragha ila ahlihi* also bears the meaning that Hadrat Ibrahim [A.S.] went inside his home to make arrangements for the feast without informing any one lest the guests should feel informal or forbid preparation of food for them for fear of causing inconvenience to the host. In that case, it would not be possible for the host to entertain his guests.

Hadrat Abu Shariah, in his report of the manner in which the Holy Prophet [S.A.W.] has urged the Muslims to show hospitality to their guests, states as follows:

> *"I saw with my two eyes and heard with mine two ears when the Holy Prophet [S.A.W.] was delivering this counsel: "The people who believe in Allah and Day of Judgement should show hospitality to their guests. The first night and first day of his stay is the prized day and night for you."* *(Bukhari, Muslim)*

To attribute 'Inam' (reward) to the first night and first day of the guest's stay implies that as the munificent feels spiritual contentment on giving away (reward) with deep sentiments of joy and love, similar behaviour should be displayed by the host towards the guest on the first night and first day of his stay with him. Likewise as the beneficiary receives the (reward) with joy and happiness deeming it as his rightful due and appreciates the munificence of his benefactor, a similar attitude should be adopted by the guest towards his host during the first night and first day of his stay with him. The guest should not stand on formality and ought to accept the offerings of the host with sentiments of joy and close fellowship considering the host's hospitality towards him as his rightful due.

4. As soon as the guest arrives, think first of his natural human needs. Make discreet enquiries as to whether he wishes to use the toilet or bathroom. Arrange a bath for him, if it is required. Even though it may be a late hour for meals, ask your guest if he wants to eat or drink in such a discreet manner that he should not decline as a matter of formality. Show your guest his bedroom where he is to stay.
5. Do not pester your guest with your constant company. Similarly do not keep him awake late in the night talking or discussing matters. Allow him sufficient time to rest so that he may not feel inconvenient. When the guests paid a visit to him, Hadrat Ibrahim [A.S.] left them alone for a while and went inside his home to prepare a feast for the guests.

6. Do feel pleasure when the guests are dining with you. Do not show any signs of stinginess, annoyance or weariness. The guest is not a burden, but a source of blessing, grace and Divine favour. Whomsoever Allah sends to you as a guest, He sends provisions for the guest also. The guest eats with you whatever was decreed for him; he does not eat your share of the Divine bounty. The visit of a guest adds to your honour and dignity.
7. Protect the honour and dignity of your guest and consider his honour and dignity as vital as your own. In case any one poses a threat to the honour of your guest, you should consider it a challenge to your own honour and conscience.

The Holy Quran affirms that when the people of the habitation assaulted the guests of Hadrat Lut [A.S.] with evil intentions, Hadrat Lut [A.S.] rose up in their defence and declared: "These people are my guests. Do not disgrace me by treating them offensively. I hold their disgrace as an offence against my own person."

"He said:

*Lo! they are my guests. Affront me not! And fear Allah and shame me not."* *(22: 68-9)*

8. Observe all the etiquettes of hospitality with deep enthusiasm and eagerness for three days. The guest has a right over you to entertain him for three days and a believer should always be extremely generous in discharging their obligations. On the first day the guest should be shown special hospitality. Hence make sumptuous arrangements for the entertainment of your guest. On the subsequent two days it does not matter if that level of sumptuous entertainment cannot be maintained. The Holy Prophet [S.A.W.] has observed:

*"And hospitality is ordained for three days. Later whatever entertainment the host offers to his guest is a charity on his part."* *(Bukhari, Muslim)*

9. Consider rendering service to the guest as your moral duty. Do not consign your guest to the care of your servants and children. Instead devote yourself personally to the service of your guest. The Holy Prophet [S.A.W.]

used to look after the entertainment of the guests personally. When Hadrat Imam Shafii [R.T.A.] paid a visit to Imam Malik [R.T.A.] he was received with every mark of honour and respect due to a guest and was lodged in his bedroom to sleep for the night. At dawn Imam Shafi heard a knock on the door and a voice said in affectionate tones: "May Allah show you His Mercy! Arise, the hour of prayer has come." Imam Shafi at once got up and found Imam Malik standing on the door with a vessel full of water in his hand. At this, Imam Shafi [R.T.A.] felt some embarrassment, noticing which Imam Malik [R.T.A.] remarked in deep affection "Never mind, brother, it is my obligation to look after the guests."

10. Having lodged the guest, tell him the location of the toilet; provide him with a vessel of water; point out the direction of the Qiblah, and supply him with a prayer-mat. The servant of Imam Malik [R.T.A.], having lodged Imam Shafi [R.T.A.] in a room submitted to him: "Hadrat! This is the direction of the Qiblah; the vessel of water is placed here and the toilet is located this way."

11. At dinner time wash your hands first and reach the table before your guests wash their hands. When Imam Malik [R.T.A.] observed this etiquette, Imam Shafi [R.T.A.] asked him the significance of this gesture. Thereupon Imam Malik [R.T.A.] observed, "Before starting the meal the host should wash his hands first and reach the dining place before his guests in order to greet them at the meal. At the end of the meal, however, it is the guests whose hands should be washed first and the host should wash his hands last of all lest some more guests should drop in before the host gets up from the dinning place."

12. The quantity of food and the number of plates should be somewhat in excess of the actual number of guests. It is possible that someone might turn up during the meal. In that case, the host will have to get up and take the extra trouble of making further arrangements. If the provisions and plates are already there the new guest will be saved from embarrassment and will rather feel happy and honoured.

13. Show selflessness and sacrifice in the case of a guest. Provide comfort to him at the cost of your won convenience.

One day a person came to the Holy Prophet [S.A.W.] and submitted: "O Prophet of Allah [S.A.W.]! I am in a terrible agony of hunger." The Holy Prophet [S.A.W.] sent word to one of his holy wives [R.A.A.]: "Send whatever food is available," The answer he [S.A.W.] received was: "In the name of Allah Who has sent you as His Apostle, there is nothing except water available here." The Holy Prophet [S.A.W.] thereupon sent the same message to a second wife and received the same reply. The Holy Prophet [S.A.W.] made enquiries from each of his wives, but answer was invariably the same. The Holy Prophet [S.A.W.] then turned towards his companions [R.A.A.] and observed; "Who among you will accept this man as his guest for tonight?" A companion [R.A.A.] from among the Ansar submitted: "O Prophet of Allah [S.A.W.], I accept this man as my guest."

*The Ansari [R.A.A.] thereupon took the guest to his house and told his wife: "I have brought a guest from the Holy Prophet [S.A.W.] with me. Show him some hospitality." The wife answered: "I have just enough food for children and no more." The illustrious companion said: "Put the children to sleep by diverting their attention to some thing else and when you serve the meal before the guest, extinguish the lamp on some pretext and sit down beside the guest so that he may feel we are sharing the meal with him." In this manner, the guest ate to his fill, but the hosts passed the night on an empty stomach. Next morning when this illustrious companion [R.A.A.] reached to the presence of the Holy Prophet [S.A.W.], the Prophet [S.A.W.] on beholding him observed: The goodness both of you displayed towards your guest has won you the immense pleasure of Allah."* *(Bukhari, Muslim)*

14. Even if your guest has treated you with bad manners and given you a cold shoulder on some occasion in the past, behave towards him with generosity, liberality and magnanimity.

*Hadrat Abul Ahwas Jashmi [R.A.A.] relates about his father that once he submitted to the Holy Prophet [S.A.W.]: "If I come across someone and he does not perform his duty of hospitality and entertainment towards me and later if he happens to meet me, is it obligatory upon me to show him hospitality? Or should I act towards him in the same impolite and indifferent manner? The Prophet [S.A.W.] observed: "No, you should perform your obligation of hospitality towards him in any case."* *(Mishkat)*

15. Make a request to your guest to offer a prayer invoking the favour and grace of Allah on you, especially when the guest is a man of piety, a devotee of religion and a person of excellent faith. Hadrat 'Abdullah b. Busr [R.A.A.] reports: "The Holy Prophet [S.A.W.] once stayed as a guest with my father. We presented to him a dish of 'Harith'. The Holy Prophet [S.A.W.] ate some of it. Afterwards we offered some dates. The Holy Prophet [S.A.W.] ate the dates and taking the kernels between the two forefingers of his hand, cast them away. Finally we presented a drink. He [S.A.W.] took some draughts of it and passed it on to the next person sitting on his right. When the Holy Prophet [S.A.W.] got up to leave, my father took hold of the bridle of his horse and submitted: "O Prophet of Allah [S.A.W.]! Pray for us." Thereupon the Holy Prophet [S.A.W.] prayed for him.

*"O Allah! Bless the provisions you have vouchsafed to them with Thy increased bounty, grant them salvation and show them Thy Mercy."* *(Tirmidhi)*

## CARE FOR THE GUEST

1. When you pay a visit to someone as a guest, do take some gifts for the host or for his children according to your means. Keep in mind the taste and liking of your host while choosing gifts for him. Exchange of presents and gifts augments sentiments of love and promotes intimate relationship. The gift creates a soft corner in the heart of the receiver for the donor.

2. Do not stay for more than three days as a guest with any one, save under special circumstances or when the host insists on your staying with him for a longer period. The Holy Prophet [S.A.W.] affirms:

*"It is not permissible for a guest to stay so long with the host as to cause him trouble." (Al-Adab-ul-Mufrad)*

'Sahih Muslim' reports:

*"It is not permissible for a Muslim to stay so long with his brother as to make him a sinner." The people submitted: "O Prophet of Allah [S.A.W.]! How will a Muslim make his brother a sinner in this manner?" "By staying so long with his brother that his brother may be exhausted of all means of entertaining him."*

3. Do not always be a guest of others. Invite others also to be your guests and entertain them liberally.
4. When you go to stay as a guest with somebody, take necessary baggage and bedding etc. according to the season along with you. In winter, especially, never forget to take the bedding with you, otherwise the host will be put to extreme hardship. It is highly improper that the guest shall in any way become an unbearable burden for the host.
5. Keep in mind the engagements and duties of your host. Take care that your host's occupation, duties and engagements are not in any way disturbed by your presence as a guest with him.
6. Do not make all sorts of demands on your host. Be content with whatever provisions he makes for your comfort and entertainment and thank him for this. Do not put him in any extraordinary trouble.
7. If your host's women are not your close or blood relation, avoid entering into conversation with them without reason. Do not eavesdrop on the mutual conversation of your host's women. Behave yourself in such a manner that your conversation or conduct does not become a nuisance for them. Do not violate the privacy and the limitations of Purdah in any case.

8. If for some reason you do not wish to eat with your host, or you are observing a fast, excuse yourself politely and say a prayer invoking the Grace and Blessings of Allah upon your host.

When Hadrat Ibrahim [A.S.] presented a sumptuous meal to his venerable guests and the guests would not partake of it, Hadrat Ibrahim [A.S.] said to them: "Gentlemen, why don't you eat?" In a bid to put Hadrat Ibrahim at ease the angels submitted: "Please do not take it ill. As a matter of fact, we cannot eat. We have come only to convey the glad tidings of the birth of a talented son to you."

9. When you attend a feast, say a prayer at the end of the meal invoking Allah to bless the host with extensive means, grace, favour, salvation and His Mercy. Hadrat Abu Athhim b. Tahan [R.A.A.] once invited the Holy Prophet [S.A.W.] and his illustrious companions [R.A.A.] to a feast. When the meal was over, the Holy Prophet [S.A.W.] observed: "Reward your brother." The illustrious companions [R.A.A.] submitted: "How can we reward him, O Prophet of Allah [S.A.W.]?" The Holy Prophet [S.A.W.] observed:

*"When a man pays a visit to his brother and eats and drinks there, he can reward his brother by praying for Allah's favour and blessings upon his brother:*

*(Abu Daud)*

The Holy Prophet [S.A.W.] once visited the house of Hadrat Saad b. 'Ubadah [R.A.A.]. Hadrat Saad [R.A.A.] presented to the Holy Prophet [S.A.W.] bread and olive oil. The Prophet of Allah [S.A.W.] took the meal and then prayed for him:

*"May the fasting people break their fasts with your provisions! May the pious partake of your meals and may the angels pray for Allah's Mercy and forgiveness for you."* *(Abu-Daud)*

## THE CONFERENCE

1. Try to keep company with persons of good character.
2. Join in the conversation that is going on among those present in the company. To exclude yourself from the conversation and to sit in company with a frowning face

betrays a haughty attitude. The Holy Prophet [S.A.W.] used to take an active part in the conversation among his illustrious companions. Do not adopt a gloomy attitude or a posture of depression while sitting in a company. Wear a smile on your face and sit in the company in a fresh and joyous mood.

3. Try that the remembrance of Allah and the life in the Hereafter should form part of discussion in each of your meetings. When you feel that the interest of the participants is lagging in conversation on religious matters, change your topic to worldly issues. Later when a suitable opportunity arises make a discreet effort to bring the talk round to religious topics again.
4. When you go to a meeting take seat wherever you find room. Do not make a bid to move ahead by pushing through or jumping over the heads or shoulders of the people. Such conduct causes inconvenience to those who came early and took their seats first and the man who indulges in such impolite behaviour reflects a sense of self-importance and haughtiness.
5. In a meeting, do not try to dislodge a person from his seat in order to occupy it yourself. This is a very bad habit. Such conduct provokes hatred and ill-will in the hearts of others and betrays a sense of self-assertion and a haughty attitude towards others.
6. In a meeting where people are sitting around in a circle, do not sit in the centre of the circle. Such a behaviour is not only ridiculous, but extremely improper. The Holy Prophet [S.A.W.] has cursed such defaulters.
7. Do not try to grab the seat of a person who leaves his seat for a while. Keep his seat reserved until he returns. However, if it is known that the person will not return, you are free to take the seat previously occupied by him.
8. Do not separate two persons sitting together in some gathering without seeking their permission. They might be sitting together because of intimacy, love or for some other reason and separation may hurt their feelings.
9. Avoid sitting at a place of distinction in a gathering. If you pay a visit to somebody's house, don't by to take a

seat of distinction, save in case the host himself insists on your taking such a seat. Always sit in the meeting in a respectful manner. Do not spread your feet or stretch your legs.

10. Do not make a bid to always sit near the person presiding the meeting. Sit wherever you find room, and leave space for those who arrive after you to find a place to sit conveniently. In case a greater number of people arrive to attend the meeting, you should try to adjust yourself in a smaller space and generously leave room for the new comers to find a seat.
11. Do not stand before or around someone, even to show respect as it is against Islamic etiquette.
12. No two persons should talk to each other in confidence in a gathering or sitting. This annoys others and creates a feeling that they do not deserve to be taken into confidence. It may also create a misunderstanding among others that the two persons are perhaps engaged in backbiting against others present over there.
13. Seek the permission of the chairman before you say anything in a meeting. While you speak or take part in question and answers, do not assume such role as if you are presiding over the meeting. It may be taken as an attempt to impose yourself upon others as well as an insult to the chairman of the meeting.
14. Only one man should speak at a time. Each one should be heard with full attention. Eagerness to express himself first in a meeting may create chaos and pandemonium.
15. The matters discussed in confidence in the meeting must not be spread everywhere. The participants are under obligation to guard the secrets of the meeting.
16. Do not broach another issue until the meeting concludes discussion about the matter under consideration. Do not interrupt a speaker in order to start speaking yourself. In case, it is imperative for you to speak up at once, you should do so with the permission of the speaker.
17. In the course of the proceedings, the Chairman of the meeting should pay equal attention to all members. He

should address the meeting turning towards right and left so that each side receives the benefit of attention. The Chairman should allow the participants a right to express their views.

18. Say this prayer before dispersing the meeting. The meeting should not end without offering this prayer:

*"Allah, grant us Thy Fear and Mercy which may stand betmean us and disobedience to Thee. Vouchsafe to us that devotion which may entitle us to Thy Paradise. Give us such deep Faith which may render all worldly losses as worthless for us. Allah, grant us the favour of utilising our sense of hearing, sight and physical strength to our advantage and continue this favour even after we are no more. Take our revenge from him who oppresses us. Grant us victory over him who shows enmity towards us. Do not put us to trial concerning religion. Do not make worldly goods the chief objects of our lives. Do not make this world the limit of our knowledge and wisdom, nor entrust us under the charge of a person who shows no mercy to us." (Tirmidhi)*

## HAPPY GREETINGS

1. Say 'Assalamo-Alaikum on meeting a Muslim brother in order to express your feeling of attachment and felicity.

The Holy Quran affirms:

*"And when those who believe in our revelations come unto thee say: Peace be unto you." (6: 45)*

This verse which is addressed to the Holy Prophet [S.A.W.] indirectly teaches a moral etiquette to the entire Ummah i.e. whenever two Muslims meet each other, they should exchange feelings of love and felicity with each other, and the best means of doing this is that they should pray for the salvation and well-being of each other. One should say Assalamo-Alaikum; the other should respond with 'Wa 'Alaikumus salam'. Offering the salam is a means of maintaining and augmenting love and affection. The Holy Prophet [S.A.W.] affirmed:

*"You cannot enter Paradise until you acquire piety and you cannot attain piety unless you learn to love each other. Let me tell you a novel way. If you practice it, you*

*will learn to love each other. Make the practice of offering salam to each other common among you." (Mishkat)*

2. Always say 'salam' after the Islamic fashion. In personal conversation or in correspondence, you must use these words of greeting which have been prescribed by the Holy Quran and Sunnah. Do not avoid the usage of this Islamic etiquette of greeting, nor use substitute words or expressions prescribed by modern society. This Islamic mode of greeting is not only very simple, meaningful and impressive but also a comprehensive prayer for salvation and peace. The significance of your offering a salam to your Muslim brother is very vast. 'Assalamo-'Alaikum' implies 'May Allah bless you with all kinds of peace and salvation'; 'May Allah protect your life and property'; 'May Allah protect your hearth and home'; 'May He keep your family and relations in safety'; 'May Allah safeguard your faith and belief ; May you live in peace in this world and in the world Hereafter'; 'May Allah vouchsafe to your graces of which I know and graces of which I have no knowledge'; I bear deep sentiments, good-will, love and sincerity, safety and peace for you. Hence do not have fear on my account. You will never come to harm from any deed of mine'. By adding 'Alif and 'Lam' to the world '*salam*' and saying *'Assalamo-'Alaikum'* can be used for expressing heartfelt felicity, sincerity, love, goodwill and devotion to the person whom you meet, provided these words are uttered with full awareness of their significance. When you greet your brother with the words 'Assalamo-'Alaikum', you in fact invoke the blessings of Allah to protect your brother; you invoke the blessings of Him Who is the Fountain of all good and Whose Being is synonymous with peace and salvation. 'Assalam' is one of the attributes of Allah and a person can attain peace and salvation only at the goodwill of the Almighty and whomsoever He denies salvation is deprived of it in both worlds.

The Holy Prophet [S.A.W.] has affirmed:

'Assalam *is one of the attributes of Allah. It has been sent unto the world for the benefit of the people. Hence*

*make the use of Assalam common among you."*
*(Al-Adad-ul-Mufrad)*

*Hadrat Abu Hurrayrah [R.A.A.] has reported that the Holy Prophet [S.A.W.] observed: "When Allah created Hadrat Adam [A.S.], He ordained that Adam [A.S.] should approach a group of angels and offer them 'salam'. Allah also counselled Adam [A.S.] to listen carefully the answer given by the angels and to remember it, because the same prayer would be prescribed for Adam [A.S.] and his progeny. Hence Hadrat Adam [A.S.] approached the angles and said: 'Assalamo-'Alaikum'. The angels in reply said: 'Assalamo-'Alaikum Wa Rahmatullah." In other words, the angels in their answer added the words 'Rahmatullah' to '*Assalamo-'Alaikum'. *(Bukhari, Muslim)*

The Holy Quran affirms that when the angels come to extract the souls of the believers they say 'Salamu 'Alaik' on their arrival:

Thus Allah repayeth those who ward off (evil).

*"Those whom the angels cause to die (when they are) good. They say: Peace be unto you! Enter the garden because of what ye used to do."* *(16: 31, 32)*

When these God-fearing people will arrive at the gates of Paradise, the sentinels of Paradise will accord them a magnificent welcome with the same words:

*"And those who keep their duty to their Allah are driven unto the gardens in troops till when they reach and the gates thereof are opened and the warders thereof say unto them: Peace be unto you! You are good so enter you (the garden) to dwell therein forever."* *(39: 73)*

And when they shall have entered Paradise, the angels will enter from all the Gates of Paradise and say 'Assalamo 'Alaikum' to them.

*"And the angels shall arrive to offer them welcome from each Gate of Paradise and say to them: Salamun-'alaikum. This is the recompense for your patience and steadfast conduct. Hence how excellent is this eternal home."*

The people of Paradise will also greet each other with the same words:

*"And therein their tongues shall pronounce. "O Allah! Thou art Pure and Supreme" and they shall pray for each other in these words: "Salam be on you."*

*Even Allah shall send them greetings of 'Salam' and 'Blessings'.*

*"Lo! those who merit paradise this day are happily employed, they and their wives in pleasant shade on thrones reclining! Theirs the fruit and theirs that they ask; the word from a Merciful Lord is peace!"*

*(36: 55-58)*

In reality, there shall be greetings of 'Salam' for the believers from all sides in Paradise.

*"They shall not hear improper absurdities there, nor (talk) of sin. There shall only be greetings of 'Salam" 'Salam', on all sides."*

In view of these clear injunctions and evidence of the Holy Quran and Sunnah, it is not lawful for a believer to forsake the manner prescribed by Allah and His Prophet [S.A.W.] under any circumstance and adopt other modes of expressing love and felicity.

3. Say Salam to every Muslim, whether you have a prior acquaintance or connection with him or not. The condition that he is your Muslim brother suffices for establishing a relationship or making an acquaintance and a Muslim must cherish sentiments of love, sincerity, goodwill and loyalty for his brother Muslim. A person submitted to the Holy Prophet [S.A.W.]: "What is the most commendable deed in Islam?" The Holy Prophet [S.A.W.] observed:

*"To feed the poor and to offer Salam to every Muslim, whether you have a prior acquaintance with him or not."* *(Bukhari, Muslim)*

4. On entering your house, say 'Salam' to members of your family. The Holy Quran affirms:

*"But when ye enter houses salute one another with a greeting from Allah blessed and sweet."* *(24: 61)*

*Hadrat Anas [R.A.A.] reports that the Holy Prophet [S.A.W.] had advised him: "Dear son! On entering your house, you should first say 'Salam' to members of your family. This is an act of goodness and blessings for you and your family." (Tirmidhi)*

*Similarly, when you call at somebody's house, say 'Salam' before entering the house. Do not go into the house without saying 'Salam' first. "O ye who believe! Enter not houses other than your own without first announcing your presence and invoking peace upon the folk thereof." (24: 27)*

When the angels called on Hadrat Ibrahim [A.S.] as his venerable guest, they offered 'Salam' and in response Hadrat Ibrahim [A.S.] also said 'Salam' to them.

5. Say 'Salam' to small children also. This is the best means of teaching the children the manner of offering 'Salam' as well as an observance of the Sunnah of the Holy Prophet [S.A.W.]. When Hadrat Anas [R.A.A.] passed near the children, he said 'Salam' to them and observed that the Holy Prophet [S.A.W.] used to do the same." (Bukhari, Muslim)

*Hadrat 'Abdullah b. 'Umar [R.A.A.] used to write* 'Salam' *in his letters to children also. (Al-Adab-ul-Mufrad)*

6. Women can offer 'Salam' to men; likewise men can offer '*Salam*' to women. Hadrat Asma Ansaria [R.A.A.] states: "I was sitting among my lady friends when the Holy Prophet [S.A.W.] passed by us. He [S.A.W.] offered 'Salam' to us. (Al-Adab-ul-Mufrad)

*Umme Hani [R.A.A.] states: "I came to the presence of Holy Prophet [S.A.W.]. He [S.A.W.] was taking a bath at that time. When I offered 'Salam' to the Holy Prophet [S.A.W.] he en quired about me. I submitted: Umm Hani. The Holy Prophet [S.A.W.] said: "Most Welcome." (Al-Adab-ul Mufrad)*

7. Accustom yourself to say 'Salam' as often as possible and never miss the opportunity of saying 'Salam'. Say 'Salam' to each other as often as possible. The act of offering 'Salam' promotes love and in recompense for this act, Allah grants protection from all pain or loss.

The Holy Prophet [S.A.W.] has affirmed:

*"Let me tell you a device, which will promote love and friendship among you. Say Salam to each other as often as possible."* *(Muslim)*

In addition, the Holy Prophet [S.A.W.] also observed:

*"Make the practice of offering 'Salam' common among you. Allah shall grant you salvation in recompense."*

Hadrat Anas [R.A.A.] reports that the illustrious Companions of the Holy Prophet [S.A.W.] used to say 'Salam' to each other very often. So common and widespread was the practice that if at times a Companion went out of sight behind a tree and appeared in view again, he offered 'Salam' again. The Holy Prophet [S.A.W.] has observed:

*"Any person who meets a Muslim brother should say* 'Salam' *to him. Later if one of them goes out of sight behind a tree, wall or a stone and reappears, he should offer 'Salam' once again on seeing his brother."* *(Riyad-us-Salihin)*

Hadrat Tufail [R.A.A.] reports:

*"I used to call on Hadrat 'Abdullah b. 'Umar [R.A.A.] often and also accompanied him on his trips to the bazar. When both of us went to the bazar it was the common practice of Hadrat 'Abdullah ibn 'Umar [R.A.A.] to say 'Salam' to every passerby, may he be a junk-man, a shopkeeper or a poor or destitute person. In fact he invariably offered 'Salam' to every person whoever he may be."*

One day when I called on him, he said:

*"Let us go to the bazar." I submitted: Hadrat what will you do in the bazar? You never stop to make any purchases, neither enquire about any goods; nor strike a bargain; nor attend any company in the bazar. Come, sir, let us sit here and talk." Hadrat Tufail [R.A.A.] observed: "O Abu Batan (fat-bellied)! I go to the bazar merely to offer 'Salam'. Whoever happens to meet me I say* 'Salam' *to him."* *(Muwatta Imam Malik)*

8. Beware that each Muslim has a right over you to offer him 'Salam'. Discharge this obligation towards a brother

Muslim open-heartedly and never miss an opportunity to say 'Salam' to another Muslim.

The Holy Prophet [S.A.W.] has observed:

*"Each Muslim owes an obligation to another Muslim to offer him 'Salam' when ever they happen to meet."* *(Muslim)*

Hadrat Abu Hurrayrah [R.A.A.] states:

*"The most niggardly person is he who lets go an opportunity to say 'Salam'."* *(Al-Adab-ul-Mufrad)*

9. Always be the first to say 'Salam'. If, Allah forbid, you are not on good terms with someone, even then you should take the initiative in offering 'Salam' and making up the quarrel.

The Holy Prophet [S.A.W.] observed:

*"He who takes the initiative in offering 'Salam' is the nearest to Allah."* *(Abu Daud)*

Furthermore, the Holy Prophet [S.A.W.] affirmed:

*"It is not lawful for any Muslim to severe all connections with his brother Muslim for a period of more than three days to such extent that if they happen to come across each other, one should turn towards one side and the other should change his course towards the other side. Between these two, he is the superior who is the first to say 'Salam' to the other."* *(Al-Adab-ul-Mufrad )*

Someone submitted to the Holy Prophet [S.A.W.]:

*"When two persons happen to meet each other, who should say* 'Salam' *first?" The Holy Prophet [S.A.W.] observed: "He who is better than the other in the eyes of Allah."* *(Tirmidhi)*

Hadrat 'Abdullah b. 'Umar [R.A.A.] was so much particular in being the first to offer 'Salam' that no one ever succeeded in beating him in this respect.

10. Do offer the 'Salam' by word of mouth and say Assalamo-*'Alaikum* in a distinct voice so that the addressee may hear it clearly. There is nothing wrong with making a sign with your hand or nodding your head if need be along with saying the *'Salam'*. For example if the person

to whom you wish to offer *'Salam'* is out of the reach of your voice, or he is unable to hear your because of deafness, you must make a gesture of 'Salam' along with uttering *Assalamo-Alaikum*.

Hadrat 'Abdullah b. 'Umar [R.A.A.] has observed:

*"When you offer 'Salam' to someone, make sure that he hears it, for* 'Salam' *is the purest and the most blissful prayer vouchsafed by Allah to man."*

*(Al-Adab-ul-Mufrad)*

Hadrat Asma, daughter of Yazid, [R.A.A.] has reported:

*"One day the Holy Prophet [S.A.W.] passed near the mosque where a group of women were seated. While passing by the Holy Prophet [S.A.W.] offered 'Salam' to the women with a gesture of his holy hand."*

It is evident that the Holy Prophet [S.A.W.] made a gesture of the hand along with uttering the words Assalamo-'Alaikum. The Tradition recorded in the Abu Daud also confirms this point. Hadrat Asma [R.A.A.] states that when the Holy Prophet [S.A.W.] passed by us, he offered us *'Salam'*." It is proper, therefore, to make a gesture of the hand or nod the head if need be, but the words of 'Salam' must be uttered all the same.

11. Be particular in offering *'Salam'* to your elders. If you are walking along and some people are sitting on the way, you should be the first to offer them 'Salam'. When you are part of a small group and your small group comes across a large number of people, the smaller group must take the initiative in saying the 'Salam'. The Holy Prophet [S.A.W.] has affirmed:

"A Muslim has five rights over another Muslim:

(i) To make a response to the 'Salam'.

(ii) To visit him if he is lying ill.

(iii) To join in the funeral procession.

(iv) To accept the invitation.

(v) To respond to a sneeze.

Furthermore the Holy Prophet [S.A.W.] enjoined: "Avoid sitting on the road sides." The people submitted: "O Holy Prophet [S.A.W.]: It is an unavoidable necessity for us to sit on the roadside." The Holy Prophet [S.A.W.] observed: "If it is unavoidable for you to sit on the roadside, then you must discharge certain obligations concerning the roadside." The people submitted: "What are those obligations concerning the roadside? O Prophet of Allah [S.A.W.]?" The Holy Prophet [S.A.W.] observed: "To keep your eyes cast down, not to cause inconvenience, to respond to the 'Salam, to preach piety and to forbid people to indulge in wicked deeds."

18. In response to 'Salam" do not just confine yourself to saying 'Wa Alaikumus salam, but utter the words *Wa rahmatullahi Wa barakatuhu.*

The Holy Quran affirms:

*"And when ye are greeted with a prayer greet ye with a better prayer than it or repeat it."* *(4: 86)*

*The implication is that you should never miss the opportunity of responding to the 'Salam'. Say a better prayer in response by adding more words to the 'Salam', or at least utter the same words. In any case a response to 'Salam' must be made. Hadrat 'Imran b. Haseen [R.A.A.] relates: "The Holy Prophet [S.A.W.] was seated when a man came and said* Assalamo-'Alaikum. *The Holy Prophet [S.A.W.] responded to the 'Salam' and observed: 'Ten' (in other words the man had earned ten virtues). Than a second man arrived and said,* Assalamo-Alaikum Wa Rahmatullah. *The Holy Prophet [S.A.W.] responded to the* 'Salam' *and observed: `Twenty' (in other words the man had earned twenty virtues). Later a third man came to the presence and said:* Assalamo 'Alaikum Wa Rahmatullahi Wa Barakatuhu. *The Holy Prophet [S.A.W.] responded to him and observed 'Thirty' (in other words that man had earned thirty virtues).* *(Tirmidhi)*

Hadrat 'Umar [R.A.A.] has reported:

*"Once I was riding behind Abu Bakr [R.A.A.] and Abu Bakr said:* Assalamo 'Alaikum *to every one whom we passed by and every one responded with the words* Wa 'Alaikum Assalam Wa Rahmatullah. *And when Abu Bakr [R.A.A.] said: Assalamo 'Alaikum Wa Rahmatullah, the people responded with the words:* Wa

'Alaikum Assalam Wa Rahmatul lahi Wa Barakatuhu. *Thereupon Abu Bakr [R.A.A.] observed: Today the people have surpassed us in excellence to a great extent.*

*(Al-Adab-ul-Mufrzd)*

19. On meeting someone say 'Assalamo 'Alaikum' first. Do not start conversation straight-away. Start conversation only after offering the 'Salam'

The Holy Prophet [S.A.W.] has enjoined:

*"Do not respond if somebody starts talking before saying the* 'Salam'.

20. Avoid saying 'Salam' under the following conditions:
    - (i) When people are engaged in reading, listening to or teaching the Holy Quran and Hadith.
    - (ii) When some one is either delivering a sermon or is listening to it.
    - (iii) When some one is announcing *'Adaan'* or *'Takbir'*.
    - (iv) When a religious topic is being discussed in a meeting or some one is telling what Allah has ordained to us.
    - (v) When the teacher is engaged in giving a lesson.
    - (vi) When somebody is relieving himself of excretions.

Moreover, under the following conditions, you should not only avoid saying 'Salam' but also express your unconcern and spiritual agony in a discreet manner:

- (i) When somebody is engaged in licentiousness and evil acts or mercy-making such as is forbidden by Shariah and is thus guilty of contempt of religion.
- (ii) When someone is defaming religion by uttering abuses, mean and sameless talk, fabricated lies and nonsense or is indulging in obscene jokes.
- (iii) When someone is propagating views and philosophies which are repugnant to religion and is trying to proselytise people or inciting them to anti religious activities and immoral and unethical manners.
- (iv) When some one is desecrating religious beliefs and manners and is indicating his inner wickedness and

hypocrisy by making fun of the principles and injunctions of the Shariah.

21. Do not take the initiative in offering 'Salam' to the Jews or Christians. The Holy Quran affirms the fact that the Jews are the worst nation as regards their disbelief, denial of truth, tyranny and savagery, falsehood and deception. Allah showered countless bounties upon this nation, yet they always displayed ingratitude to Him and persisted in their foul practices. It is the same nation which assassinated the venerable Prophets sent by Allah. Hence the believer should eschew all such conduct which shows even the slightest trace of respect or esteem for the Jews. On the other hand, the believers should adopt such conduct towards the Jews that they should be repeatedly reminded of the fact that recompense for offering the most hideous opposition to Truth is always disgrace and humiliation.

The Holy Prophet [S.A.W.] has observed:

*"Do not take the initiative in saying 'Salam' to the Jews and Christians. When you meet them on the way, force them to move over to the edge of the road."*

*(Al-Adab-ul-Mufrad)*

The implication is that you should walk with such dignity and in a stately manner that the Jews and Christians should move over to the edge leaving the road open for you.

22. However, say 'Salam' on arrival at a mixed meeting of the Muslims and polytheists. The Holy Prophet [S.A.W.] once passed near a meeting in which Muslims and polytheists were all taking part. On that occasion the Holy Prophet [S.A.W.] had said: 'Salam' to the whole meeting." (Al-Adab-ul-Mu frad)

23. In case an occasion arises to greet a non-Muslim with some words of respect, do not say Assalamo-'Alaikum. Use words like-'Adab Arz; 'Taslimat' (respect or honour to you) etc. Do not make a gesture of your hand or nod your head or make any other sign which is repugnant to the tenets and spirit of Islam.

The letter which the Holy Prophet [S.A.W.] had addressed to Heracles contained the following words of greetings:

*"Salam be on him who follows Guidance (of the Allah)."*

24. Do shake hands after saying the 'Salam' in order to express feelings of love, felicity and reverence. The Holy Prophet [S.A.W.] himself used to shake hands with people and his illustrious companions [R.A.A.] also used to shake hands whenever they met each other. In fact, the Holy Prophet [S.A.W.] had enjoined upon his Companions [R.A.A.] to adopt the custom of shaking hands with each other, and had explained the merits and importance of this etiquette in many different ways.

*Hadrat Qatada [R.A.A.] enquired from Hadrat Anas [R.A.A.]: "Was the custom of shaking hands current among the illustrious companions [R.A.A.]?" Hadrat Anas [R.A.A.] replied: "Yes, it was." (Bukhari)*

Hadrat Salama b. Dardan [R.T.A.] states: "I saw that Hadrat Malik b. Anas [R.T.A.] was shaking hands with people. He asked me `Who are you?' I answered: "I am the slave of Bani Laith." Thereupon he passed his hand three times over my head and observed: "May Allah bless you with goodness and bounty."

On one occasion when some visitors from Yemen arrived, the Holy Prophet [S.A.W.] observed to his illustrious companions [R.A.A.]:

*"The people of Yemen have come to you and they deserve handshakes more than other visitors." (Abu Daud)*

*Hadrat, Hudhaifa b. Yaman [R.A.A.] reports: "The Holy Prophet [S.A.W.] observed: When two believers meet each other and after exchanging 'Salam' shake hands with each other they are shorn of their sins as dry leaves fall off from the trees." (Tibrani)*

Hadrat 'Abdullah b. Masud relates: "The Holy Prophet [S.A.W.] affirmed: "To shake hands is to complete your Salam."

25. When a friend, near relative or elder returns from a journey, embrace him in greeting. On reaching Medina Hadrat Zaid b. Harith [R.A.A.] went to the Holy Prophet's

[S.A.W.] house and knocked at the door. The Holy Prophet [S.A.W.] dragging his covering sheet behind him reached the door and embraced him and kissed his forehead." (Tirmidhi)

Hadrat Anas [R.A.A.] states:

*"When the illustrious Companions [R.A.A.] happened to meet each other, they shook hands and when any of them returned from the journey he was greeted with an embrace."* *(Tibrani)*

## ATTENDING A PATIENT

1. You must enquire after the health of the patients. To visit a patient is not only a social requirement or a means of promoting mutual cooperation and sympathy, but it is also a right of a Muslim over another and an essential prerequisite to devotion to Allah. He who is devoted to Allah cannot remain unconcerned with the creation of Allah. To evade the obligation of offering sympathy, consolation and assistance to the sick is tantamount to forsaking the remembrance of Allah.

The Holy Prophet [S.A.W.] has affirmed:

*"On the Day of Judgement Allah shall ordain: "O son of Adam! You did not visit me when I was ailing?" The man will submit: "O Creator! You are Lord of the whole universe. How could I dare enquire after your welfare!" Allah shall ordain: 'Such and such person from among My creatures fell ill and you did not enquire after his health. If you had gone to enquire after his welfare, you would have found Me there. (In other words you would have earned My Favour and Blessing)."* (Muslim)

In addition, the Holy Prophet [S.A.W.] observed:

*"A Muslim has six rights over another Muslim." The people submitted: "O Holy Prophet [S.A.W.]! What are those rights?" The Holy Prophet [S.A.W.] affirmed:*

(i) Say 'Salam' to your brother Muslim whenever you meet him.

(ii) Accept the invitation of your brother Muslim whenever he invites you.

(iii) Offer proper advice with all sincerity to your brother Muslim whenever he seeks your good advice.

(iv) When your Muslim brother sneezes and says *'Al-Hamd-o-Lillah'*, respond with saying *'Yar hamokallah'*.

(v) Visit your brother Muslim whenever he falls ill and enquire about his health.

(vi) When a Muslim brother dies, join in his funeral procession." (Muslim)

Furthermore, the Holy Prophet [S.A.W.] affirmed:

*"He who enquires after the health of an ailing Muslim brother will find a dwelling place on the highest level of Paradise."* *(AI-Adab-ul-Mufrad )*

Hadrat Abu Hurrayrah [R.A.A.] has reported that the Holy Prophet [S.A.W.] observed:

*"When a person goes to enquire after the health of a Muslim brother or just pays a call on him, a caller from the Heaven pronounces, "You have done well; your walking is propitious; you have earned a dwelling place in Paradise."* *(Tirmidhi)*

2. Sit towards the head of the patient, pass your hand over his head or body and utter words of sympathy and consolation, so that the patient may start thinking about the reward and recompense awaiting him in the eternal world; and he may abstain from uttering any remarks showing impatience, or feelings of anguish and complaint.

Hadrat 'Aishah bint Saad [R.A.A.] reports that her father related: "Once while in Mecca I fell gravely ill. The Holy Prophet [S.A.W.] came to enquire after my health. I submitted: "O Holy Prophet [S.A.W.]! I am leaving behind a great deal of wealth and I have only one daughter. Should I will away two-third of my wealth and leave one-third for my daughter?" The Holy Prophet [S.A.W.] observed: "No." I submitted: "Should I then will away half of my property and leave half portion for my daughter?" The Holy Prophet [S.A.W.] observed: 'No'. Thereupon I submitted: "O Holy Prophet of Allah [S.A.W.]! Should I then will away one third of my wealth?" The Holy Prophet [S.A.W.]

observed: "Yes, will away one-third of your wealth and this is enough." Afterwards, the Holy Prophet of Allah [S.A.W.] placed his hand on my forehead and passed it over my face and belly and then said the following prayer:

*"O Allah, bless Saad with health and complete his Hijrat." Since then whenever I recall to mind that moment I feel the soothing sensation of the holy hand of the Holy Prophet [S.A.W.] to the depth of my inner-self."* *(AI-Adab-ul-Mufrad)*

Hadrat Zaid b. Argam [R.A.A.] relates:

*"Once my eyes became sore. The Holy Prophet [S.A.W.] visited me to enquire after my health and said: "Zaid, what do you do when you are suffering from sore eyes." I submitted: "I endure this illness with patience." The Holy Prophet [S.A.W.] observed: If you observe patience and endurance while you are afflicted with sore eyes, Allah shall admit you into Paradise as a reward for this."*

Hadrat Ibn 'Abbas [R.A.A.] states: "Whenever the Holy Prophet [S.A.W.] visited a patient to enquire after his health, the Prophet [S.A.W.] used to sit at the head of the ailing person and repeated the following prayer seven times:

*"I beseech Allah Almighty Who is the Lord of Exalted Heavens to grant you health!"*

*The Holy Prophet [S.A.W.] observed:*

*"The patient will certainly be restored to health if this prayer is offered seven times, except in case the hour of his death has come."* *(Mishkat)*

*Hadrat Jabir [R.A.A.] reports that the Holy Prophet [S.A.W.] paid a visit to an old lady Umm-as-Saib [R.A.A.] to enquire after her health. Umm-as-Saib [R.A.A.] was shivering with intense fever. The Holy Prophet [S.A.W.] enquired: "How are you feeling?" The lady submitted: "May Allah curse this fever which is oppressing me." On hearing this, the Holy Prophet [S.A.W.] observed: "Don't curse the fever. It purges the pious of sins just as the furnace smelts the iron and purifies it of rust."*

*(Al-Adab-ul-Mufrad)*

3. When you visit a patient, enquire about his condition and pray for his recovery. Whenever the Holy Prophet [S.A.W.] visited a patient he first enquired about his health and then used to observe: *L basa tuhurun insha Allahu*. "There is no need to worry. By the Will of Allah, this illness will disappear and will prove a means of purging you of all sins." Afterwards, the Holy Prophet [S.A.W.] used to pass his right hand over the region of pain and discomfort and say this prayer:

*"Allah! Remove this pain. O Lord of mankind, grant health to this person. You are the Healer. There is none from whom we expect recovery from illness save You alone-Grant such recovery that this disease may be completely uprooted."*

4. Do not sit beside the patient for long, nor make noise near him. However, if the sick person is your intimate friend or a near relation and himself insists on your sitting beside him for a longer time, you should comply with his wishes.

Hadrat 'Abdullah b. 'Abbas [R.A.A.] states:

*"It is part of the Sunnah not to sit for long beside a patient, nor to make noise near him."*

5. Do ask the relations of the patient about his condition and express your sympathy. Offer them all possible assistance or cooperation. For example, fetch the doctor, or convey a message about the condition of the patient, or fetch medicines etc. or if required, extend financial help also.

Hadrat Ibrahim b. Abi Habla [R.A.A.] relates: "Once my wife fell ill. In those days I used to pay frequent visits to Hadrat Umm al-Darda [R.A.A.]. Whenever I called on her, she used to enquire: "Say, how is your wife?" I answered: "She is still indisposed." Thereafter, she used to send for food. I sat down and dined at her home and then came back. One day, when I called on her and she enquired about my wife's health, I replied: "By the grace and favour of Allah, she has nearly recovered from her illness. "Hadrat Umm-al-Darda [R.A.A.] thereupon observed: "When you used to say that your wife was unwell I used to arrange a meal for you. Now that she has gained her health, I need not arrange a meal for you."

6. Do visit a non-Muslim patient to enquire after his condition. Whenever you get an opportunity invite his attention towards Islam in a discreet manner as illness makes a man more inclined towards Allah and he gets more receptive to the truth.

Hadrat Anas [R.A.A.] reports:

*"A Jewish boy used to attend on the Holy Prophet [S.A.W.]. Once he fell ill. The Holy Prophet [S.A.W.] visited him to enquire after his health. The Holy Prophet [S.A.W.] sat at the head of the boy and conveyed to him the message of Islam. The boy looked to his father, who was standing nearby, as if to seek his opinion. The father said to the boy: "My son, submit to what Abul-Qasim says." So the boy accepted Islam. The Holy Prophet [S.A.W.] came out of his house saying. "Thanks Allah Who saved the boy from Hell-Fire." (Bukhari)*

7. When you visit the house of a patient to enquire after his health, avoid-looking about in the house. Sit in a manner that the inmates of the house, particularly the women are not within your sight.

Once Hadrat 'Abdullah bin Masud [R.A.A.] went to the house of an ailing person to enquire after his health. He was accompanied by some others also. One of his companions started gazing a lady of the house. When Hadrat 'Abdullah [R.A.A.] perceived it, he observed to his companion: "It would have been better for you to gouge out your eyes."

8. Do not go to enquire after the health of those who openly indulge in sinful acts and flout the Commands of Allah unashamedly and obstinately.

Hadrat 'Abdullah b. 'Amr [R.A.A.] observes:

*"When the drunkards fall ill, do not go to enquire after their health."*

9. When you go to enquire after the health of a patient, request him to pray for you also. It is recorded in Ibn Majah: "When you visit a patient to enquire after his health, request him to pray for you. The prayer of a

patient is as much effective as the prayer offered by angels." (The implication is that the angels offer prayers only at the Command of Allah and hence their prayers are always granted).

## THE GET-TOGETHER

1. Whomsoever you meet, greet him with a smiling face. Express your sentiments of felicity and take initiative in offering Salam. It will invoke great blessings of Allah on you.
2. Use no words of greeting other than those enjoined by the Holy Prophet [S.A.W.] i.e., 'Assalamo-'Alaikum'. Shake hands if possible and enquire after his health as well as the welfare of his family. The greetings 'Assalamo-'Alaikum' taught by the Holy Prophet [S.A.W.] are comprehensive in their connotations and cover all the blessings of this material life as well as our spiritual life and religion. These words signify complete peace and salvation. While shaking hands with somebody, keep it in your mind that the Holy Prophet [S.A.W.] never withdrew his hand first, but waited for the other one to release his hand.
3. Put on a clean dress when you go to call on someone; do not go out in dirty dress nor wear expensive garments while going to visit someone in order to impress him with your costly dress.
4. When you intend to visit someone, make an appointment with him first. Never visit anybody at inconvenient hours. Such a visit is not only an interference in others' engagements but also degrades you in their eyes.
5. When someone calls on you, greet him with an affectionate smile. Offer him a seat in a respectful manner and entertain him according to the occasion.
6. When you call on someone, confine yourself to talking about useful matters. Do not waste time in useless conversation, otherwise the people will dislike and avoid you.
7. When you call on somebody's house, stand outside the gate and ask for permission to enter. When permitted

to enter, say *'Assalamo-'Alaikum'* and enter the house. If you get no response after pronouncing *'Assalamo-Alaikum'* three times, don't mind it and return cheerfully.

8. While visiting somebody, do not forget to carry some suitable gifts with you. Exchange of gifts deepens feeling of mutual love and affection.
9. If a needy person calls on you, try to fulfil his need to the extent of your means. If he requests you to recommend his case to someone, do it. However, if you cannot comply with his request, you should decline in a polite manner. Do not keep him in hopeful illusions.
10. If you call on someone to seek his assistance in need, tell him your requirement in a courteous manner. If he fulfils your need, thank him. But if he declines, never mind, say *'Salam'* to him and return cheerfully.
11. Do not always expect others to call on you. You should also pay visits to others off and on. It is the most pleasant thing to develop social relations and to serve others in need. Keep in your mind that brothers in faith always develop relations for good ends.
12. If you notice a little straw or any other thing clinging to the face, beard or clothes of the person whom you happen to meet, remove it with your own hands. If the other persons does the same for you, thank him and pray for him:

    "May Allah remove all such things from you as are displeasing to you."
13. When you visit someone at night, be mindful of his comfort. Do not sit with him for long. If you come to know that he has gone to bed return cheerfully without feeling resentment.
14. When a group of people call on someone, the man who is talking should represent all his companions. Never try to press your importance or give prominence to your own self ignoring the presence of your other companions.

## TALKING TO EACH OTHER

1. Always speak the truth. Never hesitate speaking the truth even at the greatest risk.

2. Speak only when you must, and always talk with a purpose. Too much talk and useless conversation betrays lack of seriousness. You are accountable before Allah for every word you utter. The angel of Allah records.

   "A supervisor remains vigilant to preserve on record every speech that is uttered by his tongue."

3. Always speak politely. Wear a smile on you face and a sweet tone in your speech. Always speak in a moderate voice. Do not keep your voice so low as to be inaudible to the addressee, nor raise it so loud that the addressee might be over-awed by your voice. The Holy Quran affirms:

*Lo! the harshest of all the voices is the voice of the ass."*

*(31: 19)*

4. Do not spoil your tongue with dirty talk. Do not speak ill of others. Never indulge in backbiting. Do not complain against others. Never indulge in mimicking others to ridicule them. Do not make false premises. Never laugh at others, nor boast of your own superiority or indulge in self-praise. Never get unreasonable and rash in conversation. Do not pass remarks on others or satirize them. Do not call someone by a disgraceful name. Avoid swearing frequently.

5. Always say what is just and fair regardless of any loss to your self, your friend or relative.

   "And when you say something, speak what is just even if you are talking about your relative."

6. Be soft-spoken, reasonable and sympathetic in your conversation. Do not utter sharp, harsh and teasing remarks.

7. When women happen to talk with men, they should speak in a clear, straight and rough manner. They ought not speak in delicate, sweet tone lest the listener should entertain any foul expectation.

8. If the impudent wish to entangle you in dialogue or altercation offer them 'Salam' politely and leave them. Those who indulge in loose talk and absurd conversation are the worst lot of the Ummah.

9. Keep in view the mental level and outlook of the man you are talking to so as to make him understand. If the addressee cannot hear or is unable to catch your meaning, repeat what you have said before without any resentment.
10. Always be brief and to the point in your talk. It is unfair to prolong discussion without rhyme or reason.
11. When you wish to explain the tenets of Islam; want to speak on the teachings of Islam be simple and clear and speak in a passionate and heart-warming style. To seek reputation through oratory, to try to impress people with flowery language, to seek popularity among people, to adopt a proud and haughty mien, or to deliver speeches only for the sake of fun or recreation all these are the worst habits that corrupt the man to the core of his heart.
12. Never indulge in flattery, nor ingratiate with anybody. Always mind your honour and respect and avoid any thing below your dignity.
13. Do not interrupt and interfere in others' conversation without their permission, nor intercept others' conversation in order to say something yourself. If, however, you must speak, do so with the permission of other.
14. Speak slowly in a proper and dignified manner. Do not speak in a hurried manner nor indulge in fun and jokes all the time as it degrades you in the eyes of others.
15. If somebody puts a question to you, listen carefully to him and make an answer after careful thought. It is simply foolish to answer the questions without due consideration. If the questions are being put to somebody else, do not be so officious as to give answers yourself.
16. When someone is narrating something, do not say 'we know already'. May be he reveals something new and impresses you by his sincerity and piety.
17. When you talk to someone, give due regard to his age, status and his relationship to you. Do not talk with your parents, teachers and elders in a manner in which you

would talk to your friends. Likewise, when you are talking to youngster, speak with affection and elderly dignity.

18. While engaged in conversation, do not point out towards any one lest he should conceive any misunderstanding or suspicion. Abstain from eavesdropping on others.
19. Listen more and talk less. Do not reveal your secrets to others. Once you disclose a secret to someone, never expect it to remain a secret any more.

**LETTER WRITING**

1. Always begin your letter with the words.

   In the name of Allah the most Beneficent, the most Merciful

   If you wish to use an abbreviation, you may write.

   In the name of Allah, the Exalted

The Holy Prophet [S.A.W.] has affirmed: "Any undertaking, which does not commence with utterance of the attribute of Allah 'Bismillah' remains incomplete and unblessed." Some people write the numerals 786 in place of the words. This practice should however be avoided, because it is the words that carry blessings not the number.

2. Do write your own address in each letter. Never omit your address under the impression that the addressee already knows your address. Your address may not be necessarily preserved by the addressee nor can you be sure that the addressee remembers your address.
3. Write your address on the right hand side leaving a little space in between the margin and the lines of the address. Write your address clearly and take care that it is correct and the spellings of each word are also correct.
4. You must indicate the date below your address.
5. After indicating the date, write a brief 'salutation' to the addressee. Keep your 'salutation' brief and simple, such as may communicate feelings of sincerity and close relationship. Avoid words of salutation, which smack of artificiality and convey a formal sense. Along with the

salutation or on the next line after it write *'Salam Masnoon'* or *'Assalamo-'Alaikum'*. Do not write words like *'Adab'* or *'Taslimat'*.

6. If you are sending a letter to a non-Muslim, write words like 'Adab' or `Taslimat' instead of 'Assalamo-'Alaikum' or *'Salam Masnoon'*.
7. After the salutation, write down your message or purpose which you wish to convey to the addressee. Close your letter with a suitable compliment which indicates your relationship to the addressee such as yours obediently, yours sincerely, yours truly etc.
8. Your letter must be legible, clear and simple, so that it may be easily read and understood, and may impress the addressee.
9. Use fluent and polite language in your letter.
10. Be brief, but never miss necessary details to make your point clear.
11. Throughout the letter, from the salutation to the complimentary close, pay due regard to the status of the addressee.
12. Start with a new paragraph for every new point.
13. Adopt a serious style in correspondence and avoid frivolity.
14. Avoid writing letter in hot temper. Never write anything offensive. Always adopt a courteous style in letters.
15. Do not discuss secret matters in general correspondence.
16. Put a dot at the end of each sentence.
17. Do not read a letter addressed to someone else without his permission. This is a grave violation of trust. However, the elders and guardians should, as a matter of duty, go through the letters written or received by their children so that they may correct and guide them. Islam does not give free licence to the teenagers to indulge in activities that do not conform with the norms and ethics of Islamic society. Before marriage, boys and girls, having no blood relations, are not allowed to mix freely or to write private letters to each other. Hence

it is the responsibility of the parents to keep an eye on the letters written to or by their children till they are married.

18. Keep up a regular correspondence with your relatives and friends conveying to them your welfare.
19. When someone falls ill, or, Allah forbid, is injured as a result of an accident or some other calamity, do send a letter of concern and sympathy to him.
20. On occasions of ceremony, festivity or any happy development, do send letters of congratulation and joy.
21. Always use blue or black ink for the purpose of writing letters. Do not use a pencil or red ink for correspondence.
22. When some one gives you a letter for the purpose of posting it, never forget to post it without delay. Negligence and delay in such matters speaks of irresponsibility.
23. Send a return card or stamp to those with whom you are not familiar.
24. If you wish to cancel a portion of what you have written already, just cut it with a faint line.
25. While writing a letter, keep in view the interest of the addressee as well, and do not concentrate on the matters of your own choice and interest. You should not only communicate news of the peace and welfare of your own family but enquire about the peace and welfare of the family of the addressee and do not make too many demands even in letters. A man who makes too many demands degrades himself.

## THE DEALINGS

1. Conduct your business diligently and with interest. Earn your living by the sweat of your own brow and do not live as a parasite on others. On one occasion, a man from the tribe of Ansar came to the Holy Prophet [S.A.W.] and begged for assistance. The Holy Prophet [S.A.W.] enquired: "Do you have anything at home?" The companion [R.A.A.] submitted: "O Holy Prophet of Allah [S.A.W.]! We have two things only —a canvas which we

use as bedding as well as a covering sheet and a bowl for drinking water." The Holy Prophet [S.A.W.] commanded: "Bring those two things to me."

The companion [R.A.A.] at once brought both the things to him. The Holy Prophet [S.A.W.] auctioned them for two dirhams and handing over the money to the companion, observed: "Go, buy some food for one dirham and leave it with your family, and buy an axe for the other dirham."

The Holy Prophet [S.A.W.] fused a handle to the axe with his own auspicious hands and observed to the companion: "Go to the jungle daily, cut some wood and sell it in the bazar. Come back after fifteen days and report your condition to me." At the end of a fortnight when the companion [R.A.A.] returned, he had accumulated a sum of ten dirhams. The Holy Prophet [S.A.W.] was overjoyed and observed: "This hard earned income is better for thee than begging from others which might leave a stigma of begging on thy face on the day of Judgement."

2. Carry on your business in right earnest and earn as much as you can so that you may be free from dependence on others. Once the people submitted to the Holy Prophet [S.A.W.]: "O Holy Prophet of Allah [S.A.W.]! Which is the best form of earning?" The Holy Prophet [S.A.W.] observed: "Earning with your own hands and income from the business which is free from dishonesty and fraud." Hadrat Abu Qalaba [R.T.A.] observed: "Conduct your business in right earnest in the bazar. This is the way to remain attached to religion and free from all dependence upon others."
3. Promote your business by truthful means. Strictly avoid swearing falsely in the name of Allah. The Holy Prophet [S.A.W.] affirmed: "On the Day of Judgement Allah shall neither address, nor look at, nor admit that man to Paradise after purging him of sins who endeavours to expand his business by swearing falsely in the name of Allah." (Muslim). Moreover, the Holy Prophet [S.A.W.] observed: "Avoid swearing falsely in order to sell your goods. Apparently it looks like promoting your business but in fact it lets your business down and damages the goodwill of your business." (Muslim)

4. Be honest and trustworthy in business dealings. Do not turn your lawful earnings into unlawful income by supplying defective goods or by indulging in profiteering. The Prophet of Allah [S.A.W.] has affirmed: "A truthful and honest trader will be a companion of the Prophets, the righteous and the martyrs on the Day of Judgement." (Tirmidhi)
5. Try to supply the best quality of goods to the customers. If a customer seeks your counsel, give him the best possible advice.
6. Take your customers into confidence so that they may trust you as their well-wisher who will never deceive them. The Holy Prophet [S.A.W.] has observed: "He who lived on lawful earnings, observed my Sunnah and did not cause mischief to the people will be admitted to Paradise." The people submitted: "O Holy Prophet [S.A.W.]! There is a great number of such people at the present time." The Holy Prophet [S.A.W.] observed: Such people will exist even after me." (Tirmidhi)
7. Be punctual. Arrive at your place of business in time and remain there steady. The Holy Prophet of Allah [S.A.W.] has observed: "Set out in search of livelihood and lawful earnings early in the morning, for work in the morning is auspicious and brings prosperity,"
8. Work hard and demand hard and sincere work from your employees. Discharge your obligations towards your employees with selflessness and generosity and in a liberal and polite manner. Avoid scowling at them frequently or adopting an attitude of suspicion towards them in every matter. The Holy Prophet [S.A.W.] observed: "Allah never blesses a nation with piety where the weak do not get their right."
9. Be polite and liberal to your customers. Never be harsh to those who ask for loan from you neither disappoint them, nor press them unduly hard for return of your loan. The Holy Prophet [S.A.W.] has affirmed:

*"May Allah bless the person who observes politeness and courtesy in business dealings and in demanding his money back."* *(Bukhari)*

Moreover, the Holy Prophet [S.A.W.] observed:

*"Any person who craves for the protection of Allah against the affliction and oppression of the Day of Judgement should allow enough time to the hard-pressed debtor or relieve him of the burden of debt altogether."*

*(Muslim)*

10. Avoid concealing the defect of the goods and making false representations to the customer. You should openly declare the defects or inferior quality of your goods to the customer. Once the Holy Prophet [S.A.W.] passed by a heap of grain. The Holy Prophet [S.A.W.] put his hand into the heap and felt that his fingers had caught some dampness. The Prophet of Allah [S.A.W.] enquired from the grain dealer, "What is this?" The dealer submitted: "O Holy Prophet of Allah! Some rain poured over this heap." Thereupon the Holy Prophet [S.A.W.] observed: "Why did you not put the wet grain on top of the heap so that people may readily notice it. The man who deceives people has nothing to do with me."
11. Do not hoard foodstuffs anticipating a rise in prices. Strictly avoid causing distress to the people by such a vicious act. The Prophet [S.A.W.] observed: "The hoarder is a sinner." On another occasion, the Holy Prophet [S.A.W.] observed: "How wicked is the hoarder! When Allah makes goods cheap, the hoarder is afflicted with sorrow, and when the prices go up, he rejoices." (Mishkat)
12. Give the customer full value of his money. Be honest in weights and measures. Stick to one standard of give and take. Addressing the dealers on weights and measures, the Holy Prophet [S.A.W.] warned:

*"You have been charged with two duties while the people before you have perished only because they failed to fulfil these duties:*

The Holy Quran affirms:

*"Woe unto the defrauders; those when they take the measure from others they demand it full, but if they measure unto them or weigh for them they give less. Do such (men) not consider that they will be raised again*

*unto an awful Day, the day when (all) mankind stand before the Lord of the Worlds?"* *(83: 1-6)*

13. Do compensate for lapses of business ethics and give away in cash and kind as much as you can in the name of Allah without fail. The Holy Prophet [S.A.W.] enjoined upon the traders:

*"O traders and businessmen! There is every chance of exaggeration and lie in selling your commodities. Hence compensate (your faults) by spending as much as you can (to help the poor and needy).* *(Abu Daud)*

14. And never lose sight of that business which will secure you from the fearful tortures in the life Hereafter and pay you in terms of eternal prosperity, peace and pleasure. The Holy Quran affirms:

*"O ye who believe! shall I show you a Commerce that will save you from a painful doom; ye should believe in Allah and His Messenger and should strive for the cause of Allah with your wealth and your lives. That is better for you, if ye did but know."* *(61: 10, 11)*

## BIRTHS

### *The Announcement*

- If it happens that someone is the first to know of the birth of a baby to a friend, then he should take the initiative and bring the news to him.
- News of the birth of a girl should be welcomed exactly as news of a boy's birth and one should be grateful to God.
- The first thing to be done for the baby is to chant the adaan, the call to prayer, in its ear.
- The second thing, though not compulsory, is to chew a date until it is fine pulp and then place some of the liquid in the baby's mouth, afterwards saying a prayer for the baby. This is known as tahnik and it was sometimes done by the Prophet.
- The necessity of naming the child as quickly as possible should be emphasized.

- If the child is hermaphrodite, it is given a name which can belong to a boy as well as to a girl.
- If the child is born dead, it is nevertheless given a name.

***Congratulations and Visits***

- Congratulating the parents upon the arrival of a new baby is a sign of sharing the joy of the birth with them. Congratulations can be expressed in any form, but should include wishes for blessings upon the baby, and upon the parents the blessing of being able to thank God for the birth.
- It is completely un-Islamic conduct to express congratulations and good wishes on the birth of a boy, but to refrain from doing so on the birth of a girl.
- The response to congratulations is to say thanks and add, 'May God show His blessing to you and grant you a child too.'

***Seventh-Day Celebration:*** The family celebrates the birth of a new baby on the seventh day after its birth. This celebration has two major elements-slaughtering an animal and shaving the child's head.

***Slaughtering an Animal:*** To acknowledge God's blessing and to ask Him to protect the newly born child, the family slaughters an animal. The tradition enjoins the following rules:

- The rightful way is, to slaughter an animal on this occasion and not to give its value in alms.
- The animal should be a sheep, goat, cow or camel, male or female.
- The requirements in choosing the animal are the same as for the Feast of Sacrifice.
- It is recommended that one sheep or goat be slaughtered in the case of the birth of a girl and two sheep or goats in the case of the birth of a boy.
- The person slaughtering the animal should say: Bismillah, Allahumma, hadha minka wa ilayka (In the name of Allah. O God, this is done for Your sake only).
- It is completely forbidden to splash the child's head, the walls or anything else with the animal's blood.

- The animal's meat may preferably be divided into three lots-one to be consumed by the family, the other two may be distributed among relatives, neighbours and the poor.
- The animal's skin, head or limbs may not be sold or given to the butcher or the cook to meet fees.
- Some relatives and friends should be invited to dine with the family.

***Shaving the Child's Head:*** On the seventh day after birth the child's head should be shaved. It is recommended that the hair then be weighed and the equivalent weight in silver given as alms to the poor and needy. On the same day, and after shaving, saffron, if available, may be rubbed onto the child's head.

Piercing the ears of female babies, so that they may wear ear-rings later, is allowed.

***Circumcision Ceremony***

- Every Muslim boy should be circumcised. This tradition in Islam is traced back to the Prophet Ibrahim, (peace be on him).
- The duty of performing circumcision should be entrusted to someone well qualified to carry out this responsibility.
- In a circumcision the foreskin must be removed in order to expose the head of the penis; it is not necessary, however, for the foreskin in its entire length and breadth to be removed.
- If a boy is born without a foreskin, there is naturally no reason for circumcision.
- If the child's health or condition do not permit the circumcision to be carried out, then it must be postponed to a later date.
- It is recommended that circumcision be performed on those who embrace Islam, whether they be young or old unless it endangers their health.
- It is preferable that circumcision is carried out as soon as possible after birth. However, the advice of a physician should be taken if it is believed that the operation should be delayed on medical grounds.

- Godparents and other elements of 'christening' are forbidden in Islam.

## DRESS

Though clothes are an important element in the expression of human personality and social exchange, they remain, from the point of view of Islam, only a means, and should not become an end in themselves. The purpose of clothes is primarily to cover the human body and to protect it from heat or cold.

There is no special fashion to which all members of the society should adhere. On the contrary, to adhere to one type of fashion is not according to the teachings of Islam. However, general guidelines are laid down concerning dress. Some of these guidelines are common to both sexes, others relate specifically to men's or to women's clothes.

### *Common Principles*

- Muslims should distinguish themselves in dress from other nations. They should also not imitate non-Muslims in their dress or in any other way.
- A clear distinction should be observed between male and female dress. No man may dress like a woman, nor any woman like a man.
- Wearing such clothes as demonstrate arrogance and haughtiness is forbidden. In fact, arrogance and pride in any respect are not permitted. Of course, beauty and smartness of appearance do not necessarily imply arrogance. It is acceptable to wish to please God and thank Him through one's appearance.
- A man's clothes should cover his body from at least his navel to his knees. A woman's clothes should cover the whole of her body except hands and face.
- Clothes covering the above-mentioned parts of a woman's body, or a man's body should not be diaphanous or transparent.
- Uniforms are not forbidden: professionals (soldiers, policemen, etc.) may dress to declare their profession or job. However, the '*Ulama*' or the scholars of Islam, should not distinguish themselves by dressing in a special

uniform. Islam forbids anything that might contribute to the setting up of a clergy.

- It is not important to wear new clothes so much as to wear clothes that are clean. Clothes should be kept clean by washing them frequently, and dirty clothes should never be worn.
- Clothes need not be of a certain colour. The ideal colour for a Muslim's clothes is white.
- Clothes should be worn that are easy to put on and take off.
- When a Muslim buys new clothes, he must thank God for granting him the means to have them.
- When putting on clothes, one should begin with the right side, and when taking them off, begin with the left side, mentioning God's name in both cases, and then hang or fold them up.

***Men's Dress***

- Notice must be taken of the common guidelines of dress which have already been explained.
- Wearing silk, brocade, embroidered silk or a garment hemmed with silk of more than four finger's breadth, is forbidden for men. Licence, however, is given for men to wear them on medical or health grounds.
- Men should also avoid dressing in clothes dyed with saffron or with a reddish-yellow dye. There is no harm, however, in women wearing these colours.
- Wearing clothes of a non-Islamic character constitutes a kind of imitation of other nations, which is forbidden.
- Men's dress consists of the following:
  (a) Undershirt worn against the skin and made mainly of cotton.
  (b) Underwear to cover the lower part of the body.
  (c) Suit of clothes consisting of two pieces, a lower garment to cover the lower part of the body and an upper garment for the upper half of the body. No part of the lower garment should reach below the ankles. The sleeves of both undershirt and upper

garment should not be wide nor extend below the wrist, if this is done for arrogance.

(d) Headgear in the form of a turban or cap.

- Sport and swimming wear. Sportswear for men should conform to the common rule for covering nakedness, the part of the body from the navel to the knees; these parts should not be exposed to others. So sports may be played in a special type of shorts which should be ample enough hot to exaggerate or otherwise show the man's form.

***Women's Dress***

- The common guidelines on dress should be taken note of.
- A woman's dress must conform to several requirements simultaneously, namely:

(a) It must cover and conceal the whole of her body except the face and hands.

(b) The garments should not be so thin or transparent as to reveal her body.

(c) The main garment must be a 'flowing' one, that is, the woman must avoid tight or clinging clothes which exaggerate or show her figure, or any part of it, such as breasts, legs or arms.

(d) Muslim women, in order to safeguard their cultural identity, are discouraged from imitating the dress of non-Muslim women.

(e) In order to maintain their feminine identity women are forbidden to imitate men in dress.

(f) It is necessary to avoid clothes that attract the attention of others.

(g) Wearing perfume on clothes either outdoors or when meeting strangers indoors should be avoided.

- A Muslim woman's dress consists of three pieces: a shift, a veil and a cloak.

***Shift:*** a garment covering the whole body except head, face and hands. It must be long enough so that the woman's feet are entirely covered. The shift should cover the whole body. Therefore, to limit it to the knees and cover the legs with long stockings is not allowed. The sleeves of the shift should not be wide.

***Veil:*** the head-dress, is a covering to protect and conceal the woman's head and neck. It cannot be of fine net but may be made of any other material. It also cannot be of transparent material unless the folds make it opaque.

***Cloak:*** a garment to enwrap the body, rests on the top of the head and the shoulders. This helps to conceal the size of the woman's head and shoulders.

### *Shoes*

- Shoes designed or made to be used by men may not be used by women, and vice versa.
- New shoes should be bought as often as needed, if the buyer is financially able, provided that this is done without extravagance and that the purpose of doing so is not arrogance.
- Shoes should be kept tidy and clean, though they should not receive excessive attention.
- The right shoe should be put on first, and when taking them off, the left one first, mentioning God's name in both cases.
- When putting on shoes, they should be checked to ensure that no harmful insect has hidden in them during the night or while they have not been in use.
- When taking off shoes, they should be placed where they are not likely to disturb others through any unpleasant odour.

## THE ACCESSARIES

### *The Housing*

- A dwelling is one of the most important necessities of life. The fact that it is essential, but it does not mean that a Muslim should spend large sums of money on building beautiful houses, concerning himself with matters of secondary importance, such as ornamentation and unnecessary rooms. The sole purpose of the dwelling should be to protect the occupant from extremes of weather and to guarantee needed privacy.

- It is essential that bedrooms should be of two kinds, separated from one another; one for the parents, the other for the children. Girls and boys should sleep apart from the age of ten.
- Since Muslim women are not allowed to bathe in common baths, the dwelling must contain a room for bathing.
- It is preferable to have the lavatory separate from the bathroom.

***The Neatness***

- The cleanliness and pleasant smell of the house are matters of great importance.
- Refuse and garbage should be kept outside the house, so that bad smells will not disturb the residents and visitors.
- Attention should be paid to the cleanliness of the courtyard, its entrance and the garden.
- Muslims should not be influenced by non-Islàmic beliefs, such as for example, that sweeping the house at night might harm the jinn or lead to poverty, or that sweeping the house following the departure on a journey of a member of the family might harm him.

***Decoration and Beauty:*** By following and implementing the general principles of Islamic conduct, especially the principle of beauty, cleanliness and moderation in expense, the characteristics of the Muslim dwelling can be imagined-tidiness, cleanliness, simplicity, a pleasant odour, modesty.

***Cautions Efforts***

Islam recommends the following before going to bed:

- All doors are closed.
- Food pots and drinking vessels are covered.
- All sources of fire, such as gas cookers, etc. are turned off.

## CEMETERY ARCHITECTURE

***Location:*** Locations distant from towns and villages are pointless for it makes the practice of visiting graves difficult.

Cemeteries should be reasonably close to towns. With expansion of towns they may eventually become a part of the town and may if necessary be made use of for further building, planting or other useful purposes, but only if the dead have decayed to soil. The principle to be kept in mind is that people should organize their affairs without harming the dead. Cleanliness in Islam is required for the living and for the dead, so cemeteries should be kept clean.

***Interior Grave Design:*** It is not desirable for anyone to have his own grave dug and prepared before he is dead, as some people do. The grave must be dug deep and made spacious. There are two ways of digging a grave, both of which are permissible, but the first is preferable. The first is to make a niche in the side of the grave facing the Qiblah. The second is to excavate downwards in the middle of the grave.

***Exterior Grave Design:*** Islam has a unique style in building graves and cemeteries that is characterized by humility, in-extravagance and economy in costs and that avoids glorifying the dead in elaborate monuments. The height of the grave should be only about a hand-span above ground level. That serves to sufficiently distinguish the grave for it to be recognized as such and maintained. Graves should not be raised above dug soil that remains after burying. No form of construction should be erected on graves. If, however, having the graves clayed to maintain and keep them raised to within permissible bounds, so that wind or rain cannot damage them, that undoubtedly is permissible because it realizes a permissible objective. Exceeding the bounds of the permissible and/or any intent to decorate or other such vanities, are not allowed. Upright tombstones on the grave itself are forbidden. Graves must not be plastered with gypsum, paint or such like decoration, which are wholly inappropriate for a dead body decaying to soil. Writing is not to be made on graves except for the name of the dead and that only for identification purposes and not for decoration.

4

# Routine Manners

## THE OUTFIT

***Appropriate Dress:*** The dress you put on should meet the requirements of modesty, self-respect and moderation. It should protect your body and cover concealable parts adequately, and may reflect your culture, elegance and beauty. This has been enjoined in the Holy Quran in these words:

> *"O the offsprings of Adam, We have bestowed upon you garments to cover such parts of your body which need covering, and also to protect them (from vagaries of the seasons) and which may also serve as a piece of decoration."* *(7: 26)*

***Purpose of Clothing:*** The purpose of clothes is, no doubt, the garnishment and gracefulness of one's person and to protect him from the effects of the seasons. But the foremost use of the clothes is to provide covering for those parts of human body which have to be covered. The tendency to be modest and not to exhibit one's private parts is inherent in human nature. When Adam and Eve were stripped off their heavenly dress, they at once covered their bodies with the leaves of the tree of the paradise. Therefore while, choosing a dress one should keep these requirements in mind. Also one should not use an apparel which may make a fool of him.

***Clothes a gift from Allah:*** While putting on your dress you must bear in mind that clothings are a gift from Allah, which have been bestowed upon humans only and no other creatures. Therefore, you must express your gratitude to Allah for this favour.

***Clean and Pious Dress:*** **The best dress is to be pious.** The dress of piety also means inner cleanliness or sanctity of soul and apparent saintliness. This means that one should wear such clothes which may conform to the principles laid down by the Shariah, and which may not reflect ostentation and false pride. The dress should present the person as devout and God-fearing person.

***Thank Allah for New Dress:*** When you put on a new dress express your pleasure and gratitude to Allah for this favour. Imbued with thankfulness recite the following prayer which the Holy Prophet (S.A.W.) used to recite while putting on a new apparel:

"Allah! All praise belongs to Thee, Thou hast given me this dress. I pray for the goodness of this dress and the goodness for which it has been made. I seek Thy refuge against all evils that may be in this dress and from the evils for which it has been made."

***Giving Old Clothes to the Poor:*** Hadrat Umar (R.A.A.) reports that the holy Prophet (S.A.W.) had said:

> *"A person who is putting on a new dress may present his old clothes to a poor person, if he can afford to do so; and he should recite this prayer while putting on a new dress.*
>
> *"All praise and eulogy is due to Allah, who has bestowed upon me this apparel, without any ability or power on my part." Anybody who recites this prayer while putting on new clothes will remain under the protection of Allah in this world as well as in the next world.*

***Start from the Right Side:*** While putting on clothes be careful to start from the right side. That is, if you have to wear a shirt, kurta, sherwani or coat, insert your right hand into the right sleeve first and then the left hand into the left sleeve. In the same way when wearing a pyjama or pant, put your right foot first and the left foot afterwards. The Holy Prophet (S.A.W.) used to wear clothes in this way. While putting on shoes he (S.A.W.) would put his right foot into the right shoe first and then left foot into the left shoe; and while disengaging his feet, he would take away his left foot first and then the right foot from his shoes.

***Precaution Against Insect Bites:*** While putting on your clothes, shoes and socks you must take care to" thoroughly shake them, lest some venomous insect or worm may be hidden in them and may cause you harm.

***White Dress:*** If possible, use white clothes. This colour is good for males. The Holy Prophet (S.A.W.) has said, "Wear white clothes. This is the best. Only white clothes should be worn in lifetime, and in a white shroud one should be buried."

***Holy Prophet (S.A.W.) Preferring White Dress:*** According to Sahih Bukhari, the Holy Prophet (S.A.W.) used to wear clothes of white colour. He (S.A.W.) not only himself used such clothes, he (S.A.W.) exhorted the male members of his ummah to use them.

***Avoiding Arrogance through Show of Dress:*** You should not use pyjamas, trousers, etc., which have long sleeves and touch the ground. The Holy Prophet (S.A.W.) has condemned such persons who, in order to show off their arrogance and haughtiness, deliberately allow their trousers or gramments covering their lower body, to fall below their ankles and touch the ground. He (S.A.W.) has declared them as "unsuccessful and unfortunate and deserving severe punishment," He (S.A.W.) further holds "There are three kinds of persons, with whom Allah will neither talk nor look at them, and also will not purify them and allow them to enter the paradise on the Day of Judgement. They will rather get a severe punishment."

Hadrat Abuzar Ghifari, a companion of the Holy Prophet (S.A.W.) sought a clarification from the Holy Prophet (S.A.W.) on this point, who elucidated by saying:

> *"Firstly that person who allows the garment of his lower body to fall and touch the ground as an indication of pride and arrogance; secondly the man who recounts the favours done by him to somebody; and thirdly the person who tries to develop or flourish his business on falsehood."* (Muslim)

***Arrogant Persons not to Enter Paradise:*** Abdullah bin Masud quoted the Messenger of Allah (S.A.W.) as having said "Whoever has a grain of vanity, will not enter paradise. A person said that every one desires that he should have good clothes, fine shoes, etc. The Prophet of Allah (S.A.W.) replied,

*"Allah is beautiful and likes beauty. Putting on fine clothes is not pride. In reality arrognace is disregard of truth and contempt for others."* *(Muslim)*

***Following the Holy Prophet in Dress:*** Hadrat Ubaid Ibn Khalid recounting an incident says: "Once I was passing through a street in Medina when I heard a voice from my rear, saying "Raise your Tahmad (sheet for the lower part of body)-this helps a man to protect himself from all visible and invisible impurities. I turned back and saw it was the Holy Prophet (S.A.W.). I said "O Messenger of Allah! It is an ordinary piece of cloth which I have put on. How can it reflect arrogance and pride?' The Holy Prophet (S.A.W.) remarked: "Is it not your duty to follow me?" On hearing this I at once glanced on the Tahmad he was wearing then I noticed that his garment did not go beyond half the length of his calf."

***Raising the Ends of Trousers:*** The instruction of the Messenger of Allah (S.A.W.) for raising the pyjama, pant or loin cloth up to your ankle-joints to guard you from all internal and external impurities, is very significant. It means that when the cloth trails on the ground, it will be spoiled by the filth lying on the ground. This is against the etiquette of cleanliness purity and decency. Moreover, this is an indication of pride and arrogance which is internal impurity. Besides whatever is commanded by Allah's Messenger (S.A.W.) is to be obeyed because in him we have indeed

*"the best pattern (of conduct)."* *(At Quran, 33: 21)*

***Punishment:*** On another occasion the Prophet of Allah (S.A.W.) had announced a very horrible punishment for this dereliction. He has said:

*"The tahmad (piece of cloth round the waist) of the believer should be up to half of his shin. There is no harm if it is upto his ankle joint. But whatever portion trails below the ankle joint that cloth will burn in the (Hell) Fire. Anybody who keeps his cloth trailing on the ground exhibiting pride and arrogance, Allah will never cast His sight on him on the Day of Resurrection."*
*(Abu Daud)*

***Prohibition for Silken Cloth:*** Do not wear silken clothes as these are meant for women. The Messenger of Allah (S.A.W.)

has strictly prohibited the use of womanly dress by males and thereby to assume a womanly appearance and vice-versa. Hadrat Umar (R.A.A.) narrated that the Messenger of Allah (S.A.W.) has said:

> *"Do not put on silken dress: one who (man) wears it, will not be able to wear the same in the Hereafter."*
>
> *(Bukhari and Muslim)*

***Proper Use:*** Once Ukaider, the Ruler of Dommah sent a piece of silken cloth to the Holy Prophet (S.A.W.) as a gift. The Holy Prophet (S.A.W.) asked Hadrat Ali to cut this silk cloth into short pieces and distribute them among the following three ladies who bear the name of Fatima. (Muslim)

1. Fatima Zohra, daughter of the Messenger of Allah (S.A.W.) and wife of Hadrat Ali. 2. Fatima bint-e-Asad severed mother of Hadrat Ali. 3. Fatima, daughter of Hadrat Hamzah, uncle of the Prophet of Allah (S.A.W.),

It is clear from the above, that the Prophet of Allah (S.A.W.) liked only the women-folk wearing silken clothes. For this reason, the Prophet of Allah (S.A.W.) directed that the shawls should he made of the silken cloth, else that same could have been utilized for other purposes.

***Dress for Women:*** Females should put on neither such fine clothes through which their bodies may be visible, nor their dress be so tight as to make their bodies more attractive and charming and as such they may appear naked even though dressed. The Holy Prophet (S.A.W.) has cautioned women of doubtful character of their dreadful end in these words: "Such coquettes are doomed to hell who look naked even though they appear to be dressed: they entice others, and are enticed by others; their heads are filled with pride and are crooked like the humps of Bukhti camels. These women will not enter paradise nor will have even a smell of the same, although the fragrance of the paradise comes from afar." (Riaz-us-Sali-heen)

Once Hadrat Asma (R.A.A.) appeared before the Prophet of Allah (S.A.W.) dressed in fine clothes; but he (the Prophet) turned his face from her and said, "O Asma! It is not permissible for a woman, after having attained the age of puberty, that any part of her body except her face and hands could be seen (while she is out among strangers)."

***Proper Way:*** Pyjama, pant or cloth worn round the waist should not be used in a way as to expose some part of the body.

The Prophet of Allah (S.A.W.) has said:

*"Do not walk wearing a shoe in one foot only, while wearing the cloth round the waist, do not sit in a posture that may expose some part of your body; and do not wrap your shawl in a manner that you may not be able to move your hands in prayers or daily work, etc., nor lie down flat on the back, keeping your foot on each other."*

***Separate Dress for Men and Women:*** The males and, females should not adopt opposite sex's style in dress or manners. The Prophet of Allah (S.A.W.) has said:

*"Allah has cursed those men who like to adopt womanly ways and also cursed the women who imitate the ways and manners of men."* *(Bukhari)*

Once a person reported to Hadrat Aishah (R.A.A.), "There is a woman who wears the shoes meant for men." She said, "The Prophet of Allah (S.A.W.) has cursed such women, who try to imitate men."

Ladies should be very particular to cover their heads and bosoms with a shawl. It should not be so fine as to allow their hair to be seen. The purpose of shawl is to cover their beauty spots and decorations. In the Holy Quran, Almighty Allah says, "To draw their veils over their bosoms." (24: 31)

Once a piece of Egyptian soft muslin was presented to the Prophet of Allah (S.A.W.), who gave away some of its portion to Dehya Kalbee (R.A.A.) and said:

*"Out of this make a long shirt for yourself and give the other part to your wife for her shawl, but ask her to have another cloth beneath it so that the form of her body may not be visible."* *(Abu Daud)*

Keep in view the clear directive of the Holy Quran and Sunnah and the purpose of the Divine commandments and do not make a fun of these orders by putting a small piece of cloth round your neck.

Hadrat Aishah (R.A.A.) is reported to have said:

*"When this commandment was revealed, the u )menfolk made their shawls (sheets of cloth for coverage of the body) from coarse cloth and abandoned finer varieties."* *(Abu Daud)*

***Dress According to Status:*** Always dress yourself according to your means and status. The dress should be neither ostentatious as if you are running down others by an extravagant show of your wealth nor it should be beyond your means to make you a spendthrift; or put on such dress that may make you appear indigent, needy and poor. Always dress yourself in a proper, clean and neat manner, of course, according to your position and capacity.

***Ungratefulness to Allah:*** According to some, it is a sign of ungratefulness to put on old, tattered and worn-out clothes: over and above this, they consider those persons who use neat, decent and proper clothing as running after the world and ostentatious. This is absolutely an erroneous view of religion and piety.

Father of Abul-Ahwas states that once he presented himself before the Prophet of Allah (S.A.W.) with ordinary clothings. The Holy Prophet (S.A.W.) asked him, "Have you sufficient means?" He replied, "Yes sir." The Holy Prophet (S.A.W.) enquired, "What type of riches have you?" He replied, "Allah the Exalted has given me all kinds of wealth-camels, cows, goats, horses and slaves." The Prophet of Allah (S.A.W.) said: "Since Allah has graced you by granting you wealth, your physical body should reflect the effects of His bounty and benevolence." Meaning thereby that when Allah has given His bounties to you, then why you assume the role of the indent and the down-trodden. This is clear ingratitude to Allah, the Almighty.

***Allah Likes Fine Taste:*** Once a person said to the Prophet of Allah (S.A.W.) "O Messenger of Allah, I wish that my dress should be decent, neat and clean; hair of the head properly oiled; my shoes be fine and shining," and in this way he named many other articles. He even desired that his whip might also be extremely nice. The Prophet of Allah (S.A.W.) heard his talk and said: "All these are approved and Allah likes this fine taste," (Mustadrak Hakim)

***Full Dress in the Mosque:*** According to Hadrat Abdullah bin Umar (R.A.A.), the Messenger of Allah (S.A.W.) has said,

> *"Put on both the pieces of clothes during prayers (adorn yourself with full dress while praying) as it is most befitting that His servant should appear before Him well dressed and chic."* *(Mishkat)*

***Good Taste:*** Follow the proper etiquette in the use of clothes and decorum in dressing. To go about with open skirt of the shirt, uneven buttons or keep one leg of the trousers up and the other down, wearing shoe in a foot and keeping the other bare, or having dishevelled hair, are all against etiquette, and good taste.

***Well-Dressed Hair and Beard:*** Once the Prophet of Allah (S.A.W.) was sitting in the mosque, when a man with twisted hair and knotted beard came. The Holy Prophet of Allah (S.A.W.) rasied his hand meaning thereby that he should go and get his hair and beard trimmed. The person went away and returned having his hair and beard duly put in order. Thereupon the Prophet of Allah (S.A.W.) said, "Is this adornment and orderliness not better than the disarranged and twisted hair, which gives one the appearance of a devil." (Mishkat)

***Improper for Men:*** Red, bright, and dark-coloured and glittering clothes, black or saffron-coloured dress should be shunned by men. 'These are meant for females only, and that too within limits. To wear long, black robes and yellow costumes trailing the ground, is to emphasise one's superiority over others and is a sure sign of arrogance and conceit. So also do not use such unusual clothes which may make you the laughing-stock of the people.

***Simple and Appropriate:*** Always use simple, civilized and dignified dress, and be always moderate in expenses on your garments. Avoid elegance and delicacy in dress. The Messenger of Allah (S.A.W.) has said: "Be away from ease and comfort because the pleasure-loving persons are not the beloved ones of Allah. (Miskhat)

***Simplicity in spite of Means:*** The Prophet of Allah (S.A.W.) also said: "Anybody who adopted simplicity in his dress in spite of his means and affluence, only on account of humility and modesty, Allah Almighty will adorn him with the raiment (clothing) of nobility and wisdom." (Abu Daud)

***Sign of Faith:*** One day, when the companions of the Holy Prophet (S.A.W.) were talking about the affairs relating to this world, the Holy Prophet of Allah (S.A.W.) remarked, "Simplicity in dress is one of the signs of faith, (Iman) in Allah." (Abu Daud)

***Reward for Providing Clothes:*** To express thanks to Allah for this bounty of (decent) clothings bestowed upon you, you should also clothe the indigent and needy persons who have nothing to put on. The Messenger of Allah (S.A.W.) said,

> *"A Muslim who clothes another Muslim, shall be clothed with a green heavenly dress by Allah on the Day of Judgement."* *(Abu Daud)*

The Holy Prophet (S.A.W.) has also said:

> *"So long as the clothes given by a Muslim to his fellow Muslim brother remain on his body, Allah will keep in safety the provider of the same."* *(Tirmidhi)*

***Social Equality:*** Provide clothing for the servants, serving you day and night, according to your status. The Prophet of Allah (S.A.W.) has said,

> *"Slaves are like your brothers, whom Allah has placed under your control. It is your responsibility to give them the food you eat, the clothes you wear, and make them work according to their capacity. If a slave is not able to do his master's work, the master should give him a helping hand."* *(Bukhari and Muslim)*

## DRINKING AND EATING

***Etiquette of Eating and Drinking:*** Be punctual and regular in taking meals. Avoid gluttony and incessant eating. Eat only when you feel hungry and stop eating when some hunger is still left; and under no circumstances do not resort to overeating. The Holy Prophet (S.A.W.) has said:

> *"A believer eats in one intestine and a non-believer, in seven intestines."* *(Tirmidhi)*

***Healthy Stomach:*** Good health depends upon the health of the stomach. Overeating harms the digestive system. The Holy Prophet (S.A.W.) has elucidated this point as follows:

*"The stomach is like a reservoir for the body. The veins and arteries receive their supply of life—blood from this reservoir. As such, if the stomach is in good health, they will receive healthy material and if the stomach is unhealthy, they will circulate unhealthy material."*

*(Baihaqi)*

***Under-eating Encouraged:*** Encouraging under-eating the Holy Prophet (S.A.W.) has also said.

"A meal of one person should suffice for two."

***Prefer Simple Fare:*** Always have a simple fare; use bread made from flour containing roughage. Avoid food containing too much spices, and unnecessarily very tasty dishes. The food should be easily digestible which may furnish energy and health to the body. Don't go after very much savoury meals.

***Unsieved Flour Preferred:*** Our Holy Prophet (S.A.W.) preferred bread made of unsieved flour. He did not relish a thin loaf or one prepared from fine flour. Similarly, he did not like very hot and teaming food and waited till it got cool. About hot food, he often said, "Allah has not given us fire to eat," and occasionally he would say:

"There is nothing divine in a hot food."

He was fond of meat specially forelegs, pieces of neck or collar and back. In fact, meat is an essential diet for supplying energy to the body, and developing the spirit of a chivalrous Mujahid. And a Muslim should always keep his heart full of the spirit of a Mujahid.

A meal should be taken in a serene and peaceful mood; each morsel should be thoroughly chewed. Refrain from eating while you are in a state of gloom, anger or agitation. Food eaten in a placid and unperturbed state is wholesome, and that taken under some strain and stress of sorrow, concern and disturbance adversely affects the belly, and does not supply sufficient energy to the body. As such do not sit on the dining table while in a state of gloom or dullness. Exhibition of too much joviality causing loud giggle sometimes proves fatal. One should enjoy ones meal cheerfully and may cut jokes moderately. Do not forget to thank Allah for gifts and favours bestowed by Him. If and when you feel sick, be very careful about your diet.

***Be Careful in Eating While Sick:*** Hadrat Umm Munzar says that once the Holy Prophet (S.A.W.) visited her house. This was the time when date trees had borne fruits and bunches of dates were hanging from the trees. The Holy Prophet (S.A.W.) plucked some fruits and started eating. Hadrat Ali, who accompanied him, followed suit and also started eating dates. Since he had recently recovered from sickness, the Holy Prophet (S.A.W.) forbade him from eating dates as the same would have harmed him. Hadrat Ali accordingly stopped eating dates. The Holy Prophet (S.A.W.), however, continued eating.

> *In the meanwhile, the distinguished hostess prepared a fare with barley and beet root for the August visitors. The Holy Prophet (S.A.W.) this time invited Hadrat Ali to partake of this preparation saying, "Ali, take this, it will do you good."* *(Shamail Tirmidhi)*

***Entertaining a Guest:*** Whenever the Holy Prophet (S.A.W.) had a guest at meals with him, he (S.A.W.) used to be very solicitous and called upon the guest to eat to his fill, and when the latter had eaten to his satisfaction, the Holy Prophet (S.A.W.) then only would refrain from pressing him to eat. It was the Practice of the Holy Prophet (S.A.W.) that he used to talk with those who joined him (S.A.W.) in eating, in a happy and cordial atmosphere.

***Siesta after Mid-day Meal and Stroll after Dinner:*** After mid-day meal, take a short nap; and after the evening dinner, go for a walk. Do not take up any hard physical or mental work after meals. According to an Arabic Hakim, 'Take rest after mid-day meal and go out for a stroll after evening meal."

Wash your hands before starting to eat. The norms of personal hygiene and cleanliness requires this. It is natural that one should be mentally satisfied about the cleanliness of his hands which are going to touch the food-stuff.

***Begin Eating with the Recitation of:*** *Bis-mil-laah ir-rah-maa-nir-ra-ha-heem* i.e. in the Name of Allah, the Most Compassionate the Most Merciful. If we forget to recite it, we may recite the following words as soon as we are reminded of it. *Bis-mil-laahe Awwa-lo-hoo wa aa-khiro-hoo,* i.e. in the name of Allah from beginning to end.

Remember that the meals upon which the name of Allah has not been recited, turns into devil's food. Do not take recourse to a prop while eating; sit in an unassuming style with your knees pointing outwards, or with one foot up and the other down, because the Prophet of Allah (S.A.W.) sat like this while eating. However, if you have to sit on a chair, sit straight without leaning while eating.

Always eat with your right hand using the left hand only when necessary. Eat with three fingers only if necessary, use fourth one, except the small one. Do not soak the fingers to their roots in the soup etc.

***Moderate Size Morsels:*** Do not take too big or too small morsels; take the next morsel, only after swallowing the first one.

***Do not Wipe your Fingers with Loaves:*** This is a very dirty habit.

Eat from the corner of the plate facing you neither eat from the middle of the plate nor from the other side.

***Wash the Fallen Morsel:*** If a morsel falls down, clean it, if necessary by washing, and then eat it.

Eat collectively along with others, as eating in company generates mutual love and affection and mates the meat enough and to spare. Never find fault with the food if you do not relish, leave it. Avoid laughing very loudly and too much talking at meals.

***Eat and Drink in a Sitting Posture:*** Fruits, desserts and drinks can be taken in a standing position, if necessary.

***Clean the Plate:*** Drink off the left-over from the plate, if liquid; and clean the same with a finger, if thick, and lick the finger.

Do not blow your breath on the food as the breath coming out of your mouth is putrefying and poisonous.

Take water in three breaks as it will slake the thirst and is more convenient to the person drinking water; whereas gulping it off in one breath may lead to complications.

***Consideration for the Company While Eating:*** While eating in company, be considerate to both slow eaters and fast eaters. Make allowance for both and leave the dinner-table along with others.

***Etiquette While Eating in Company:*** Do not smell the food unnecessarily. It is a bad habit. Neither open your mouth too often during the course of eating so as to make the chewing matter visible; nor put your finger frequently in your mouth for picking the teeth as it is repulsive to other participants of the meal.

***Don't Go Uninvited, but Do Go if Invited:*** The Holy Prophet (S.A.W.) has said: "Anyone who has been invited but has rejected the invitation has transgressed the commands of Allah and His Prophet. He who has gone to a party uninvited, has in reality entered as a thief and come out like a robber (from there)."

***Take one Piece at a Time:*** While eating fruit, do not pick up two slices together nor pick up two fruit pieces at a time.

Do not drink water directly from the tap or, faucet, waterspout or a long-necked vessel. Take water in a widemouth utensil or tumbler, so that it may be visible and no impurities may slip into the mouth.

Having finished the food, recite the, following prayer:

"All praise for Allah who has fed us, given us drinks, and has made us Muslims."

## NIGHT AND DAY

***Children to be Called in Before Nightfall:*** When the sun is setting, the children should be asked to come in and they may not be allowed to remain outside. However, they may go out, if necessary, only after a part of night has passed away. The Holy Prophet of Allah (S.A.W.) has said:

> *"Keep the children at home when the evening has fallen, as satanic forces descend (on earth) at this time. But if some night has passed, they might be allowed to go out."*
>
> *(Sihah-Sitta quoted by Hisn-e-Haseen)*

***Prophet's Evening Prayers:*** The Holy Prophet of Allah (S.A.W.) used to recite the following prayer at evening and taught the same to be read out by his followers:

*"O Allah (only) with Thy grace we could pass evening and (only) with Thy help we will pass morning. We are living with Thy favour and will die when Thou so command. And at last long, we shall return to Thee."*
*(Tirmidhi)*

The following supplication is to he recited at the time of the Adaan (the call for prayers) of Maghrib (evening) prayers:

*"O Allah this is the moment of the arrival of Thy night and the departure of Thy day and the time of the Calls of Thy Muazzins (the persons who call the Muslims for prayer) and the presentation of prayers to Thee. So forgive me."*

Avoid going to sleep before 'Isha prayers as there is likelihood of the same being missed. The Holy Prophet of Allah (S.A.W.) did not go to bed before 'Isha prayers'.

The house should be lighted up as soon as the night falls. The Holy Prophet of Allah (S.A.W.) avoided sleeping in a house that was not lighted.

***Day Sleep No Substitute for Night Sleep:*** Sleep early in the night and also rise early in the morning. Do not make up the deficiency of late sleeping in the night by sleeping in the day. Allah has created night for rest and peace, and the day is meant for work for the necessities of life.

***The Holy Quran says:*** "And it is He (Allah) Who has made the night a covering for you, and deep (a means of) repose and tranquillity and made the day for rising (work)."
(25: 47)

And also at another place, it is said:

*"And We have made sleep (as a means) of rest and peace for you, and have made the night as a cover, and the day for the struggle for the livelihood." (78: 9 to 11)*

Again in Soora 'An-Namal, it is said:

*"Have they not observed that We have made the night dark so that they may rest therein and the day alight and brilliant (so that they may struggle and work for their livelihood). Certainly there are indications (in this arrangement) for the believers to ponder." (27: 86)*

The idea behind making the night dark and a time for refit and the day bright for toiling and working is that one should take rest in the night and engage himself in the business of daily life in the light of the day till his body begins to feel tired and he may get peaceful and soothing sleep in the night. At dawn, we should get up duly refreshed and reciting the name of Allah ready for our work. The persons who sleep during the day due to sluggishness or keep awake in the night for enjoyment and pleasure, act contrary to the law of nature, and harm their health and life. Those who sleep during the day, do so at the cost of their daily obligations and deprive their body of natural rest and relaxation, as sleep of the day is no substitute for a night's sleep. The Holy Prophet (S.A.W.) has not even liked that a man should pray the whole night and place himself under undue ordeal.

The Messenger of Allah (S.A.W.) once asked Hadrat Abdullah bin 'Amr:

> *"I have been told about your fasting during the day and offering optional prayers throughout the night. Is it correct?" Hadrat Abdullah said: "O Prophet of Allah (S.A.W.), it is true." The Holy Prophet (S.A.W.) thereupon said: "Do not act like this. Keep fast occasionally and at times eat and drink. Similarly go to sleep and offer prayers, for your body too has right upon you: the eyes as well have their privilege."* *(Bukhari)*

Please do not use too comfortable and cosy bed. The Momin (believer in Allah) should shun worldy comforts, self ease and luxury. For him, the whole life is a Jihad (continuous struggle).

***Holy Prophet's (S.A.W.) Bedding:*** Hadrat Hafsah (R.A.A.) was asked by someone as to the nature of the bedding of the Holy Prophet of Allah (S.A.W.). She replied:

> *'It was made of a coarse jute cloth that we used to fold twice and spread under the Holy Prophet (S.A.W.). One day I thought that it could be a little more comfortable if it were folded four times. So I did the same. Early in the morning the Messenger of Allah (S.A.W.) asked: 'What had you spread under me last night?' I replied, 'The same piece of jute cloth was your bedding but I folded it four times instead of two foldings so that it*

> *may become a little cosier.' The Messenger of Allah (S.A.W.) said: 'No, let it remain twice folded only. The softness of the bedding was a source of hindrance in getting up for the Tahajjud (after mid-night prayer) last night.* (Shamail-e-Tirmidhi)

***The Holy Prophet (S.A.W.) disliked a cosy bed:*** Hadrat Aishah narrates: "Once an Ansar lady came and saw the bedding of the Holy Prophet (S.A.W.). On reaching home she prepared a very soft bedding for the Holy Prophet (S.A.W.) stuffing it with wool and sent it for his use. When the Holy Prophet (S.A.W.) saw this he enquired, 'What is it?." I said, 'O Messenger of Allah, the Ansari lady who had come 'to see you had noticed your (hard) bedding. She prepared a soft one and has sent it for you." The Holy Prophet (S.A.W.) said; 'No, return it to her." Hadrat Aishah further stated,

> *"I liked the bedding very much and wanted to retain it, but the same had to be returned due to the insistence of the Holy Prophet (S.A.W.)."* (Shamail-e-Tirmidhi)

***Hereafter Preferred to This World:*** Once the Holy Prophet (S.A.W.) was sleeping on a (bare) mat. This mat had caused some impressions on his body. Hadrat Abdullah Bin Masud says: "On seeing this, I began to weep." The Holy Prophet (S.A.W.) saw me weeping, so he asked, "Why are you weeping?" I submitted, "O Messenger of Allah, Emperors of Rome and Iran sleep in the soft cushioned beds of silk and velvet and the Holy Prophet of Allah (S.A.W.) on a mat (of date-palm leaves)." The Messenger of Allah said, "This is not the point to weep; for them is this world only, and we have the Hereafter."

***Any Day May be Doomsday:*** The Holy Prophet (S.A.W.) once remarked:

> *"How can I pass a life of comfort, ease and leisure when Hadrat Israil may blow the trumpet which is ever ready on his lips, and his ears are all attentive to the command of Allah to announce the Doomsday."* (Tirmidhi)

This excellent pattern of conduct of the Holy Prophet (S.A.W.) demands that the Muslims should lead a hard and strenuous life, avoiding pleasure-seeking and luxuriant way. Before going to bed, perform ablution (wudu) and go to sleep duly cleansed and purified. Any fat or grease sticking to the hands should be well washed off. 'The Holy Prophet of Allah (S.A.W.) said: "If anyone goes to bed without washing his hands and removing the greasy material from them, and he suffers on this account (bitten by some insect or animal) he should reproach none but himself (why he slept without washing his hands?)" It was the routine of the Holy Prophet of Allah (S.A.W.) that he performed wudu (ablution) before going to sleep.

When the Holy Prophet (S.A.W.) intended to go to bed while obligatory bath was due, he used to wash away the filth from its place and then went to bed after performing wudu (ablution).

***Close Doors, put out Light and Fire and Cover Pots before Retiring:*** Before retiring to sleep, shut the doors of your house, cover up the utensils containing eatables; put out the candle or lantern and extinguish the fire burning in the kitchen, etc. Once, a fire broke out in one of the houses in Medina, thereupon the Holy Prophet (S.A.W.) said: "Fire is your enemy, extinguish it when you go to bed." The Holy Prophet (S.A.W.) also said, "While shutting the door, putting out the light, closing the mouth of the water-bag (or pot), covering the kitchen utensils containing foodstuffs, recite Bismillah (in the name' of Allah). If there is no cloth to cover the utensils they should be covered with something else."

***Requisites for the Bed and Bedside:*** The following articles should be kept ready at hand near bedside: water for drinking, a jug and a tumbler, a stick, a match-box or a torch for light, and a towel. If one is putting up as a guest, he should ask about the location of the toilet so that he may be saved from the inconvenience of not knowing the same at night, if necessary.

***Holy Prophet's (S.A.W.) Routine:*** The Holy Prophet (S.A.W.) kept the following articles by his bedside: (a) a bottle of hair oil, (b) a comb, (c) a collyrium container and stick, (d) a pair of scissors, (e) one miswak, (f) a mirror, and (g) a small stick such as one used for scratching the head, etc.

Clothes and shoes should be kept nearer to your bed, so that on waking up, you may not have to look for them. The shoes should not be put on immediately on getting up from the bed. Shake up the shoes and clothes before using them.

The bed should he shaken up before going to sleep and also whenever one leaves it momentarily for some work, he should shake it up again. The Messenger of Allah (S.A.W.) said "If anyone gets up from the bed and goes to it again, he should sweep it with a piece of cloth, as he is not aware as to what may have crept into the bed in his absence."

***Bedtime Prayers:*** When going to bed, the following prayer should be recited. It has been reported by Hadrat Anas, the chief attendant companion of the Holy Prophet (S.A.W.) that while going to sleep he (S.A.W.) used to say:

> *"All praise is for Allah, who gave us food and water, helped us fully in our chores and labours, gave us shelter for living. There are numerous others, who have nobody to help them or to accommodate them."*
>
> *(Shamail-e-Tirmidhi)*
>
> *According to Hadrat Abu Hurrayrah (R.A.A.), the Messenger of Allah (S.A.W.) used to recite the following prayer before going to bed:*
>
> *"Allah with Your name, O my Lord, I have put my side on the bed and with Your help shall raise it from the bed. Have mercy on me if You will to take away my life at night and if You grant further reprieve it be under Your protection as You guard Your pious servants."*
>
> *(Bukhari and Muslim)*
>
> *The following short prayer can also be recited in place of the above: "O Allah, with Your name, I go into the fold of death, and in Your name shall I rise alive."*
>
> *(Bukhari and Muslim)*

***Bedtime Recitation from the Holy Quran:*** While going to sleep recite a passage from the Holy Quran. The Messenger of Allah (S.A.W.) invariably recited a portion of the Holy Quran before going to bed. The Holy Prophet (S.A.W.) has said, "When a person in bed recites a surah (chapter) from the Holy Quran, Allah sends an angel who guards him against all evils till he gets up."

Further, the Messenger of Allah (S.A.W.) said: "When a person goes to his bed, an angel and a Satan come up to him. The angel says, 'Let your actions come to an end with virtuous deeds'. Satan says, 'Be through your deeds with something bad.' If the person goes to sleep remembering Allah, the angel guards him the whole night."

*Hadrat Aishah narrates: "When the Prophet of Allah (S.A.W.) went to bed, he used to combine and stretch his hands as in prayers and used to recite the three surahs of the Holy Quran i.e., Al-Ikhlas (112) Al-Falaq (113) and An-Naas (114). Having recite d these, blew his breath upon both hands beginning from head, face and front portion of the body. He repeated this routine thrice."*
*(Shamail-e-Tirmidhi)*

***Mode of Sleeping:*** When you intend to sleep, lie on the right side and put the right hand below your right cheek. Hadrat Baraa' narrates:

"When the Prophet of Allah (S.A.W.) used to repose, he would put his right hand below his right cheek and recite the fo.lowing supplication:

*"O Allah: save me from: Thy punishment on the Day when Thou will resurrect Thy servants before Thee (for reckoning)." It is reported in Hisn-e-Hasin that the Holy Prophet (S.A.W.) recited the above words three times.*

Avoid sleeping flat and lying on the left side. Father of Hadrat Maeesh, Taf-khatul-Ghifaree narrates:

*"I was lying in the mosque with my belly touching the ground, when somebody shook me by the foot and said:*

*"Allah does not like this mode of sleeping." When I looked up, it was none but the Holy Prophet of Allah (S.A.W.) himself."* *(Abu Daud)*

The sleeping room should be airy; place for sleeping not accessible to fresh air should be avoided. While sleeping do not cover the face. It adversely affects the health. Always sleep with uncovered face so that you may get fresh air.

Sleeping on an open roof without railing or protective wall should be avoided. While coming down the stairs, arrange for light. Sometimes a minor slip results in considerable suffering.

Burning Coal or Lantern in the Sleeping Room: In spite of intense cold one should not sleep in a closed f room with the coal burning in a grate, or a lantern on, as the gas thus released, is harmful to health and might result in death.

***Cultivate the Habit of Tahajjud (Late Night Optional) Prayer:*** It is highly commendable to get up towards the end of the night, for Tahajjud (Optional) prayers. In order to discipline yourself and to develop concord with Allah, it is essential to wake up towards the close of the night and offer prayers. Allah has spoken of this distinctive quality of his beloved servants, that they rise up in the night, pray and prostrate to Him and beg forgiveness of their sins. It was usual with the Holy Prophet (S.A.W.) that he went to sleep early and prayed towards the close of the night.

On waking up, the Holy Prophet (S.A.W.) used to recite the following prayer:

> *"All praise and thanks are for Allah who gave us life after death (sleep) and surely we are to be resurrected before Him (on the Day of Judgement)."*

## SEEING GOOD VISION

Praise Allah and consider it as good tidings for the future. The Prophet of Allah (S.A.W.) has said, "Out of Prophethood, nothing has remained now except good tidings." The companions of the Prophet of Allah (S.A.W.) enquired, "What is meant by good tidings?" The Messenger of Allah (S.A.W.) replied, "A good dream" (Bukhari)

> *And the Messenger of Allah (S.A.W.) also said, "One Who is more truthful among you, will see truer dreams." And the Messenger of Allah (S.A.W.) furthermore advised his followers, "Whenever you see a good dream, glorify your Lord (Allah) and describe it to your friend only.' Whenever the Prophet of Allah (S.A.W.) saw a dream, he used to mention it to his companions and also advised his companions to mention dreams to him so that he would interpret the same.* *(Bukhari)*

***Vision of the Holy Prophet (S.A.W.):*** Recite Darood or Salat (invoking blessings of Allah and offering salutations) to the Holy Prophet (S.A.W.) as much as possible. It is quite likely that Allah Almighty may graciously enable you to see the vision of the Holy Prophet (S.A.W.) in dream. The Prophet of Allah

(S.A.W.) is reported to have said "Whosoever saw me in the dream, he did actually see me in the vision, as the Satan cannot impersonate me in dream."

God forbid, if you see an unpleasant dream, do not mention it to anybody. Seek the protection of Allah from its evil effects: God Willing, you will remain immune from its adverse effects. Hadrat Abu Salam said that he often remained sick due to harmful effects of dreams. One day he complained about it to Hadrat Abu Qatadah who narrated the following Hadith of the Holy Prophet (S.A.W.) "A good dream is divine (from Allah): if anyone of you sees such a vision, he should mention the same to none except to a sincere friend; but perchance one sees a disquiet dream, it should never be told to anyone, but on the other hand immediately after awakening, he should recite thrice:

*Aoo-zubillaa-hi minash-shai-taa-nir-rajeem.*

*"I seek refuge with Allah from (the mischief) of the Satan, the cursed" and should spit three times on the left side and also change his side on the bed; and thus he shall be safe from the-evil effects of the dream.*

*(Riaz-us-sali-heen, Muslim)*

***Do not Concoct Imaginary Dreams:*** Hadrat Abdullah Ibn Abbas.narrates the Messenger of Allah (S.A.W.) as having said, "Whosoever narrates false dreams, will be asked by way of punishment to knot together two pieces of barley grains which he will never be able to do." And the Holy Prophet (S.A.W.) also said: "It is a big calamity to describe a scene which one has not witnessed."

***Interpretation of Dreams:*** When a friend narrates his dream, that should be interpreted favourably and blessings of Allah be invoked for him. Once a person narrated his vision to the Prophet of Allah (S.A.W.) who said: "You have seen a good dream and it will augur well."

The Prophet of Allah (S.A.W.) used to sit with folded feet (cross-legged) on the floor of the mosque after the morning prayers and would ask his companions to narrate their dreams if any and recite the following prayer before hearing them:

*"May you be blessed with the good of this dream and be immune from its evil. It may be a blessing for us and*

*a curse for the enemy. All praise is for Allah, the Creator and Sustainer of the worlds."*

***Pray on Seeing a Nightmare:*** If one had an evil and horrifying dream, the following prayer should be recited. Grown-up children in the family be asked to memorise it. Hadrat Abdullah Ibn-i-Amr bin-Al 'Aas narrated that the Holy Prophet Muhammad (S.A.W.) recommended this prayer to him to be recited whenever he had a nightmare:

*"I seek shelter in the perfect words of Allah; from His wrath, from His punishment, from the evil of His creatures, from the instigations of the Satans and from their advance towards me."*

## TRAFFIC RULES

One should walk with a moderate speed neither so swiftly that he should become a spectacle for the passers-by nor as slowly as if crawling and may look like a sick person, and the people may stop and enquire after his health. The Holy Prophet (S.A.W,) always walked steadily with long steps and never dragged his foot.

One should walk with decorum keeping his eyes downwards, and not glancing here and there unnecessarily. Casting eyes at random is against good manners. The Holy Prophet (S.A.W.) walked carrying his weight forward as if descending from an elevation. He walked gracefully with a slightly swift step with the body kept compact and collected, never looking sideways.

Walk modestly without making any noise or ostentation. One should never strut. It is impossible for anybody to rend the ground he walks upon, nor scale the mountain peak. Then why to swagger and show off?

***Avoid Walking Barefooted:*** Shoes offer protection against gravel, thorns and other dangerous things, insects and crawling creatures.

The Holy Prophet (S.A.W.) said: "Put on footwears as far as possible. One who uses footwear is a sort of rider."

Walking with one shoe is a ridiculous practice, unless some special circumstance has made it unavoidable. Have due regard for good manners and decorum.

*The Holy Prophet (S.A.W.) has said "Never wa.k with one shoe on. Walk either with bare feet or with both shoes on. (Shamail-e-Tirmidhi)*

The garments should be gathered and collected while walking. The Holy Prophet (S.A.W.) walked with his shirt slightly raised.

One should always walk with the spirit of companionship and informality with his friends, and not try to be ahead of them, as if to have himself singled out as superior to others. It is better to be fraternal and walk hand-in-hand with friends. The Holy Prophet (S.A.W.) walked thus and never tried to make his presence felt. He often walked behind the companions, and occasionally clasped their hands.

## DUTY ON THE ROAD

It is not proper to stand or sit on the road and stare at the passers-by. If one by necessity has to stall himself on the roadside or sit thereon, one should have the following rules in mind.

(i) To keep the eyes down.

(ii) To remove impediments that might prove troublesome to others, from the roadside.

(iii) To offer greetings.

(iv) To preach good and to check from doing evil things.

(v) To guide those who have gone astray from the proper road.

(vi) To help one who needs one's help.

***Good Company on the Road:*** It is advisable to have the company of good people on the roadside and to shun the undesirables.

***Men and Women should not Walk Together:*** Women should walk on one side of the road and men should keep themselves at some distance from them. The Holy Prophet (S.A.W.) said: "It might be tolerable for one to collide with a filthy pig smeared with mud, but not that the shoulders of a man should brush against a stranger woman." Noble ladies while walking on the road, should cover their dress and all articles of decoration and put veils over their faces.

Ladies should not walk with such ornaments on their bodies which may give out jingling sound. They should rather walk softly so that their walking may not attract the attention of strangers. Ladies should avoid the use of strong and enchanting perfumes before going out in the street. The Holy Prophet (S.A.W.) has condemned this practice vehemently.

Recite the following prayer when leaving home:

*"In the Name of Allah (I have stepped out) and Him alone 1 trust. There is no power nor strength except in Allah."*

While Going to the Market recite the following prayer:

*"In the name of Allah (I enter the market place), I beg for the good of this market and the good of all that is in it and seek Thy shelter from the evil of this market and from the evil of all that is in it, and seek Thy protection from taking a false oath here, or from entering into a bargain that may result in a loss."*

***Another Prayer:*** According to Hadrat Umar Ibn Al Khattab (R.A.A.), the Holy Prophet (S.A.W.) said that anyone who recites the following prayer while stepping into the market, shall have a million blessings credited, and a million sins debited in his account, and further he will be elevated by a million grades.

*"There is no God except Allah, His is One: He has no partner and His alone is the sovereignty. He alone is deserving of all thanks and praises. He is Who gives and takes life. He is Everlasting. He will never die. All that is good is in His possession and He has authority over everything."*

## ON A JOURNEY

One should start on a journey at such a time that he may have to spend the least period in travelling and may be able to offer his prayers in time. The Holy Prophet (S.A.W.) whenever undertook a journey or sent someone on it, regarded Thursday as the most appropriate day for the same. Travel in company as far as possible. One should arrange for a company of at least three persons. Such a company will provide means of looking after the luggage, ensure mutual cooperation and safety from dangers. The Holy Prophet (S.A.W.) has said: "If people know the dangers inherent in travelling alone that I know, then even a rider would not negotiate a journey at night."

*If a group of persons is travelling, then they should appoint one of them as their leader. Nevertheless, each member of the party must retain his travelling documents, ticket, etc., some cash and other essential articles with him. Once a traveller who was proceeding on a journey to a distant place came to the Holy Prophet (S.A.W.). When asked as to who was accompanying him, he said, "None". Thereupon the Holy Prophet (S.A.W.) said: "A single rider is a Satan, two riders are also satans, but three riders are riders." (Tirmidhi)*

A woman should always travel with someone (i.e. *Mahram*) whose company is permitted by the Shariah. She can, however, travel alone if the journey is of half a day's or one day's duration. But discretion requires that she should not travel unaccompanied. The Holy Prophet's (S.A.W.) Tradition is:

*"A woman who believes in Allah and in the Day of Judgement is not permitted to travel alone for a period of three days or more. She can undertake such a long journey only if she is accompanied by her father, brother, spouse, son, or someone who is Mahram." (Bukhari)*

*On one occasion he even said: "A woman should not go alone on a journey extending over one day and one night." (Bukhari, Muslim)*

***Prayers on Starting on a Journey:*** The following prayer should be recited on boarding a vehicle or mounting an animal and when it starts moving.

*"Glorified be Allah who enabled us to keep in control this (animal or vehicle) although we were not in a position to control it. Verily, we are to return to our Lord."*

***Consideration for Fellow-travellers:*** It is necessary to care for the convenience of fellow travellers during journey. A companion during the journey has a right upon the fellow-travellers. The Quran says: "Treat your companion in the flank well." A companion in the flank means a person who becomes one's companion during the course of a journey anywhere, any time. Such a companion deserves all courtesies and help, and every effort should be made not to cause him any mental or physical harm. The Holy Prophet (S.A.W.) has said:

> *"The leader of the people is their servant. The person who tries to serve others the best, is only second to a martyr."* *(Mishkat)*

***Prayers at the Beginning and End of a Journey:*** On starting for or on returning from a journey two rakats of prayers in thanksgving to Allah should be offered. This was the practice of the Holy Prophet (S.A.W.). One should stay at night at a place which is safe from thieves, robbers and harmful animals.

***Quick Return from Journey:*** As far as possible, you should return home after having completed your business. Do not unnecessarily prolong your sojourn.

***Convenience for Animals Accompanying the Traveller:*** If animals or cattle accompany a traveller or a rider is keeping company, every convenience and protection should be provided to them. While travelling during cold weather take necessary bedding and clothes with you so that the host is not unnecessarily inconvenienced. Carry a pot for water and a prayer carpet with you, so that you may not be inconvenienced when necessity for toilet, ablutions, prayers and drinking may arise.

***Prayer to be Recited if Night Falls En Route:*** The following prayer is to be recited if night falls during the journey:

> *"O earth, thy Sustainer and mine is Allah. I seek the protection of Allah from three evils and that which is in thee, and from the evils of creatures which Allah has created in thee, and from the evils of the creatures that crawl and walk on thee. And I seek the protection of Allah from the lion, the black python, serpent, the scorpion, the inhabitants of this land, and the evils of every begetter and which is begotten in this land."*

On returing home from journey recite the following prayers:

> *"We return to Allah penitents, worshippers and adorers of our Lord."*

When seeing off someone, you should accompany him up to a reasonable distance. At the time of departure he may be requested to offer the following prayer and you should also recite this: "I commit to Allah's care your faith, your trusts and the consequences of your actions." A person returning from a journey should be welcomed with words appropriate to the occasion. He should be greeted with a handshake, or, if the occasion so dictates, an embrace as well.

## TABLE MANNERS

***The Meal:*** To prepare a good table, it is necessary to concentrate on cleanliness, tidiness and moderation concerning the amount of food and the variety of dishes.

- Food should be prepared from only lawful ingredients. Pork, alcohol, anything containing gelatine taken from a pig, sweets made with alcohol, blood, animals forbidden in Islam such as snake and frog, animals slaughtered in a non-Islamic way are Haram, unlawful to consume.
- Cooking vessels belonging to non-Muslims should be thoroughly cleaned before use. This is because Muslims have special instructions on cleanliness and food, which others are not expected to follow.
- Cooking a little extra broth is recommended since it will help to feed more people. Also, filling vegetables, such as squash, may be prepared, since this is an economical way of enlarging a meal and so satisfying the hunger of more people.
- If onions or garlic are liked they should be used in cooking, but should not be eaten raw as this gives rise to mouth odour which is unpleasant for others.
- Using silver or gold tableware is forbidden.
- Milk and honey are the best foods. The best part of an animal is the meat from its back.
- Food should preferably be taken while sitting on the floor, as this is a sign of humility.
- Considering the consumption of meat (including beef) to be forbidden is itself forbidden.
- Setting the table in Islam differs from the method used in other cultures. The Islamic table is characterized by cleanliness, simplicity and moderation; beauty is also a

recommended characteristic, provided it does not result in a waste of time and energy, as is often the case in Western etiquette. Meals should be considered a means of nourishment and not an end in themselves.

### Sitting Down to Eat

- A Muslim should be humble to God while sitting to eat, respecting His Grace. Although there is not a particular prescribed form of sitting, there are conditions, of which humility is the most important.
- A Muslim should not eat while lying on his back or stomach and should avoid eating while standing or walking.
- When eating, a Muslim should be properly seated and should not lean on a cushion or on his hand.
- Sitting to eat should be so arranged that excessive amounts of food and of time are avoided.
- He who misbehaves while eating, such as by eating with his left hand or using foul language or eating from other people's side of the platter, should be reprimanded.

### Proper Table Manners

- There is no objection to taking meals alone, thought it is better if the family gathers together for dining because, it is believed, food tastes better when the family eats from a common platter.
- It is a noble attitude of mind to not disdain to eat with others, poor or rich, young or old.
- Those who have bodily defects are allowed and entitled to eat with healthy and sound people, provided there is no possibility of contagion or the defects are not of a horrifying nature.
- Hands should be washed before and after a meal.
- There should be no hurry to take or swallow food while it is still hot; it is better to wait until it has cooled somewhat. Breathing or blowing on food in order to cool it should be avoided.
- On eating, a Muslim should start by saying: Bismillah al-Rahman al-Rahim (In the name of Allah, the Merciful,

the Mercy-giving). The following invocation may also be said: Allahumma barik lana fima razaqtana wa qina 'adhab al-nar (O God, bless this food and protect us from Hell).

- If a Muslim forgets to mention God's name over the food when he begins eating he should say: Bismillahi awwalahu wa akhiruhu (In the name of God at the beginning and at the end) of the meal.
- It is not enough that one of the group at a meal mention God's name. It is the duty of everyone present to do so.
- Food should not be taken from all sides of the platter, but eaten from that which is nearest. If, however, the platter contains fruits or dates, then selection may be made from any side.
- If a Muslim is served with food and the time for prayer comes, he should first have his food and not hasten to prayer until he has finished eating, provided there is no danger that the time for the prayer will elapse before he finishes eating. The purpose of this is to help him to concentrate on his salat, something that cannot be achieved when thinking of food.
- Eating should be done using the right hand only, using a spoon, or using three fingers of the right hand after washing them, if spoons are not available.
- Food should be eaten slowly and not greedily.
- If the person who is eating likes the food, then he may express approval and admiration, otherwise he should never be disrespectful and criticize or express disapproval of it. In the latter case he may say, 'I do not want any' or 'I am not used to this kind of food.'
- Eating cold and hot food at the same time is not recommended as it might be harmful to the teeth and stomach.
- Talk should be light, neither controversial nor provocative, and should avoid at all costs anything involving distasteful descriptions, for this may upset others.
- It is bad manners to speak with a mouth full of food.
- If some food falls from the mouth while eating, it should be cleaned, if possible, and eaten. This is because

wastefulness is forbidden. This applies also to leaving large remnants of meat on the bones, which is also wasteful.

- It is permissible to greet people engaged in eating, but is impolite to shake hands with them.
- A Muslim should not eat a great amount of food. He should stop eating before his stomach is full. Voracious eating is an un-Islamic habit.
- Going to sleep immediately after eating is unhealthy.
- Unconsumed food should not be left on the plate.
- When a Muslim has finished eating, he should praise God for the food by saying: Alhamdu lillahilladhi atamana wa saqana wa jaalana minal muslimin (Praise be to God who has given us food and drink and made us Muslims). He can also praise God by saying: Allahumma barik lana fihi wa atimna khayran minhu (Praise be to God in abundance, bless us with food and give us better to eat).
- Hands and mouth should be washed after eating. Washing is especially necessary after greasy food. After the meal, a toothpick should be used to clean food remnants from teeth. This helps to maintain healthy teeth.
- Politeness requires that children do not start eating before their parents and members of the family do not eat before guests. Respect for elders is one of the principles of Islam.
- If a fly falls into food or drink, it should be pushed down until it is submerged and then drawn out and thrown away. The reason for this, as given in an authentic Hadith, is that every fly carries on one wing malady and on the other remedy.
- A Muslim should try to ensure that everything he eats outside the home is halal (food permitted for Muslims).
- Newspapers or correspondence should not be read at meals if this leads to spending a great deal of time over the meal.

### *Drinking*

- Intoxicating beverages of all kinds are forbidden.
- Drinking out of silver or gold vessels is forbidden. Any other kind of vessel may be used.
- Drinks should be kept clean, especially water, and the containers should be covered, especially at night.
- A vessel should be checked before drinking to make sure that nothing has fallen into it.
- The right hand should be used for drinking, and not the left hand unless there is a necessity.
- God's name should be mentioned upon drinking by saying: Bismillah al-Rahman al-Rahim (In the name of Allah, the Merciful, the Mercy-giving).
- Drinking directly from the mouth of a bottle, jug, water skin or leather container should be avoided.
- A cup with a broken edge should not be used for drinking.
- When drinking one should not breathe into the vessel. One's thirst should not be quenched in one gulp. The cup should be removed from the mouth, a breath taken, and then a further drink.
- If drinking from a spring, river or pool, the drinker should avoid putting his mouth to it while lying on his stomach; he should use his hands instead, after washing.
- It is recommended to drink quietly, not gulping, from a cup or glass. In the course of drinking the vessel should be removed from the mouth and a breath taken. This should be repeated three times during the drink, dividing it into three sections. This is more thirst-quenching, healthier and wholesome.
- One should not drink while standing, reclining or lying down. Drinking should be carried out while sitting unless there is a necessity, for instance when drinking from a water fountain.
- When a Muslim finishes drinking, he should praise God and thank Him for it. After drinking milk, there is a special thanks: Allahumma barik lana fihi wa zidna minhu. (O God bless us with it and prosper us from it) for the benefit contained in the milk.

- When a group of people drink, the one on the right should drink first, regardless of age; that is, the vessel should actually be passed to the right. One should ask permission of the one sitting on one's right to interrupt passing to the right so as to give the drink to another person.
- When a person distributes something to drink among a group of people he should give it to whoever is on his right, then proceed along to the right, even if there is on his left an old person. Preference should always be given to those on the right. The drink should be passed with the right hand.
- If a Muslim is offered something to drink by someone, he should not forget to thank him and pray God to bless him.
- If something is drunk which contains fat or sugar acid, such as milk, then the mouth should be rinsed afterward in order to keep it clean and healthy.
- A hot drink should not be blown on to cool it; it is better to wait until it has cooled.
- If a dog drinks from a vessel, then it must be washed seven times with water, including once with clay if available, otherwise with soap. Such washing is specifically for dogs' saliva (not for other animals).

## MANNERS FOR JOURNEY

Travelling is not easy, but rather tiring and often complicated. Thus, Islam enjoins certain rules for travel to make it as light and enjoyable as possible;

- When intending to travel, a Muslim should say two rakats (*istikhara* prayer), if possible, and seek proper guidance from God.
- Certain superstitious beliefs and practices, observed by some people when a relative travels (such as refraining from cleaning the house immediately after the person's departure lest that might harm him) are completely forbidden, as Islam rejects all kinds of superstitions.
- A Muslim should not refrain from travelling when he thinks he has seen a sign or omen against it.
- It is better to take a companion when travelling, and to avoid travelling alone.

- It is better to start a journey at the beginning of the day. And, if possible, to set out on a Thursday.
- It is permissible to start a journey on any day and at any hour. The idea that one should not travel on Fridays is not in accordance with the teachings of Islam.
- The ideal company while travelling consists of four people.
- When getting in or on his conveyance, a Muslim is recommended to mention this phrase: *Subhanal-ladhi sakhkhara lana hadha wa ma kunna lahu muqrinin wa Inna ila Rabbina la munqalibun* (Glorified be He Who has subdued this to us, and we were not capable of subduing it. And to our Lord, surely, we are returning).
- On bidding farewell, a Muslim should say, while shaking hands with the traveller: *Astawda' Allah dinaka wa amanataka wa Khawatima amalika* (May God preserve your faith, religious duties and conclusion of your deeds).
- If a group of three or more are travelling together, one should be chosen as the leader, to organize the trip.
- All those taking part in a journey should listen to and obey the leader. Disobedience to him and disagreeing with him could lead to arguments with undesirable consequences for all.
- If a Muslim has more than one wife, then the only to decide which wife accompanies him on a journey is to let them draw lots.
- The same rule, as 12 above, should be observed when leaving to perform *hajj* or *Umrah*.
- It is not advisable for a Muslim to take with him the Quran or portions of it if he is travelling to countries which might dishonour it.
- Women are not allowed to travel long distances unless accompanied either by mahrams or their husbands.
- To be polite, kind, helpful and cooperative to travelling companions is recommended. As is being solicitous to serve others and not allowing them to do everything.
- It is the duty of a traveller in company to look after any member of the group who falls ill.

- The expectation that those who travel to other countries should, upon their return, bring presents for relatives or friends makes travelling more difficult and more expensive.
- If the journey is a long one, then the traveller is advised not to exert himself, but to take a rest whenever necessary.
- If stopping for any reason, then it is a traveller's duty not to park his vehicle on the road or occupy a part of the road, for such action could hinder traffic and might also endanger his life and the lives of others.
- When stopping or sleeping outdoors, the traveller should avoid places where there could be harmful creatures, especially at night.
- When travellers stop, to take a rest or for any other reason, they should not divide themselves into groups or separate from one another, but rather gather in one group.
- It is the duty of a Muslim traveller, to help those whom he meets who are in need of his help, by providing them with water or fuel, by repairing their vehicle, giving them a lift, or any other kind of possible assistance, irrespective of the religion, race or nationality of the person needing help.
- Fasting during Ramadan while on a journey is allowed. If a Muslim feels able to fast while travelling he is allowed to do so, if not, he is allowed to break it.
- For the ease of the traveller, it is permitted that he combines the noon and the afternoon prayers, and also the sunset and the evening prayers.
- While on a journey, a Muslim may pray from his vehicle or astride his riding animal, in whatever direction he is travelling.
- Prayers consisting of four rakats are shortened to two rakats on a journey.
- The traveller is recommended to take advantage of the night hours for travelling.

- It is recommended that a Muslim returns home as soon as the purpose of his travel is accomplished, especially after hajj.
- When returning from a journey, arriving home at night should be avoided.
- The first thing that a Muslim should do on returning to his home town is to go to the local mosque and pray two rakats.
- It is recommended to greet the traveller on his return with an embrace. A man may embrace another man, a woman another woman.
- When about to enter a village, town or residential area, a traveller should pray by saying: *Audhu bi kalimate Allah al-tammat min sharri ma khalaq* (I seek refuge with the perfect words of Allah from the evil of what He has created).
- Praying while travelling is recommended. In fact, the supplications (dua) of a traveller are of special importance. Prayer here does not refer to the five obligatory daily prayers (salat), rather to spontaneous remembrance of God, asking Him for perfection, guidance, and help.
- Saying Allah-o-Akbar (God is great) as he climbs an ascent, and Subhan Allah as he makes the descent, are recommended of a Muslim when travelling.
- Among the good manners expected of a traveller is to overlook and forget his companions' mistakes, chat with them kindly, share food and drink with them, and avoid disputes.
- When travelling on a riding animal and passing through an area where there is grass and water, the traveller should proceed slowly; when passing through a barren or desert area, he should proceed quickly.
- It is not recommended for Muslims to go to non-Islamic lands and live there permanently. If a Muslim travels to a non-Islamic country there should be a good reason.

# Bibliography

Abbas Hashmi : *Rasul (PBUH)*, Adam Pub., New Delhi, 2001.

Abdali, M.R. : *Scientific Thought in Islam*, Pious Publications, Hyderabad, 2001.

Abdul Qadir : *Criminal Law of Islam*, Kitab Bhavan, New Delhi, 1999.

Abdul, H.S.: *The Life of Muhammad (PBUH)*, Islamic Pub., New Delhi,1997.

Abdullah Enan : *Decisive Moments in the History of Islam*, Islamic Book Company, Delhi, 1996.

Adil, H. M. : *Letters of Hadrat Usman Ghani (R.A.A.)*, Kitab Bhavan, New Delhi, 1992

Ahmad, Ilyas : *Sovereignty, Islamic and Modern*, Allies Book Corporation, Karachi, 1965.

Ahmad, Imtiaz : *Ritual and Religion among Muslims in India*, Manohar Publishers, New Delhi, 1984.

Ahmed, Hasanuddin : *Islamic Economics*, Goodword Books Pvt. Ltd., New Delhi, 1991.

Ali, Ameer : *Muhammadan Law*, Kitab Bhavan, New Delhi, 1986.

Arnold, T. W. : *The Caliphate*, Routledge & Kegan Paul Ltd., London,1965.

Asghar, Ali : *Islam : Women and Gender Justice*, Gyan Books Pvt. Ltd., New Delhi, 2001.

Ataur-Rahim : *Jesus a Prophet of Islam*, Idara Ishaat-e-Diniyat Pvt. Ltd, New Delhi, 1995.

Azam, Zaki : *The Ideas of Arab Nationalism*, Cornell University Press, New York,1956.

Baral, Raj : *Regional Migrations : Ethnicity and Security*, Popular Prakashan, Bombay, 1995.

Beverly, Milton : *Islam and Politics in the Contemporary World*, Blackwell, New York, 1987.

Bosworth, C.E. : *The Legacy of Islam*, Oxford University Press, New York, 1979.

Carl, W. : *Teaching of Sufism*, Deep & Deep, New Delhi, 2000.

Charles Howard : *The Constitutionalism*, Great Seal Books, New York, 1947.

Chave F. : *Islamic Histroriography*, Cambridge University press, New York, 1990.

Daniel, N.A. : *Islam and the West : the Making of an Image*, University Press, Edinburgh, 1962.

De, Laet : *The Political Systems of Empire*, Oxford, New York, 1963.

Edwin, Elliot : *Worship in Islam*, University of Madras, Madras, 1925.

Fauzi M. : *The Islamic State : a Study in Traditional Politics*, Oxford, New York, 1967.

Gardet, Louis : *Mystique Musulmane*, Allen & Co., Paris, 1961.

Gellner, E. : *Post-Traditional Forms in Islam : the Turf and Trade*, Oxford, New York, 1982.

Ghulam Sarwar : *Muhammad (PBUH) the Holy Prophet*, Dar-ul Ishaat, Karachi, 1997.

Gibb, H.A.R : *Studies in the Civilization of Islam*, Beacon Press, Boston,1962.

Glubb : *The Story of Arab Legion*, Feroz Pub., Lahore, 2000.

Gulzar Ahmed : *The Prophets (PBUH) Concept of War*, Aziz Pub., Islamabad, 2000.

Herbert, Friedman : *The Amazing Universe*, National Geographic Society, Washington D.C., 1980.

Husaini, S.A.Q : *The Pantheistic Monism of Ibn al-Arabi*, Feroz Pub., Lahore, 1970.

Hussain, Ahanger : *Customary Succession among Muslims*, Uppal Publishibng House, New Delhi, 1997.

Hussain, M. : *Imam Abu Hanifah : Life and Work*, Kitab Bhavan, New Delhi, 2001.

Hussain, S. : *Human Rights in Islam*, Kitab Bhavan, New Delhi, 2001.

Ikbal Ali : *Islamic Sufism,* Idarah-I-Adbiyat-I-Delhi, Delhi, 1979.

Ikram, S.M. : *Muslim Civilization in India,* Oxford, New York, 1981.

Jafar Sharif : *Islam in India,* Atlantic Publishers, New Delhi, 1999.

Jafar, Sharif : *Islam in India,* Oxford, New Delhi, 1972.

James, Piscarton : *Islam in the World of National States,* Macmillan, New York, 1982.

Jean-Baptiste : *Travels in India,* W.Crooke, London, 1925.

Jha, V. : *Indian Society: Historical Probings,* Rawat Pub., Delhi, 1974.

John L. Esposite : *Islam in Transition,* Oxford, New York, 1969.

John Surowiecki : *The Pulse of the Planet,* Crown Publishers, U.S.A. 1972.

Kalim Bahadur : *Domestic Conflicts in South Asia,* South Asia Publishers, New Delhi, 1986.

Kalim, M. Siddiq : *Studies in Pakistan Culture : an International Perspective,* Manohar Publications, New Delhi, 1993.

Karnal, A. : *Islam : Today and Tomorrow,* Deep & Deep Pub., New Delhi, 1989.

Katharine, Scarfe : *Perception of the Islamic Word,* Cambridge University Press, New Delhi, 1992.

Kaur, R. : *Islamic Co-operation and Unity,* Deep & Deep Publications, New Delhi, 1993.

Kazim Munishi : *Alamgir-Nama,* A.B.C. & Co., Calcutta, 1865.

Khaduri, M. : *War and Peace in the Law of Islam,* Hopkins Press, Baltimore, 1955.

Landau, R. : *The Philosophy of the Ibn Arabi,* Century Pub., London, 1959.

Lewis, Richards : *Universe,* Harmony Books, New York, 1973.

Mac, Closky : *Pacts for Peace,* New Century Pub., London, 1980.

Margery Milne : *The Nature of Life,* Crown Publishers, New York, 1995.

Mathew, Thomas : *Political Economy of Etimic Conflict,* School of International Studies, Jawaharlal Nehru University, New Delhi, 2003.

Mayne, P. : *Saints of Sind,* New Century Pub., London, 1965.

Meer, Ali : *Observations on the Musulmauns of India,* Macmillan & Co., London, 1832.

Mohiuddin, Ahmad : *Saiyid Ahmad Shahid,* Modern Pub., Lucknow, 1975.

Moreland, W.H. : *From Akbar to Aurangzeb,* MacMillan & Co., London, 1923.

Mualana, Taqi : *Fundamentals of Ijtihad,* Idaara-I-Adabiyat, Delhi, 1986.

Muhammad, Asad : *Islam at the Crossroads,* Kitab Bhavan, New Delhi, 2003.

Murtaza, G. : *Judicial System of Islam,* Kitab Bhavan, New Delhi, 1994.

Muslehuddin, M. : *Islam : its Political System,* Kitab Bhavan, New Delhi, 1999.

Nabith, A. : *The Foundations of the Articles of Faith,* Feroz Pub., Lahore, 1963.

Nicholson, R.A. : *Studies in Islamic Mysticism*, Cambridge, New York, 1967.

Nikki, R. : *Saints and Sufis, Muslim Religious Institutions since 1500,* University of California Press, California, 1972.

Noomi, Kurtha : *Prisoners of War and War Crimes,* Deep Publications, Lacknow, 1980.

Padwick, C.E. : *Muslim Devotions*, MacMillan & Co., London, 1960.

Palamer, E.H. : *The Quran,* Atlantic Publishers, New Delhi, 1996.

Peter Lambron Wilson : *Traditional Modes of Contemplation and Action,* University Press, Tehran, 1977.

Qazi A. Qadir : *The Changing World of Islam,* Royal Pub., Lahore, 1992.

Richards, J.F. : *Mughal Administration in Golkonda,* Oxford, New York, 1975.

Robert, D. : *Exploring our Living Planet,* National Geographic Society, Washington, 1989.

Rodinson, Maxime : *Islam and Capitalism,* Penguin, London,1974.

Rosenthal, E.I.J. : *Islam in the Modern National State,* University Press, Cambridge,1965.

Sardar, Ziauddin : *The Future of Muslim Civilization,* Croom Helm, London, 1979.

Sarton, George : *Introduction to the History of Science,* Carnegie Institute, Washington, 1950

Saxena, K.P. : *Human Rights: Perspective and Challenges,* Lancers Books, New Delhi, 1996.

Saxena, V. K. : *Muslims and the Indian National Congress,* Discovery Publishing House, New Delhi, 1985.

Scarman, Leslie : *Law : the New Dimensions,* Stevens and Sons, London, 1974.

Schacht, J. : *The Origins of Muhammadan Jurisprudence,* Clarendon Press, Oxford, 1953.

Schwartz, E. : *Science and Civilization in Islam,* Cambridge, London, 1966.

Seervai, H. : *Constitutional Law of India,* N.M. Tripathi & Co., Bombay, 1967.

Setalvad : *War and Civil Liberties,* Feroz Pub., Lahore, 1992.

Sharif, M. : *Islamic Social Framework,* Islamic Book Foundation, Dacca, 1980.

Sharma, S.R. : *Women's Education in Ancient and Muslim Period,* Discovery Publishing House, New Delhi, 1996.

Siddiqi, M.Z. : *Hadith Literature,* Deepali Pub., Calcutta, 1961.

Singh, Nagendar : *Human Rights and International Cooperation,* S. Chand & Co., New Delhi, 1969.

Sir William : *The Caliphate, its Rise, Decline and Fall,* Oxford, Edinburgh, 1915.

Sir, Richard : *Sind and Races that Inhabit the Valley of the Indus,* Allen & Unwin, London, 1851.

Sir, Thomas : *The Caliphate,* MacMillan, London, 1965.

Smith, M. : *An Early Mystic of Baghdad,* Cambridge, New York, 1920.

Smith, M.: *The Mystic and her Fellow Saints in Islam,* Cambridge, London, 1929.

Smith, W. C. : *Modern Islam in India : a Social Analysis*, Manohar Publishers, New Delhi, 1985.

Suhrawardi, Umar : *Awarif al Maarif bin Muhammad*, Sheikh Ghulam Shahabuddin Ali & Sons, Lahore, 1964.

Syed Husain : *Three Muslim Sages*, Cambridge, New York, 1959.

Syed, Amir Ali : *The Spirit of Islam*, Royal Pub.,Lahore, 1979.

Taqi Muhammad : *An Introduction to Islamic Finance*, Idara Ishaat-e-Diniyat Pvt. Ltd., New Delhi, 1999.

Thompson, H.R. : *Sculptures and Inscriptions of Darius the Great on the Rock of Behistan*, Oxford, London, 1907.

Valliuddin, Mir : *The Quranic Sufism*, Motilal Banarsi Das Publishers, New Delhi, 1989.

Wahed, Husain : *Administration of Justice during the Muslim Rule in India*, Ashish Publishing House, New Delhi, 1977.

Waheed, Akhtar : *Sufi Approach to the Problem of Alienation*, Wilson & Co., New Delhi, 1975.

Waheed, Mirza : *The Life and Works of Amir Khusrau*, Kaveri Pub., Calcutta, 1935.

Walker, Benjamin : *Foundation of Islam : the Making of World Faith*, Rupa & Co., New Delhi, 2001.

Watt, M. : *The Faith and Practice of Al-Ghazzali*, MacMillan & Co., London, 1953.

Watt, W.M. : *Islam and the Integration of Society*, Routledge, London, 1961.

Yazbeck, Haddad : *Islamic Values in the United States*, Oxford, New York, 1997.

Yezbeck Haddad : *Islamic Values in the United States*, Oxford, New York, 1999.

Zafeeruddin, M.M. : *System of Modesty and Chastity in Islam*, Idara Ishaat-e-Diniyat Pvt. Ltd, New Delhi, 1995.

Zahid, Malik : *Subjects of Quran*, Kitab Bhavan, New Delhi, 1998.

Zahurul Hasan : *Tarikb-i-Sufiya-i-Gujarat*, Jamil Academy, Ahmadabad, 1981.

Zaydan, Jurji : *Umayyads and Abbasides*, Luzac & Co., London,1907.

# Index

## Q



## R



## S



## T



## U



## V



## W



## Y



□□□